THE STORY OF DANCE MUSIC

The Story of
DANCE MUSIC

BY

PAUL NETTL

GREENWOOD PRESS, PUBLISHERS
NEW YORK

TO MARTHA GRAHAM
THE GREAT DANCER
OF OUR TIME

CONTENTS

FOREWORD

This highly diverting book should be of immense interest to us here and now. It is, in effect, a history of music with emphasis on those special elements which derive from the dance. And the influence of the dance on the development of music is, it seems to me, something which we of today are appreciating more and more. "Also Beethoven" says Dr. Nettl, "does not disdain to write real dance music. In the Seventh Symphony he raised the dance to a level unique in the history of music."

Dr. Nettl (with due reference to his predecessor, Dr. Curt Sachs) tells of primitive dance cults in ancient civilizations. He speaks of the "pleasurable narrowing of consciousness" brought about by the influence of monotonous rhythm, of bodily motions which, through repetition, become effortless and automatic. He compares the music of the American Indian with that of the Negro and says: "the much more passionate and less balanced gesticulations of the Negro . . . call for the more complicated rhythmic elaboration which keeps both player and hearer in continuous tension." Those of us who are interested in the music of our American Indian will be interested to learn that the famous Matachines dance derives its name from a stock character in the old Italian Commedia dell'Arte: Matacino, an awkward fellow who often appeared with accessories such as jingle bells, a sword and a helmet.

He tells of a Rabbi who, in sixteenth century Italy, wrote the first treatise on the art of dancing. We hear of English mummers who, at a somewhat later date, travelled through Germany in groups and who did much to determine the development of German dramatic art. We learn of tournaments and

ix

equestrian ballets and we learn the fact that our present day amusement-park carrousels are the only remnants thereof: for the word Carrousel originally meant Tournament. Acrobats, necromancers and dervishes flit through this book and ancient papyri, Sienese frescoes and contemporary lithographs are laid before us for inspection.

It is, indeed, a tribute to the unquenchable spirit of man, to his never ending quest for pleasure and beauty. To those of us who enjoy viewing the activities of man from an eminence, as it were, this book should bring many hours of delight. The musical illustrations are profuse and illuminating.

This is the age of Martha Graham . . . of Fred Astaire . . . of the orchestra of the Ballet Russe . . . of Cab Calloway. Copland and Leonard Bernstein have brought something new, something American, to the development of the ballet. It is well for our sensitive composers, for our intelligent lay-public, for our dancers and our musical performers generally to know how all of this came about.

FREDERICK JACOBI

New York

PREFACE

The publication of a book which has as its subject the Dance is an event of importance, not only to dancers or specialists in music but to those whose interest is man, the revelation of his processes and the fruits of his Search.

When a book treats the subject with the precise attention of the scientist and the devotion of the lover then indeed is it cause for rejoicing.

A book about an art can reveal many things.

It can reveal the foundations of that art as existing deep within the heart of man.

It can reveal as a common and honorable ancestral home that structure of art as built by countless generations of being.

It can reveal added reason for an ultimate faith in man's stubborn and lovely dream.

Finally it can reveal how very close and very like we are— that there does exist for us a common basis of understanding regardless of the differences of place and language.

Art is the expression of the hearts impulse. As such it is our common tongue.

A book which can arouse in us the delight of recognition that we have a common speech, that we need not be alone or foreign to each other, that by learning about ourselves and others through the study of the history of an art we can speak together about important matters is wise and honorable and welcome.

It is my privilege to be among the first to welcome the publication of this book in the United States.

MARTHA GRAHAM

ACKNOWLEDGMENTS

It is a great pleasure to me to express my deepest gratitude to Mrs. Margaret Bush, my friend and secretary who for many years has been my faithful collaborator. She was particularly helpful in giving shape to this book and is to a great extent responsible for its accomplishment.

I also acknowledge my thankfulness to Mrs. Rosalyn Krokover and to Dr. Franz Allers for their contribution to the last chapter, and should like to take the opportunity to thank Dr. George Amberg of the Museum of Modern Art; Mrs. Frieda Best; Mrs. Ada Bodanzky; Mrs. Elizabeth Delza-Munson; Mr. Lincoln Kirstein. Miss Marian Eames and Mr. Paul D. Magriel of "Dance Index"; Miss Liljan Espenak and Miss Rosalie Hausmann.

PAUL NETTL

CHAPTER I

CULT AND MOVEMENT.

DANCING, as regulated and orderly bodily movement, has its roots in the biological relation of the human and animal organism. The rise and the fall of the breathing lungs, the beating of the heart, these are the foundations for the movements of living organisms. Goethe in his outline of the "Science of Tone" says: "All organic movement manifests itself in systoles and in diastoles", (the expansion and the contraction of the chambers of the heart). And he adds: "The entire organism is moved thereby towards the march, towards the leap (Sprung) dance and gesture".

It is not surprising, that even in the animal world dancelike movements may be readily observed.

Mammals dance during mating time. Antelopes dance, the moose leaps with rhythmic steps around the female he is wooing. The horse learned to dance after it was domesticated and Pliny already reports of the efforts made by the Sybarites in that direction. These old forms of the horse ballets, practised by the Romans and the Arabs later were practised at the courts of the 17th century where they had their highest development in the "Balletti a cavallo" of which we shall speak later.

Primitive Man makes dancing the expression of every kind of emotions. The birth of his heir, marriage and funeral rites, the initiation of the young men of the tribe, worshipping of the gods or propitiation of evil demons, are all accompanied by appropriate dances. They dance to pay honor to the change of the seasons, while they plough the fields, when they set out for the hunt and when they return from it.

Every mother knows that children love to identify themselves with objects of the world around them and with any

1

human being. The little fellow playing with a dog imitates the dog, barking and rolling around, and he is for the moment the dog himself. Also when a child accompanies the movement of the toy train with "puff, puff", he is merely playing at being an engine. Subject and object are one and the same, and this may have held true of primitive man as well. He would as he gave a mimic representation of the quarry, act out the fall of his prey in a rhythmic dancing representation, a charm to make his hunt successful. These old charms and magic incantations of the chase have come down to our day.

When primitive huntsmen would set out to hunt, they would first make an effigy of the animal they want to kill and dance around it. Or, in a later phase of development, he himself puts on the mask of the animal and impersonates the beast, thereby obtaining power over it. In this mimic representation we have the first traces of a dramatic dance form with the power to work a charm, such as, at a later stage of development was wrought by invocation, by appellation and by symbolical gesture.

The religious cult represents one of the great roots of the dance and that at these early times in the history of mankind severe regulations governed it, constituting a "taboo", which might not be infringed without arousing the anger of the deity invoked. Many a form of primitive dancing is performed in a state of ecstasy, which takes hold of the person executing it, as he passes into a condition of veritable intoxication while approaching the divine presence, or sensing the approach of the demon. Impressionable as the unspoiled child of nature, primitive man is swayed relentlessly by every stimulus coming from the outside world; the tone of the instruments, narcotic medicines or incantations, exert their power over him and the ecstasy is often followed by veritable outbursts of insanity. And thus the dance of primitive men is a genuine dance of the possessed.

The theoreticians of the dance contrast the forms of this art and classify the various manifestations as spontaneous dancing, and imitative dancing. Curt Sachs makes a distinction between the "non-pictorial" and the "picturesque" dance. The

latter aims at giving in pantomimic portrayal the events preceding the goal desired, thus making itself an instrument by
which the purpose is to be attained. Contrasted with this are
those dances which merely accompany some parts of the cult,
or of a given ritual without making any attempt to imitate
any natural gestures or actions in pantomime. A similar
division was already made by the philosopher Wundt in his
"Voelkerpsychologie", where a distinction is made between
ecstatic and mimic dances. And we find that the two-fold
branching of the development of the dance, into ballet and
social dancing follows the same general line.

It would seem that (according to Wundt) imitative dances
originate in the sympathetic magic of the primitive peoples.
For, with his animistic concept of the world around him,
the savage sees everything as a spirit and attempts to subject
all nature to his will by a kind of incorporation. Since, however, he is incapable of incorporating all of the natural world
which surrounded him, he must content himself with "partial
magic". Not being able to consume his enemy entirely and
thus make him part of himself, he merely takes over his scalp,
his garments and his decorations. This "partial magic" has
a signal influence on the development of the dance, because it
constitutes the origin of costume and mask in dancing. In
assuming its shape, primitive man became a part of nature.
We have but a poor notion of the intensity with which a savage
man can enter into the body and the spirit of the form which
he takes over. In his reports of the "leopard men" living on
the East Coast of Africa, Albert Schweitzer tells how this tribe,
possessed of the idea that they are the animals which they
impersonate, fall upon other tribes, as if they were really wild
beasts.

This confusion between subject and object, this identification of the ego with surrounding nature, is found in all
the dances celebrating and invoking fertility, in all parts of the
world. The growth of plants and the bearing of fruit are
identified with a heightened human sexual activity. That the

fruit-bearing earth is identified with the womb of the human female is a concept familiar not only to ethnologists and psychologists, but a part of folk-lore itself. Earth is the great mother of all from whose lap we have sprung, and to whose bosom we must return, and love and death are joined insepa-rably. Love brings death, and death brings resurrection and new life. Therefore it is not strange to see funeral ceremonies of primitive peoples in which the idea of procreation and birth are the main motif. The old rite of the funeral feast, the "wake" which is still prevalent all over peasant Europe, is, according to some psychologists, a remnant of the primary ritual, when the old chief was killed and (as by the cannibals even consumed) by the young men of the tribe, in order to make way for a stronger and more valiant member of the tribe. In many parts of Europe the custom still prevails of having the band play dance music on its return from the cemetery, to which it has accompanied the hearse of the de-ceased, while playing dirges.

In his book, "Forest- and Field Rites", W. Mannhardt, the ethnologist, has shown that dances for greater fertility were performed in ancient times by persons who blackened their faces, "bugaboos", the "black men". In this same fashion foolish nurses try to force their wards into frightened obedi-ence. Some psychoanalysts believe that these blackened char-acters represent the fathers killed by their sons, returning as ghosts to impose this rule over them. Greek mythology takes over the tale of the father killed by the sons in the person of Kronos, and in later days, the cruel custom of the murdered sire is replaced by the killing of the sacrificial animal, the slaying of the "totem", which subsequently becomes the sacred beast worshipped by the tribe.

In the group of "black man" games and dances belong the so-called "Moorish dances" which, according to Franz Magnus Boehme, the great authority on dancing, prevailed for a long time in those parts of Europe where there were actual wars between the "white men" and the Arabs or Turks, that is in Spain, France, Southern Italy, 'Austria and Hungary. That the

English "Morris" dances hark back to this old form of a fertility ritual is quite apparent from the description of such a dance dating from the eighteenth century. I take my example from Chambers' "Medieval Stage": Seven persons take part in this dance, the fool, his five sons and a woman named Cecile. The sons decide to kill the father, he kneels down, makes his last will while the swords touch his throat; finally he is killed but the comic character, one of his sons called "the pickled herring", resuscitates him while the sons stamp the ground with their feet. Now a sword dance follows, while the fool and his sons court Cecile. That the father and the sons woo the same woman, that he is killed and comes to life again, and that the earth is beaten, — these are the unmistakable signs of a dance, celebrating fertility and growth. This trampling on the soil has its own ancient ritual significance, that is the bringing about of increased fertility by stamping on the ground. Occasionally an old phallic symbol, a magic wand accompanies the rite. In many regions these fertility dances have two separate phases, one of these being a procession on the field, the other the actual stamping of the soil which is to bear more fruit. Perhaps this division may help us to explain the twofold character of dancing, the two old forms of dancing: the paced slow steps, and the leaps, following in the "round". All these old dances have been preserved in various forms in many parts of Europe, in Germany and in Austria, as well as in Eastern countries overseas. The superstitious inhabitants of these parts repair to their fields in the spring, and perform high jumps and leaps in the air to charm the demon of fertility and to cause him to make the corn grow as high as their jumps into the air!

Winterstein in his psychoanalytical study on the "Origin of Tragedy" says that the beating of the earth, in other words, the stamping of the dancer, originally had a phallic meaning. The accompanying bells, part of the trappings of the dancers, are remnants of phallic dance requisites. It is not fortuitous that, in connection with the fertility rites we often find sword dances, for the sword is not merely an instrument of death, it has its own phallic meaning. It is characteristic that the sword dances, quite similar to the Moorish dances, were performed to the accompaniment of bells and in spring time. For in the primitive phase of culture the desire to fight and the sexual urge seem to have been closely related, and the ecstasy of destruction and of love were often paired in life, and therefore also in the dance. The women dance around the warriors who have returned victoriously from the battle and are carried away by emotional paroxysm. Already the Greeks and the Romans knew and practised these dances. The Romans called them "tripudia", which according to Cicero was derived from "terra pavio", stamping the earth. Tacitus tells of a dance with weapons practised by the Germans in chapter 24 of "Germania". "Naked youth, who delight in this, dance about between swords and threatening lances. This exercise makes them supple and decorous". We need not stop here to tell of the countless dances with weapons described by ethnologists and travelers in savage and half-civilized countries. In medieval times these dances become a matter of guild activity and of exhibition of skill, and later are transformed into the jousts and tournaments, culminating in modern times in the circus and variety shows.

From these fertility dances to the funeral dances there is but a small step. For, like the child, who cannot believe in the disappearance of those whom he has known and loved, primitive man expresses his belief in the life after death in his customs and habits. This desire for the return of the beloved is strangely enough often combined with a dread of his return. In many African tribes the deceased is tied to a stake, and the dancers surround him, coming ever closer and closer. While this is going on, rattles are turned and gourds are shaken (these, otherwise used to scare the demons), and by their noise the dead men are prevented from returning to life.

In the dances of some primitive peoples, all the gestures and movements of wooing, refusal and yielding are reproduced in the dances. Such a dance of the coy maidens with a subsequent yielding to the wooers is danced according to Josephat

Hahn (in his book "The Ovaherero"), by the Herero tribe in Africa. The girls of the tribe gather at evening to dance their "On tyina". They stand in a circle, clap their hands, sing and perform in pantomime. At a given signal they rush in all directions to avoid the grasp of the men who have been watching them and subsequently gather in a circle again. Though dancing and wooing are occasionally one and the same, at other times the sexual act is only symbolically represented. At about the middle of spring the Watchandie tribe of Western Australia prepare to celebrate their semi-religious festival called the Caarofeast. On the eve of the day, the men are separated from the women and children, and the former must not look at a woman until after the end of the ceremonies. A hole is dug in the ground which the men surround with wild cries and shouting as they dance. We see here, as has been said before, an identification of the human womb with the lap of the mother earth, and a fertile rite of a primitive type.

One of the most important rites of primitive cultures is the ceremony of initiation, the celebration of the coming of age of the young men. In all these rites dancing plays an important part. Here, as elsewhere, sympathetic magic expressed in the dance is to bring about the help of propitious demons during this important step in the life of the human being, and, at the same time, that evil spirits be banished and exorcised. In California, the Indians dance about the adolescent girl; in Australia, the tribesmen surround the boy growing to manhood. This figure of the magic circle appears even in the fraternity initiations of the present time. As when Masons surround the neophyte before he is admitted into the lodge. A German author, Taubert, tells in his "The Honest Dancing Master", ("Der Rechtschaffene Tanzmeister", 1717), that in the years around 1700, the newly made doctor of theology was made the center of a dancing circle consisting of the dean and the professors of the University, with the idea "that thereby some of their wisdom might be imparted to him".

From the mass of material on primitive dancing, we have chosen only the most characteristic types in order to arrive at some understanding of the cultural and philosophic background of the dance as an expression in the life of the peoples. We have noted that in every case the dance is accompanied by some special adornment of the dancer, and at times by a mask. From the colored headdress of feathers and the colorful painting of the naked body, down to the modern evening dresses of our ballrooms and the costumes of our comic operas there are countless variations of dance decoration.

In the mimic dances of the savages we may look for the origin of the mask as an aid in banishing the demon by helping the conjurer to assume the shape of the deity or the evil spirit for whom his incantation is intended. Not only were demons, gods, animals imitated and their shapes assumed, but so were the sun, the stars, the wind, in short all the phenomena of the surrounding world which were to be affected by magic. Even without a mask, the movements of the dance alone had the power to produce a state of ecstasy in the performer, to make him singleminded, or even absolutely unconscious of reality. With the mask he took on an entirely different ego, and for the moment created himself anew, becoming the demon, the deity, the animal and the natural phenomenon in person.

These masks are not measured or proportioned according to realistic standards. We find a gigantic head with an enormous beak and eyes, more like a gas mask of modern times and no less uncanny. Another mask shows a head with an outstretched arm protruding from it. Another, a deformed body, with an arm growing asymmetrically from one side. These nightmares are sometimes like high walking towers, approaching the trembling beholders, frightening them out of their wits.

Commensurate with the importance accorded to the animal in primitive life the animal masks predominate, and the animal dances have continued from the earliest times down to our own days. The comedies of Aristophanes bring us actors disguised as birds and frogs, who speak and dance in chorus. Sachs cites a number of animal dances and describes the seal dance of the Firelanders in detail: "the men, squatting on their haunches, shake up and down, scent the air about them, scratch their chests and armholes and grunt like animals". Not an easy task, even for primitive men!

In medieval times animal dances were also practised: the "Peacock's Tail", (Pfauenschwanz), — the word "tail" (Schwanz) signifies "dance"; — the "Crane's Beak", and many others. The "Pavane" of the 16th century (peacock dance) is originally an animal dance, ("pavoggionare" means to strut about like a peacock). Up to the present time the peasants in South Germany dance a "Hammeltanz", (dance of the bellwether). There is a dance called the "Hen's Scratch" (Huehnerscharre), a "Swallow" — and a "Dove Dance". In Bohemia we still find the "Rak", (crab dance), the "Krocan", (turkey dance), and the "Zaba", (frog dance). A "Cock's Dance" from the carnival in Vienna, of the year 1801, is described in a fashion journal of that period: "On the stated day of the festival, in the middle of the room where the dance is to take place, there is a large cock, decorated with flowers and bright ribbons. The girls who are to take part in the dance are given bouquets of artificial flowers to place on the hats of their partners. After having feasted and drunk well, the girl who is to lead the dance, comes with a large bouquet of flowers, and around the cock, fire crackers are set up and lighted, while the couples line up. The leader gives up her flowers to the second pair, and so on, to the end of the line, until the last cracker around the cock has gone out."

The cock has been a symbol of light and of fire from time immemorial, and in Germany the fire is also called "der rote Hahn" (the red cock), because the bird, with wings outspread and red coxcomb, resembles the rising flame. The Slavs honor the cock as the bird sacred to the Sun-God "Svantewit" (of Saint Vitus). The dance described above is accordingly not only an animal dance, but also a light and fertility dance, and it is no coincidence that the carnival time, the end of the winter solstice, was chosen to perform it.

All peoples of the earth worshipped the sun as the giver of life and light. In the famous Bulgarian fire dance "Nestinari", performers leap into the embers of a great bonfire, and dance in the ashes to the sound of bag pipes and drums, which however have no definite rhythm. Like the dervishes they arrive at a mystically ecstatic condition of trance, in which they sing and scream, beat their hands, tear off their garments, and finally semi-conscious, half dead in the confusion of the assemblage, begin to hold forth, in prophecy. It clearly points to the fact that this is a remnant of ancient Slavic sun-worship, — the tremendous fire, made of 40-50 wagon-loads of wood, and the picture of the sacred saint wrapped in a red shirt.

The Germanic "Yule Festival", the "Sunnenwende", became the Christian feast of St. John, while the Slavic "Svantewit"-feast was transformed into the dances of St. Vitus. The winter solstice is celebrated in Christian countries by the illuminated tree, while the Jews light their "Chanuka lights", around which the children dance. The poet Ludwig Boerne tells how the little Rothschild-fellows in Frankfurt placed candles on the floor and sprang over them as it was the custom among the Jewry (Sachs). In England the theme of the young girls' leap through the fire is found as late as 1686. The object of the leap is to gain wealth or love. Loving couples jump through the fire, hand in hand, and in Bavaria a short song tells how the boys sang:

> "I swing my hat, above, below,
> If you love me,
> Through fire we'll go!"

There is a saying "to go through fire and water for someone" and this test of fire is nothing new, for in the initiation of all tribes, the test of endurance by fire played an important part, even down to its artistic representation in Mozart's "Magic Flute." There Tamino accompanied by his beloved Pamina walks through the fire, not only to prove his ardent passion for her, but to prepare himself for the initiation into the sacred order of Isis.

We must not forget to mention the torch dances which were

danced in Germany, France and Sweden at weddings and were part of the ceremonial prevalent at the courts of the German princes and of the French nobility. In a short pamphlet F. O. Raumer has recorded the practice of these dances at the weddings taking place at the courts of the Prussian Electors. He tells how twelve ministers of the state advanced in pairs carrying burning wax torches before the bride and groom and after several rounds conducted them into the bridal chamber, where the pages took over the torches to light up for the couple. Sweden has a special melody for the torch dance, which is played while the bridal wreath is removed from the bride's head.

The various types of dances enumerated here should serve as a basis for the historic discussion of dance music. Before however, treating this more specifically, it might be useful to deal briefly with the sociological and psychological factors having such an important influence on cultural life, that is the matriarchate and the patriarchate. By the latter we mean that form of society in which property, inheritance and social functions are handed down through the father. Contrary to this, in the matriarchal forms of culture, inheritance through the mother was paramount. In the latter, the child belongs to the clan of the mother, and her eldest brother is its guardian, while in the former, the father's clan takes over the progeny. In our present Western culture, the patriarchal form is the predominant one, even though it has retained a number of matriarchal features, such as amongst others the guardianship of the child through the mother at the father's death. The matriarchate is not unknown in the Bible, and even in the recent giving of names among the Jews of the Eastern European countries we find definite matronymic traces.

Bound up with these forms of social organization we find specific differences in the cultural and religious life of the peoples; we see that where the father commands there is greater stress on many virtues, more aggressiveness, a tendency to nomadic life, there is cattle raising and sunworship, — in one word, — an active and initiatory state of mind. The matriarchates are characterized by sensibility, reflectiveness, agriculture, and the worship of the moon, an emphasis of the milder qualities and female virtues. Keeping in mind Jung's familiar division as he laid down in his book "Psychological Types", distinguishing between the extrovert and the introvert type, we may say that these distinctions correspond in certain ways to the two forms of social organization. The extrovert, open-minded and objective, has its counterpart in the patriarchal form; the introvert, subjective and not dependent on the outer world, leans to the matriarchal form. We may observe that groups controlled by the father tend rather to mimic representation in the dance, while those with matriarchate tendencies incline to non-mimic forms of the dance. (Sachs) The former will perform their steps more violently, leap higher, intending to symbolize and imitate, while the latter will move more soberly and their dance will appear as a mere lyrical expression of emotion. It is a truism that neither of these types of culture is to be found in pure form, but elements of both mingle in the life of all peoples.

Chapter II

THE ORIGIN OF MUSIC

In the preceding chapter we dealt with the philosophic, religious and cultural background of dancing; our next problem is to discuss the origin of dance music, that is to say the origin of music as a whole. The legends of many peoples, no less than the religious myths deal with this. But we wish to mention a number of hypotheses on this problem.

Let us take up, as a first theory, Charles Darwin, and let us not shrink back from trying to seek in his materialistic philosophy of the "survival of the fittest" the roots of music proper. Darwin bases his explanation on the dictum: that the beginning of all is sexual love, i.e. sexual attraction, not the romantic attachment of a Werther, nor the ecstatic transports of a Tristan, but such as exists in the animal kingdom, where the male seeks to charm the female, and the female prefers him who exerts the greatest "charm". For the brightly colored bird, and the most eloquent in song is usually the male, and the law of the jungle gives to the male the dominant role. The question is, however, whether we may in fact designate these tone expressions of the animal as "music". In his book on the origin of music, ("Die Anfaenge der Musik"), Stumpf says that the birds sing at other times as well as during "wooing" and that their calls are often mere signals, or, at times, the expression of an overflowing feeling of buoyancy. He also remarks that the mammals which rank immediately below humans do not sing. Besides, he says, the primitive peoples sing, not only during the time of mating, but to accompany warlike and religious activities. The most important argument against the Darwinian point of view is the recognition of the fact

13

that music does not signify merely the simple production of sounds, but implies their succession and arrangements according to certain definite laws. At this point we may have recourse to the "Gestalt-Theorie", such as it was advanced by Mach, Ehrenfels, and Wertheimer, among others. A "Gestalt" is shaped, when a number of stimuli, as for example several successive sound stimuli strike the ear, and we experience not only a number of disconnected tones, but obtain a concept of "melody", because of the certain succession of these tones. This peculiar quality, which distinguishes a melody from a mere succession of single tones, was defined as "Gestaltsqualitaet" by Christian von Ehrenfels. In laying down his principle of what constitutes a "Gestalt", he emphasized that its quality is independent of its parts, so that for example the "Gestalt" of a square is always the same irrespective of its size, its situation, and its color. The succession of the sounds C-D-E is essentially different from the succession of the sounds D-E-C or C-E-D, in spite of the fact that the same tones are used. But it resembles the "Gestalt" of C sharp, D sharp, E sharp, though on the latter the tones themselves are not the same. Only the ability to recognize a succession of tones, to be able to transpose them, is that which determines whether the producer of the music is musical or not. This ability to transpose is found among all the primitive peoples, but not• among the animals. A parrot or a trained starling are not able to transpose a melody which has been sung to them though at times slight changes in the absolute pitch are possible. The calls of the birds are usually somewhat lower in pitch when there has been fatigue but this is a purely physiological phenomenon. And music is in fact created only where a succession of tones has assumed "Gestalt", both as a creation, and as a reproduction. To create a "gestalt" is however, a purely human ability and therefore the Darwinian theory deriving music from the call of the birds has been repudiated both by philosophers and musicologists.

Another theory, propounded by Herbert Spencer, lays down as its axiom that "in the beginning was the word." Accordingly, music grew out of the accents and the rise and fall of the human voice. If there is the stress of excitement, when someone is called with a loud voice, speech turns into musical tones, and these tones severed from words are subsequently made independent and transferred to instruments. Such is the theory of Spencer. It is indisputable that primitive peoples use a kind of chant, and there are numerous instances when speech turns to song and, conversely, song becomes mere talking. Every modern opera and "lieder" singer knows that, and is aware of greater effectiveness through such alternations. (But it is a matter of common knowledge that this combination of speech and music in the so-called "melodrama" is aesthetically inferior and was not able to persist as an artistic form of musical expression.) Besides, we must never forget that the melodics of speech and those of music are intrinsically different. For in every expression of speech the scale of tones is sometimes such that the lowest tone is separated from the highest by two octaves. Note for example when the greeting "Hello" is called out. Without the least exertion of the muscles of the larynx, twelfths or double-octaves are spoken, not sung. Language has no distinct intervals like music, only sliding, gradual differences. This is the basic distinction between language and music.

In spite of this, cases may occur where music is strongly subject to the influence of words. The songs of Schubert and of Hugo Wolf, and the Wagner operas show clearly how each rise and fall of the voice in declaiming the poem, has its corresponding melodic value in the song.

The most striking example of the dependence of music on spoken words is found, strangely enough, in the dance rhythms of some nations, as for instance, in those of the Czechs. The wealth of consonants of the Czech language brings about a jerky and explosive speech. This type of voice expression in words is closely reproduced in the vivid, eruptive types of their dance themes, which we will discuss further on.

And yet, in spite of all this, music did not originate in the spoken word, for the emotion aroused by the harmonious succession or combination of thirds, fifths, and octaves, has nothing to do with the reaction, aroused by language, the intervals of which follow entirely different laws and principles.

Another axiom on the origin of music is to be sought in the words of Hans von Buelow: "Rhythm first" or rather "in the beginning was action". The economist Carl Buecher in his book on "Work and Rhythm" (Arbeit und Rhythmus) tried to find the origin of music in the rhythmically aligned expressions of sound which accompany regulated and orderly physical labor. The ethnologist Ratzel, in discussing the working methods of primitive man said that the savage does not do less work than the civilized human being, but he performs his task at random, according to his mood as it were. Guglielmo Ferrero pointed out the same as Ratzel. While cultured peoples have definite objects in view of all their activities, those of the savages — for example in their dances — are more or less automatic, requiring only the initial effort to set the muscles in motion. Once that is done, each movement will call forth another, without further directives given by the will, and the swiftness of the movements will increase automatically and proportionally with the excitement of the dancer. There is no doubt that the automatic movement at the beginning of a dance brings about a narrowing of the field of consciousness, and that the repetition of equal rhythms has the same effect on the awareness of the subject, the effect of a narcotic, tending to decrease consciousness and awareness. That decrease in the consciousness is pleasurable, is a well-known fact.

When several persons perform a dance simultaneously, imitating the movements of an animal or performing a magic rite, around a sacred object, they will tend to perform an equal gesture not only because such similarity is exacted by the traditional character of the rite, but also because a repetition of motions represent a saving of energy as well as retract the field of consciousness, therefore being pleasurable. It is easier to march "in time" when there are others also doing it, because the single pedestrian is always tempted to interrupt his pace with a rest. Buecher cites many examples where a common task performed by many in unison and in a regulated way, is much easier than when performed in an unregulated manner. Collectivism of work brings about that the forces of the weaker among the workmen grow and that thus he is compelled not only to fit himself into the whole, but also to give "the best" he can of his strength. And this is accomplished by the afore mentioned narrowing of consciousness which is the result of the narcotic influence of a monotonous rhythm. This is the origin of thousands of "work songs" which accompanied the work in the fields, the rowing, the lifting, the hoisting of anchors, the driving of nails by the smiths. There is much to be said for this theory, but one cannot designate as music the noise of the tools raised and lowered in unison, nor the sighs of the slaves driven to work by the cracks of the whip. Surely, such rhythmically organized work played its part in the foundation of musical expression but Buecher cannot tell us when "Die holde Kunst", as Schubert sings, — music as we know it — crystallized from these early beginnings. The third theory therefore must be dismissed as an insufficient explanation.

We must not forget that only a small part of the Primitives' songs and dances were work songs and dances. By far the larger part is rooted in religious practices, in the songs of the priests and medicine men, in love and wooing songs and in magic incantations.

Of all the hypotheses which have been formulated concerning the origin of music, it seems to me that the one proposed by Stumpf is the most plausible. Stumpf puts the question thus: "What do we understand by the term music?", and answers it as follows: "It is the art, the material of which consists of stable yet transposable tone intervals". If that is the case, our first question must be: "How did one ever come to transpose?" For "this question deals with the ability to abstract, to recognize impressions dealing with the time and space, irrespective of their absolute relation to each other. This ability to abstract, to form concepts, is an exclusive human quality. And together with the power to form concepts comes the power to transpose. This constitutes the general intellectual and psychological background of music". (In this respect Stumpf follows the "Gestalten Theorie").

Among the many causes that give impetus to the formation of musical tones, such as excited speaking, the simultaneous speech of many or the noise of tools at work, we also find the giving of signals. If one tries to give a signal to another person, to span a great distance, the voice rises to a high tone, which is lowered as the power of the lungs decreases from the exertion sustained.

The yodeling and hellohing of the shepherds in the mountains are examples also. If several people call at the same time because the voice of a single man is not sufficient, and if among these there are men, women, boys and girls, tones of a different pitch will arise. This is the origin of polyphony. Among these polyphonic combinations there is one, the octave, which because of the relationship of the vibration of both its tones, is the most remarkable one. Their parts are so much alike that they are almost unrecognizable. Stumpf calls this quality: "Verschmelzbarkeit". (Fusibility.) The dualism of the human body which is characterized in time by the rise and fall of breathing, in space by the symmetry of vision, finds its corresponding manifestation in the realm of sound in the basic position of the octave. Records have been made which have shown that 75% of all men consider the octave but a single tone, while only 40-60% do this in the case of the fifth, and 28-36% with regard to the fourth.

The remarkable fusibility of certain tones (when played simultaneously) is a part of their quality, quite aside from their absolute pitch, and therefore makes them particularly suitable for transposition. And Stumpf believes that as soon as the differences between these simultaneously produced sounds had been recognized, the next step was to sing them in succession (octaves, fifths, fourths, occasionally also thirds,) a tendency also furthered by the instinctive playfulness common to all men. The intervals were then bridged by interpolated sounds.

There are, in fact, primitive peoples whose entire music moves in small intervals, as for example the Veddas in Ceylon. In this case we have the distance principle of narrow intervals as contrasted with the consonant principle of wide intervals (octave, fifth and fourth).

In summing up, it ought to be granted that all the theories enumerated contribute their share to the solution of the problem involved. As the most intricate and complicated product of a complicated organism, music cannot be reduced to a simple formula of origin. Though signalling and work may play their parts in giving rise to certain musical forms, they cannot be its sole and basic foundation. Though speech cannot possibly be the mother of music, it has this in common with it, that both have been born out of the deepest districts of human expression, and sourced and dominated by nature, gods and demons.

And this brings us back to that music whose essence is incantation, and religious rite.

Among all the various appliances for religious rituals and the working of magic, musical instruments are by far the most important. Just as essential as the mask, which is used as a means of identification with the world of gods and of demons, the musical instrument is the voice, the sounding manifestation and personification of the spirit who is feared or worshipped. The tone of the instrument by itself already works the charm, it is the inexplicable miracle, the all and ever-present spirit. For in these early stages of human development the musical instrument is by no means an implement for artistic production. Its tone calls forth or banishes the spirits, it conjures up events and natural phenomena and altogether assumes an importance in the life of men which civilized beings of our own times find hard to conceive. Indeed, tone in those days had a material, not merely an aesthetic significance. If the tone is described as "hollow", it was so, not only symbolically but actually, because it was felt so, because it came from a hollow body, producing sound. The drum with its muffled tone had female significance for its hollow space was in their imagination taken for the female body. In the cultural groups emphasizing the matriarchate, the drum was beaten with the hand, not with a stick. Only in the patriarchal tribes beating with the drumstick was developed, where drumstick and phallus were related. And there the hollow, dark and muffled tone grew lighter in quality. The drum's covering of animal skin varies according to the prevalent type of culture: In the matriarchal pattern of social life we find the use of fish and serpent skins, in the patriarchal tribes of hunters and cattle-raisers we have the skins of mammals, particularly of the animal dominating the tribe, of the totem animal. Thus the acoustic mask, the instrument, acts like the facial mask, imparting magical power. And our memories which are called up by the hollow, muffled sound of the drum hark back to immemorial times when it meant death and rebirth. Up to our own day, the drum has remained the instrument of funeral music, and as we listen with deep emotion to the funeral marches in Beethoven's "Eroica", or in Wagner's "Goetterdaemmerung", we do not realize the true sources of our feelings.

In primitive times, the flute was the symbol of the Phallus and at the same time the music instrument used at the initiation rites. It was even recognized as such by Mozart and his librettist Schikaneder, when they intuitively chose the flute to become the instrument of the hero's initiation in the "Magic Flute" for the flute is to express the idea of rebirth, of revival from death, corresponding to the Masonic background of this opera.

The flute for a long time was only played by men, and in former times we rarely find girls using it, except perhaps in that Greek tale, where the goddess seeing her image in the water, as she played the flute, is shocked at her appearance, and throws it away. Today the flute is the instrument of love, of serenades, of "night music", expressive of tenderness and longing, though no one may be thinking of the original significance attached to its shape.

The hornshaped wind instruments have developed from the horns of the totem animals. The sacred and holy character of these instruments clearly come to light in the practice of the ancient Jewish rite of sounding the "shofar" on the days of the New Year and of Atonement, as well as on the days of the new moon. The new moon, that is the darkness of the moonless nights, is to be banished by the sounds of the instrument. Likewise, the walls of Jericho are to be rebuilt by the sound from seven horns, blown by priests. Here we have the struggle of light with darkness, and the triumph of light, the force incorporated in the sound of the horn, bearer of the strength of the sacred animal. In fact all these "lighter" tones of brasses, the trombones, trumpets and horns, are the typical manly ones. These instruments were later to become the heralds of kings and heroes, the beckoners to the hunt and to the tournament.

The origin of the violin is the "musical bow", a flexible bent staff, the ends of which were joined by a string. Often the bows were fixed on a hollow gourd (the holy womb of the mother). Sachs believes that the musical bow originated from the ancient, primitive ground zither, which consisted of a string strung across the membrane fastened over a shallow hole in the ground. And since the immemorial time, harps, zithers, and violins have been considered to be the soft, emotional instruments in contrast to the strong and war-like sounds of trumpets and horns. That the tremendous development of instrumental music in Western civilization is based on the sound of the strings has its deeper meaning. Namely to the fact that this our culture of refinement pays homage to women, the spirit of the gentle teachings of Christendom. We think that the delights of the spirit as expressed in philosophy and in science, cannot be expressed better than by tones of the stringed instruments.

It is clear that these differences between masculine and feminine cultures, between intro- and extrovert peoples must also express themselves in the dance. Masculine cultures, where the people indulge in war and hunting dances, are active, aggressive and bound to the material world around them, have mimic, imitative dances. Introvert, female cultures practice but less violent dances. In these latter dances imitation is negligible.

While the masculine peoples have wide and abrupt gestures, the others have restrained ones and their dances are more self-contained and slower. This duality of the dance forms expresses itself also in the melodic line of the dance. The patriarchal tribes seem to have preferred wide intervals, the matriarchal, that is the introvert ones, narrow intervals.

Stumpf gives a number of examples of these two types: The Wanyamwezi of Central East Africa dance with wild leaps and their melodies move in fourths and fifths, even sevenths and tenths are not unusual. He also states that the Pueblo Indians are extraordinarily "wide" in their melodic line.

As has been mentioned previously, the introvert peoples, like the Veddas of Ceylon, use correspondingly narrow intervals, and dance with small steps.

In the course of time, the heroic and manly brass instruments (horns, trumpets and trombones) with their wide intervals became the symbols of masculine feelings whereas, string instruments and woodwinds (the latter because of their shape originally male instruments) represented introvert (female) mentality with regard to their soft smooth and tender sound. Likewise, strong (masculine) peoples—as for instance inhabitants of mountainous countries (Bavarians, Austrians, etc.)— prefer wide steps and intervals in contrast to more introvert peoples of higher culture.

Dance forms, melodic lines and instruments keep step from the very first beginnings of culture until our own modern times of elaborate and complicated refinements of all varieties of artistic expression.

CHAPTER III.

DANCE MUSIC IN PRIMITIVE, CLASSIC, AND
NON-EUROPEAN CULTURES.

THE music of the primitive peoples, as well as that of the
highly cultivated Chinese, Japanese, Javanese, Persians and
Arabs has one characteristic in common with that of the ancient
Hellenes, that is monophony. This is true in spite of the fact
that polyphonic forms and light traces of imitations, yes, even
canons, are found occasionally in the music of African tribes
and a strange form of polyphony is noted in Javanese and in
Siamese music. As a whole this music presents a striking
contrast to the occidental polyphony as the last centuries have
shaped it. Oswald Spengler with good reason called this western art form a Faustian, Gothic, dynamic and limitless art, and
contrasted it with the static, narrowly limited art of sculpture
as it was practiced in ancient Greece. The man of this period,
knowing only a plain geometry, and seeing his gods as beings
with human qualities, painting without any application of
perspective, has music that moves along one plane, is static
and monophonic. Contrasted with this, the New Time created
the Holy Roman Empire, and turned its glance westward to
new worlds. We in the western world see how machinery is
made subject matter, integral and infinitesimal mathematics are
developed, perspective painting created, and a music of three
dimensions, a polyphonic art, based on the system of the triad.

We must guard against putting the music of the primitive
peoples into the same class as that of the Eastern civilized
nations, such as the Chinese, the Hindus and the Javanese.

23

Nevertheless, all the music systems of Western peoples have certain common characteristics. First and foremost, their music mostly is recorded by tradition, not by notation, which has brought about the eternal cleavage between the composing and the reproducing musician in the western world. The western musician creates a unique and unchangeable work of art, fixed and preserved by its notation. Not so the oriental performer, a musician who creates and executes simultaneously, and at each presentation recreates his work with renewed force, letting it dominate his whole being for the moment. To the oriental man, music is religion, magic and material life, and is as much part of him as are his customs, his headdress and his "demon". It becomes the immediate and direct expression of his character and his temperament. How definitely characteristic is the type of different racial groups. . . Anyone can remark it in watching the movements of an Italian, for example, as contrasted with those of an Englishman; or of a Hungarian in juxtaposition with those of a Swede . . . All the more this is true speaking of the primitive peoples whose folk character is so much better preserved than that of the civilized groups, where the uniformity demanded by social life has stifled development.

The music of the American Indians is a true picture of their racial character. The German ethnologist Herbert Baldus who wrote "Studies on the Indians in the Northeastern Chaco", compared the temperament of the tribes of that region with "their wild dance-leaping, the powerful swinging of rattles, and the violent singing" with that of those tribes of Indians whose dance is a "hesitating seemingly tired walking to and fro". Their musical instruments "sound muted, the flutes are never shrill, and even their war-horn never sounds louder than a child's trumpet".

Musicologists have rightly seen and ascertained that the formation of melody is closely tied up with the racial character of a people.

The following excerpt from a "Dirge of the Hopi Indians" (recorded by Stumpf) proves with its range of eleven tones and its irregularity of rhythm characteristics of wild Indian

music and ardent dances not only possess a wide range of tones, but also a most irregular rhythm; the same is true of their dancers: their movements are large, their music is performed with excessive force, and the change from loud to soft plays an important part. The voices chime in on the high notes with a fortissimo, the low notes are scarcely audible. Sometimes the musical tone passes over into a veritable cry. Wherever the voice sets in the excited breathing is definitely noticeable. To return to the problem of intervals: A true narrow melody is found on the American continent in the music of the Firelanders. In their manner of delivery the Firelanders show their kinship with that of the other Indian groups, but, whereas the majority of the American natives employ descending fourths and fifths as skipped intervals, or with one to two inserted tones, and have a large range of tones in the melody itself,—the melodic system of the Firelanders is confined to a narrow tone range. The Yamanas on Fire Islands sing and dance to this melody at the initiation rites of their young

men. They call it the "song of the shark". These Indians are still among the most primitive of their race. Non-American primitive tribes, such as the Kubu of Sumatra, or the Vedda of Ceylon have the same degree of culture, as well as the same type of music. Physically these groups have in common small stature and correspondingly a typical musical style. We might call it "dwarf music."

The following typically poor and primitive duet of the Kubu is taken from Hornbostel's "Music of the Kubu Tribe". This "eagle" melody is sung by a man and a woman in a kind of recitative, with a rhythm strongly under the influence of the prosody of the text, which possibly determines the rhythm completely. Perhaps we have here an illustration of Spencer's theory, seeking the origin of music in language.

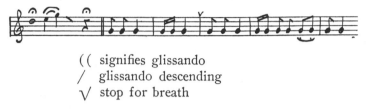

((signifies glissando
/ glissando descending
√ stop for breath

The following dance melody, poor in range of tones, is sung by the Tehueltshe Indians in Patagonia: It does not go beyond

a small third and is like the Indian melodies with its descending line. The tribe having the meagerest group of tones are the dwarfed Veddas of Ceylon. They are so undeveloped musically that they possess no instruments, not even percussion instruments. Their musical poverty may be a sign of their low development. A similar cultural phase is seen among the Andamanese and the Papuas in New Guinea, and Hornbostel believes that all these "tone-poor" tribes belong to a cultural group of which the South-Eastern Australians are the chief representatives and traces of which are found in South Asia (Andamanese), on the Fire Islands and in Central California.

The first traces of polyphonic composition are found already in the music of the Indians. Dixon writing in his "Voyage round the World" in 1789, describes a dance song of the Sitka Indians living north of Vancouver. In trading for furs

he witnessed a dance performed at the closing of the transac-
tion during which for over half an hour there was singing
accompanied by rhythmical clapping of hands and beats of a
drum, by swinging of rattles, and the gestures of the chief.
Apparently the object was to drive away the evil spirits of
a bad bargain! Stumpf considers this record of the dance

authentic and correct and we have here surely one of the oldest
records of Indian dance music. The theme of the chief is
repeated several times on lower C. The melody of the chorus
accompanies it in unison at times, at others ornaments it on a
tone sustained by the chief, descending at the same time and at
the close arriving at the lowest dominant and from that again
to the tonic. We should however be wary of using these
modern harmonic concepts in analysing primitive pieces of
music. Stumpf classified this primitive polyphonic style as
so-called "Heterophony", an early form of polyphonic treatment, in which the principal part is surrounded and ornamented
by several secondary parts.

It is interesting to note that corresponding to the simple
dance songs of the Firelanders, we find a simple treatment of

songs among the Eskimos, while, in the central regions we came upon the above mentioned abrupt and large intervals. That easier conditions of life and a higher standard of living make for a richer musical development, is quite apparent.

But let us examine briefly the music of the wild African tribes: It is definitely and often influenced by European music types, especially along the coast, and shows greater signs of progress than that of the Indians who retained, for the most part, the traditional primitive forms. The most characteristic quality of African music is the artistic form of its rhythmic polyphony, in which it often excels that of civilized peoples.

Primitive peoples, when they speak or sing, are manifesting merely constituent parts of an all-embracing motor process. When Western peoples sing, — gestures and movements are less important. Among primitives, however, tone and movement are one and inseparable. As the body moves during the dance, larynx, feet, and hands are set in motion, and stamping of feet and clapping of hands are the original and natural accompaniment, giving the rhythm. They are the ancestors of the drumbeat. The rhythmic accompaniment of Indian music is comparatively simple with the drum beating more or less ad libitum during the singing. The African negroes, however, had the xylophon imported from South East Asia and made it play an important role in the accompaniment of their songs. The following chorus is reported by Lachmann (Handbuch der Musikwissenschaft, on page 11). It is a chorus, with accompaniment of the xylophon, of the Negro tribe of Cameroon. The

unschooled listener tries to find for this phrase a rhythmic principle which he draws from his own western concepts of music. Involuntarily he tends to form some kind of larger unit from simple temporal relations, as for example, two, four or eight measures. We shall come upon such temporal relations in the music of the Chinese and we also find them in Indian music. However, these simple temporal relations are by no means a sign of "primitive form", on the contrary, they point much more frequently to a long course of music evolution. The rhythmic figures of the Negroes and of the tribes of the Near and Middle East exhibit a much more complicated relation between the various rhythmic motives. Certain simple and dignified gestures and movements of the Indians have correspondingly simple temporal relations. The much more passionate and less balanced gesticulation of the Negro, however, calls for the more complicated rhythmic elaboration which keeps both the player and the hearer in continuous tension.

The ever recurring drum themes of the Africans have been compared to the European bassi ostinati, but should properly be put side by side with the unvarying melodic skeletons of the Hindoos, which are called "Ragas" by them, "maquams" by the Arabs, and "Patets" by the Javanese. Perhaps there is some connection between these forms. All these musical forms have in common the following characteristics: music is considered by all these peoples as an elemental force, music and the mythical world of their gods are closely related. The primitive tribes believe that their instruments are sacred and the civilised Asiatic peoples consider them as the gifts of their gods. Where the savage believes that music can produce natural phenomena, the Asiatic credits melody with a cosmic power. We find traces of these beliefs even as late as in the Pythagorean doctrine of the music of the spheres.

In the writings recorded about 100 A.D. by the Chinese concerning their sacred rites, called the "Li ki", we find the following passage: "Music is that whereby everything in heaven and on earth is measured, it is the basic principle of balance and of harmony; human emotions cannot but be swayed by it". The strict observance of rules, the adherence to tradition which is the practice in the ritual dances of the Chinese, thus not only serves as a hand-maiden to the harmony of the universe, but has its task in controlling human passions. In this respect the Chinese as well as the oriental conception of music join hands with that of the ancient Greeks who considered that music was above all a matter of ethical import. Chinese authors speak of the custom to diminish the number of strings of certain instruments and the omission of certain tones when these instruments were used to accompany singing, so that the soul might not be stirred up dangerously.

The chief mark of distinction between the tone productions of the primitive peoples and that of the civilized nations of Asia, is the fact that the latter evolved musical scales and systems. This was partly due to the greater development of the instruments used, partly to the greater emphasis put on cosmic speculative thinking. The Eastern and South Eastern peoples of Asia, China, Japan, Burma, Siam and the Indian Archipelago play with scales consisting in the main of five tones, (Pentatonic scales). Added to the five melodic main tones we have five helping or transition tones, (pien). There exist a number of scales, some without half tones, (for example scales beginning with F) : that is F. G. A. C. D., others with two half tone intervals, (for example F. G. A flat, C. D. flat). A scale without half tones can be formed if one progress in perfect fifths to the fifth tone, for example: F. C. G. D. A., i.e. F. G. A. C. D. In many Scotch, Irish, Scandinavian and Slavic melodies we are apt to find such pentatonic structure.

Ancient Chinese music is no longer extant in China, except perhaps in the far-off lands, in the solemn hymns and festival choruses at the courts of Korea and of Japan. Its outlines, however, have been preserved in the melodies of the Chinese stage and of the street singers, who employ the pentatonic melody without half-tones, and the multiple rhythm of two beats. Particularly on the Chinese stage, which ought really to be designated as an operatic rather than a dramatic one, do we find these old forms with the dialogue interrupted by hundreds of arias executed to the accompaniment of flutes (Ti-tse), three-stringed guitars (San-hsien), percussion instruments and songs.

In the fifth century, down through the seventh, Japan received the basic forms of its music from Korea and from China. Instruments, tone systems, theory and melodies, as well as manner of delivery do not differ essentially from Chinese music. But the rigid and severe rules governing musical production were relaxed. The melodic system remained pentatonic,

the half-tone interval not employed in China was introduced and through the time remained a multiple of two, it was frequently interrupted by a free recitative. Both China and Japan draw a sharp distinction between sacred (gagoku) and profane music. Ritual music was to be performed by male professional musicians and female roles only played by male actors who, in taking these parts evolved that characteristic shrill and raucous tone, a falsetto, which is so characteristic of the vocalists of China and Japan. The pentatonic half-tone-scale is the

skeleton, as it were, of this piece, which is declaimed by the Samisen, the East-Asiatic guitar and around which the voice of the singer weaves its theme. This kind of interweaving and intertwining of a main part by another, this kind of heterophonic treatment, as Stumpf calls it (borrowing the expression from Plato) was already mentioned. The ear of the Western listener often finds much that is unpleasant in these combinations. But as the oriental people have no notion of the laws governing the triad system, they are not in the least disturbed by this kind of music. There is a fundamental difference between the polyphony of the Eastern and primitive peoples and that of the western world. The European combinations of tones follow one another according to the principle of dissonance and consonance, with the tension of dissonance resolved by the distension, the relief of consonance. This western harmonic system based on tension has in recent years, especially in the music called "atonal" given way to a, so to speak absolute, harmonic system. And many musicologists believe that this evolution of western music was in part influenced by primitive musical concepts.

But let us return to the dance music of the Japanese. In that country the priestesses of Shinto still perform the ancient holy Kagura dances in which old Japanese legends are represented dramatically. From these ancient religious festivals as they were practised in the 15th century there grew the so-called "No" plays. The authors and impersonators in these dramas were members of the aristocracy or of the upper priesthood. The form of these dramas is either operatic or ballet-like and they contain dialogue, music and dancing. Each of these "No" plays lasts about an hour, the actors make no attempt to be naturalistic; gesture, language and vocal music are highly stylised. Eight members of a chorus, clad in extravagant ceremonial robes advance with peculiar halting and dragging gait with flute and drum players, on to the stage and in the manner of the Chorus of Greek tragedy explain to the audience what is about to happen. Thereupon the impersonators appear in wooden masks, the design of which is laid down by tradition. In these No-plays we have the foundation of the Japanese drama, called "Joruri". Originally it consisted merely of the recitation of the poet who accompanied the rhythm of his verses by beats of the fan which he held; later the fan was supplanted by the guitar (shamisen), and the actors took over the representation of the personages. In the 17th century human impersonators were banished from the stage, which gave rise to the Japanese puppet plays.

Music plays a most important role in all forms of the Japanese drama, accompanying the whole performance. Two musicians make up the orchestra, and — hidden in the wings — they take turns at playing the various instruments. At times one of them plucks the shamisen, utters sounds that sound like a dirge, or gives commands in a military tone of voice. At times the other accompanies the appearance of the chief personages with singing, while dancing is going on, and plays on the percussion instruments. There are three drums of different sizes, (one of them called Odaiko, the other two Taikos), two gongs, (Dora), a small set of carillons, (Orimoro), a small gong, (Kaimeh), a bell shaped like our small table bells, (Wle), a pair of castanets, (Ki), and besides these a somewhat larger reed-pipe, (Takefuye), and a small metal whistle, (Musifuye). The two castanets beat together with a sharp tone, equivalent to our signals to call the actors out on the stage, and at their sound the curtain is raised or lowered.

When we come to the highly civilised cultural life on Java and the Indian Archipelago we see that it consists of several layers, superimposed on the original Malayan foundation, for since the fourth century A.D., the Hindoos held sway there, leaving behind them the mighty architectural remnants of their civilisation. From the 15th or 16th centuries the Mohammedans ruled the land, and after them, from 1597 until now, the Dutch conquerors. This counterpoint of four different cultural spheres has its corresponding form in the music of the islands, above all in the variety of their instruments and different pitches, in the wealth of specific musical forms, in the melodic treatments used, in the rhythms employed and in the polyphonic richness of their music. (Hornbostel)

The Chinese pentatonic scale, without halftones, was tempered in Java, that is: all whole tones and small third intervals were levelled off, so that all intervals became equalized (5/4 tones). Notwithstanding, we hear the intervals to which we are accustomed though they sound somewhat out of tune. The

Javanese call this mode the Slendro Mode but at the same time they also employ a heptatonic tone system "Pelog" with whole and half tones. In these modes, often used together, in which the melody is pentatonic, and the accompanying parts are heptatonic the famous orchestras of Java, called "Gamelan", play for their audience. These orchestras are adored like sacred bands, and their conductors are recruited from among the noblest families. Indeed, one may rightly call them one of the seven miracles of the East. The single voices bearing hetero-phonic relation to one another, are therefore somewhat prim-itive in their polyphony. But their charming, often magical tones, seem to conjure up some modern impressionistic tone picture, and often remind one of Debussy's music. Hornbostel gives us the orchestration of such a Javanese composition in the introduction to his collection of records.

We find Javanese culture and Javanese music in this form on the island of Bali, where we can witness ecstatic dances, as for example the "sitting dance" — Djanger, danced with ardent and exhausting passion. In this recently-introduced dance, the participants sit in rows around a square, the men opposite each other on two sides, the women on the two other sides. The leader of the dance in the middle of the hollow square glances about him wildly. In response the others throw back the upper part of their body, swaying to and fro under his hypnotic power. A monotonous motive of the drums and the dragging melody of the Rebab, the Arabian fiddle, complete the hypnosis. In broken tense rhythms the men in chorus repeat loudly a sort of song which interrupts the monotony of the instruments. Sitting dances are also the custom in Samoa.

Siam is the connecting link between Eastern Asia and the islands of the Indian Ocean. Its melodic system and its rhythms are borrowed from those of China, its tonal system, its use of instruments and of the orchestra, comes from Java. (Horn-bostel). Here we find the heptatonic scale in tempered form and the octave divided into seven equal "neutral" intervals.

In British India, however, we see the bridge between the

Near- and the Far East. We find that the original music pre-vailing here is interfused with Arabic and Persian elements and with the melodic types mentioned above as "ragas", "maquams" and "patets". On the whole oriental and all prim-itive music is governed by certain typical melodies. The musician therefore cannot dispose of the tones of his special register to form with them any and all melodic arrangements that may occur to him, although he may dispose of a limited number of different melodic types and skeleton arrangements, which are not distinguished by a definitely observed succession of tones, but rather by their movement. These various arrangements constitute the material with which he can work, and the rhythm he must use runs parallel with the given form or type. These "ragas" and "maquams", have according to the Oriental view, magic significance, and the melodic type is sacred and unalter-able. There is an Indian legend which tells of a virtuoso who recklessly broke the law of the "ragas", but was finally brought to repent of his misdeeds by the god who showed him in a dream his tortured melodies in the shape of human figures with broken limbs. The magic power of these typical melodies reaches so far that we see them indissolubly connected with certain seasons and certain hours of the day. Certain ones may only be sung in the open air, others only indoors, and woe to the artist who dares disobey the immutable law! The ancient Greeks who possessed similar ideas concerning the use of melodic types, according to the variation of the ethical signifi-cance of the melody, distinguished between the Lydian, Dorian, and Phrygian mode. And we may add to these the "neginoth" of the Jewish ritual songs. In more recent times, the trouba-dours, the minnesingers, and the mastersingers of the medieval towns, distinguished likewise between the different modes, — these were the last European remainders of the Oriental skel-etons.

Should, however, musicologists assert that the ragas and maquams are characteristic of Oriental music only, we may say that even in our modern Western musical practice there are certain observances resembling those of the Eastern musical world. For our composers, too, cannot arbitrarily decide upon the succession of tones within the limit of the tonal system, they must follow certain, in part unwritten laws of the art of forming melody. The German Bach has quite another style than the contemporary French Rameau, and the difference between them constitutes the difference in "National Style". But the German Bach writes different tone successions than the German Mozart because he is of an earlier time, and even within his own creative work, we find the same difference in style between his piano works, his organ pieces and his masses. For each work demands its own style.

But let us return to India. We know a good deal of the dances which play such an important part in Hindoo mythology, for instance the dance of the "Asparasas", the heavenly maidens, and that passionate round dance of the gods in the cosmic ocean and the cosmic matter itself. Through the wild dance of the gods the atoms were sent whirling and the world created. So great was the magic power of this dance that not only the earth appeared, but the sun hidden heretofore, now entered the universe. This is the idea of the birth of the universe from the dance. Baharata, the fabulous creator of the art of acting arranged the first dramatic representation in the presence of the gods themselves. These dramas consisted of simple dancing (nritta), of mimic dancing (nritya) — that is pantomime, and of pantomime accompanied by singing (natya). Dancing was considered part of the education of the aristocracy and at the courts of the kings there were special schools for dancing. The female dancers, however, were recruited from among the courtesans; and even now the sacred dancers (called "Dewo-dasi") serve both the deity and erotic purposes. Rooted in an early form of prostitution connected with the temples, the dance of these "priestesses" assumed ever more exhibitionistic and orgiastic forms.

We know very little of the old Hindoo dance music but we know to what kind of music people dance in India today. Just as the forms of the dances differ in the North and in the South, so does the character of the music. The North has been influ-

enced by the Islam, and the Near Eastern elements, the South
has certain points of contact with the Far East and Melanesia.
The scales approach the Arabic forms of music because of the
raising of the ascending tones and the diminishing of the
descending ones.

The following example is the instrumental prelude of a
vocal piece from North India, accompanied by string instruments
and a hand drum. It is from Lachmann's "Musik des Orients".

Indian music reflects something of the vastness of the time
element in the country's history, the immensity of the mountains and the immeasurable extent of the landscape. It is at
the same time impressive and soulful. Eternity and immorality
join with contemplative reflection and inwardness, and we find
in it a measure of introversion as we do nowhere else. Fox
Strangways in his work on the music of the Hindustani tells
of a Hindoo's opinion: "An important characteristic of Indian
music is its reserve and consequently all unhampered expression
of emotional states is eliminated. Our gay and our sad moods
are often intertwined, our passionate turns are not able to carry
away foreign hearers. It is the kind of music that may contain
deepest, heartfelt joy, but it is a reposeful, not a proclaiming
kind of music, it leads us to reflect rather than to act".

Contrasted with the pentatonic steps of the Far East we
have the diatonic-chromatic successions of the Arabs. They
divide the fourth either diatonically (A B C D), or chromatically (A - B flat, C sharp - D). This chromatic succession
gives an impression of tension because of the uneven intervals.
But these are merely the main directions of the musical system.
On the two most important instruments which these people use,
the "Ud" (a short lute), and the "Tanbur" (a long lute), the
player can dispose of a large variety of tones. The Arabian-
Islamic artistic music, more than any other music of the Orient

looks for the intoxicating and exciting, rather than for the soothing and comforting. While the ideal of the Chinese musician is to practice restraint and self-control, the Arabian tries to bring himself and his audience into a kind of fury of intoxication. This is particularly true of the dances of the dervishes. Solemnly the monks pace around a square, counter clock-wise, while they bow, turn, and make strange steps. Then they form two circles, a small and a large one, and in each of these they turn with outstretched arms on their heels, while the oldest one among them walks to and fro between them. A monotonous, fascinating and hypnotically exciting music induces a kind of trance, the dancers lose consciousness of reality, and as they invoke Allah and the Prophet, they seem to be possessed by the Spirit. The whole ceremony seems to resemble an ancient astral dance-ritual. The music for such a dance during which the dancers continue to pronounce the word Allah in a short motive, to the point of exhaustion, is recorded by Hornbostel.

The Arabs are a people particularly fond of dancing and of music. Every occasion, whether in public or in private life is celebrated with the accompaniment of music. The female dancers in the coffee houses of Cairo and of Tunis dance and sing to the sound of European Kemange and Arabian violins (Rebab), of guitars (Knitra), zithers (Qanum), tambourines (Tar), and drums (Darabukke).

Even though we are fairly informed about the dances of the ancient Greeks, we have little knowledge of the music to which these dances were performed. Of the eleven musical pieces from Hellenic times which have been preserved, the greater parts are hymns, and only two short fragments are instrumental music. We are therefore reduced to mere conjectures if we are to discuss Greek dance music.

Already in Homer, we find the round dance of the young men or the young girls described in detail. Crete seems to have been a sort of center point for the practice of dancing, and the legend tells how, on his return from Crete to Athens, Theseus danced on the island of Delos with the liberated youths and maidens in a round, using the "crane step". It is interesting to observe that in Chinese legends there is talk of a "crane dance" during which young boys and girls are sacrificed; apparently this was connected with some fertility or re-incarnation ceremonial dance, (because of the phallic symbol of the crane).

It was the Dorians who developed the dances with weapons, performed by males; these were called "Pyrrhiche" and were both combat- and diversion dances. The pantomimic dances in honor of Dionysos laid the foundation for the later forms of Greek tragedy, and the chorus both in this dramatic form, as well as in the dithyrambus, the rapturous song in honor of Dionysos, was danced to the music of the singers. In the tragedy the chorus was arranged in a square, and two rows advanced towards one another, in the latter the performers were arranged in a circle and moved in and out in curved lines. The mode of these various dances differed, that of tragedy was solemn and slow, it was called "Eumeleia"; that of the Satyrs, called "Sikinnis" was a fast, grotesque dance; the "Kordax" in the comedies was wild, burlesque and cynical, and danced only by men, while the women moved slowly in the dance of tragedy.

There is no space here to describe in detail the many varied forms of Greek dances which are preserved for us by the fascinating portrayals on vases, reliefs and other monuments of Greek art. From these pictorial records we also know about the musical instruments used in old Greece. They were the aulos, the kithara, the tympanon, the krotales, and the skabillon.

We know even less of Roman dance music; though we know that in the cult of the ancient Roman Salic priests there were lively leaping dances (these accompanied by spring processions of the priests on the freshly tilled fields and part of the fertility magic). This tradition came to them from the Greeks who also had been the first to practice the funeral procession at the obsequies of the nobles, at which the "archimimos" dressed in the garments and wearing a mask resembling the deceased, performed a mourning dance. This was surely a form of incantation to propitiate the spirit of the dead man. After the Punic Wars, when there had been contacts with various forms of other civilizations, the dance rose in popular estimation and was made part of the physical training of the young men and women. Not until the Imperium with its expansion of luxury and good living were there professional dancers and dances for the entertainment. In the days of the later Empire we hear frequently of the shameless professional women dancers, who were considered at times so lewd that the Emperor Tiberius issued edicts forbidding certain of their dances. The music for all these forms of dances has, however, not come down to us.

Just as little do we know about the actual music to which the Egyptians danced though we have stone representations of the movements. There is a relief from the tomb of Nencheftkai at Saqqara dating from about 2700 B.C., which shows us the singers making gestures in the air with their hands, to follow the rhythm of the melody. This "Cheironomia" is an important factor in the history of the notation, because from it developed the notation of the Alexandrian grammarians, and from those the "neumes" which, in their turn, became the predecessors of our modern music notation proper.

In the language of Ancient Egypt, the word "singing" signifies also making rhythmical movements with the hand. In the relief two women beat time by clapping their hands; the instruments are a long flute, a harp and a double clarinet.

Hebrew dancing and music was influenced by that of the Egyptians. Both Clemens Alexandrinus and Philo designated Moses as a music student of the Egyptians. Surely there must be some connection between the sacred bull of the Egyptians (a former "totem") and the golden calf of Biblical history. There are certain contradictions in the dance practices, as for example between the solemn dances of the Old Testament, and the ecstatic movements of David in front of the sacred Ark containing the scrolls. For while this dance made him despised in the eyes of his consort Michal because he showed his nakedness to the eyes of his men and maidservants, the King's reply was "though I be base in mine own, yet of the maidservants of which thou hast spoken, of them shall I be held in honour."

This matter of social cleavage, so often encountered in the later history of the dance throws an interesting side light on cultural and social history of the ancient world. The Bible of pre-Davidian times speaks of women as dancers, as for example of the dance of Mirjam, and the maidens of Silo. At the point of David's discussion with Michal, we might have the transition from the matriarchal to the patriarchal cult.

The dance was accompanied by the voices of the women, who were the bearers of culture in the first thousand years before Christ. They also accompanied the dance with instruments.

Hebrew dances have come down to our times, and are still danced in synagogues, particularly in orthodox Jewish congregations of Eastern Europe. The sacred scrolls are held by the dancers and often there is a procession through the temple following the dance, on to the raised platform, where usually the reading of the scriptures takes place. A melody used by these people is archaic because of its predominant range within a fifth, and points to an origin in the 17th century. We know

that the Jews were renowned in the Middle Ages as good players of dance music, and it may be noted here, that in the Middle Ages Jewish dancemasters were most important. In the Near East, as for example in Tunis, the players for dancing are largely Jews. On the European continent, it was above all Bohemia where Jewish dance music played an important part. At the wedding of the Bohemian nobleman, Peter Wok von Rosenberg, (1580) an old record tells us that "the Jews played extraordinarily well for the dance". In Prague, the Jewish musicians were so popular in the 16th and 17th centuries, that the Catholics saw themselves compelled to have recourse to law, and introduced a strict police surveillance of Jewish musicians. The files contain the accusation that these musicians "keep neither time nor rhythm, introduce a number of false notes and make the noble art of music to be despised". It was apparently the practice of the Jewish musicians to use their ancient traditional sacred melodies for profane purposes for these "false notes" for which they were blamed, were none other than the augmented seconds of the Jewish scales which resemble so closely the scales of the Arabs: (Gypsy modes) a b♭ c♯ — d e f g♯ — a. The blameworthy rubato also points to oriental origin. The German lutenist, Hans Neusiedler records in 1544 a "Juden Tantz", a grotesque piece full of dissonances which is doubtlessly the caricature of such a Jewish dance. On the other hand we find in Jewish musical manuscripts of the 17th century contemporaneous Christian dance melodies to which even religious Jewish texts were sung. In the collection "Simchat Haimefeth" (The delight of the soul) which was printed in the town of Fuerth in 1727 we find a Passover song: (which is almost word for word one of

the dances of Schmelzer who died in 1680.) The Sabbath is celebrated with a melody which returns in one of the chamber

cantatas of Caldara. This interplay of oriental and occidental musical concepts which we see in the dance music of the Jews in the 17th and 18th centuries is typical of the fluctuating interchange between West and East which may be noted throughout the entire history of music. This is true as well for the development of the various medieval modes, of Catholic church music and, in many instances, for the history of dance forms. The Jewish musicians are but one of the many examples of this cultural evolution.

CHAPTER IV.

THE EARLY MIDDLE AGES.

IN the early Middle Ages, and even in the folk dances of modern times, we find the same dance motives prevailing as outlined in the introductory chapter. All that Christianity was able to do was to blur the outlines of these motives, it could not erase them altogether. The main factor and dominating influence on all dances is the magic of the fertility rite, and the classic type of all dance festivals is the time of the Carnival, especially the night of "Mardi gras". The word Carnival has its origin in the Carrus navalis, the ship on wheels which bore the leader of the ancient chorus and dances, in the rites of the god of fertility, Dionysos, giving a dramatic presentation of his death and re-incarnation. The word itself, however, had to undergo a new etymological explanation in Christian times, becoming "Carne vale", "fare thee well, delight of the flesh". This was but one of the transformations to which heathen habits and customs were subject.

But the old, eternally persisting node of the tradition could not be stamped out. Up to our own day, on the first of May the "may-pole", ancient symbol of the tree of life is surrounded by dancers and at the time of the summer solstice the fire is circled by a magic ring of dancers. Even today, in certain parts of the world the newly married couple is "led with dances" into the bridal chamber, and sometimes funerals such as those in the French province of La Nièvre and in Auvergne are accompanied by dances of the hired mourners, costumed and stepping like the mourning women of

43

classic Greek days. The forward and backward steps of the
Jewish ritual "Kaddish", the service for the dead, are reminiscent to these ancient rites. In other parts of the world this
kind of step is called the "pilgrim's step", which Sachs describes
as being best known through the processions to the tomb of
Saint Willibald at Eschternach near Aix la Chapelle, where
the pilgrims moved forward three to five paces, and backward
one to three steps, as they approached the shrine. Similar steps
and movements are found in the regions of the Orinoco in
South America. Wherever they appear their sense is to express
death and rebirth and here as elsewhere movement, that is
dancing, expresses human wishes, emotions and thoughts about
life and death.

It is not surprising that in the Early Middle Ages the dignitaries of the Church and its councils had to place penalties
on the dances practiced at the graves of the dead in order to
show disapproval of the heathen spirit. The Roman synod
under Leo IV ordered at the beginning of the 9th century that:
"In witness of the true and living God, the devilish songs
which are heard at night on the graves of the dead are to
cease, as well as the noise which accompanies them". And a
later resolution says: "Whoever buries the dead should do so
with fear, trembling and decency. No one shall be permitted
to sing devil songs and perform games (joca) and dances
(saltations) which are inspired by the devil and have been
invented by the heathen". The primitive custom that a feast
followed the funeral was continued beyond the Middle Ages.
Occasionally, some one of the guests appeared in the garments
of the deceased and spoke to the mourners in a ghostlike voice.
This custom has come down to us in the old German "Wider-
rufe", "Recalls" as late as the 17th century when Heinrich
Albert the classic composer of the German Baroque Lied wrote
a number of such songs to be sung at the grave of the deceased

Here do I lie, my bones decaying ...

by one of his friends impersonating him. Here do I lie, my bones decaying.

The primitive peoples used the dance to banish the spirit of the dead and keep it from doing harm, while it was at the same time an invocation to the spirit of fertility calling the new life. Christianity attempted to convert the custom to its spirit. The dance remained, but the cheerfulness and gaiety attending newly awakened love of life gave way to repentance about life spent in futile toil. — All are alike before Death who takes his toll from the ranks of the living: Whether emperors, kings or knights, citizens, peasants or beggars. — From the 14th century on poets and painters have described this religious experience. In their representations and images, Death leads the endless line of the living in their dance of life and death.

A wood cut contained in Hartmann Schedel's "Weltchronik", published in Nuremberg in 1493, illustrates the ghostly dance of the skeletons following Death, who is playing his weird tunes. Three pipers play for the dancing skeletons on a wood cut of Jacob Meydenbach, made in 1491. Both suggest the very same "Danses Macabres" which Saint-Saëns imagined in his Symphonic Poem, where the dead leave their tombs at the stroke of twelve, and dance to the sounds of the xylophon. The short staccato motive is the motif of the dead; the flowing melody in the strings, the theme of the re-incarnation. Liszt, on the other hand, brings in his "Totentanz" the old sequences of the Day of Judgment, "Dies Irae".

The French musician G. Kastner has taken the old illustrations of the Middle Ages as the sources for the enumeration of the instruments of the time. In addition to singers, there were flutes, shawns and oboes, bag pipes, horns and cymbals, portable organs, percussion instruments, zithers, and guitars, harps and psalters, vielles, bassdrums, tambourines, bells, rattles, castanets and drums.

But the dance of the dead was not always a dance macabre, sometimes it was of ghostly gaiety. The following old (17 cent.) funeral dance coming from the province of Brandenburg is to be played slowly. It is remarkable that this melody

bears a strong resemblance to the old Spanish Folia which we find in the 16th century. But we must not forget that the dances of the dead had strong roots in Arabia on which Spanish culture was so dependent. Even the word "macabre" is of Arabic origin, as Kabr means tomb, and Makbara cemetery. And the verse, "Dust thou art, to dust returneth" is an Islamic motto, found on all cemeteries.

The demons of the primitive peoples appear in the Middle Ages in the dances of the devils and witches. For it was impossible for the church to eradicate the old beliefs entirely among the men of the "Middle Ages", still so very close to nature and its inexplicable forces. Neuroses of witchcraft and possession by the devil occur even in times recorded not so long ago, — in the Middle Ages they were exceedingly frequent. A strange form of eroticism imbued with religious elements caused men and women to dream of devils and witches, and to transform these dreams into real life, into dances with and for the devil. As the angels dance their heavenly rounds in honor of God, the hellish dances are performed in the "Inferno" by those who on earth indulged in sinful practices. These witch-dances of the Middle Ages, assembling in the dead of night, worshipping the devil with lewd and fleshly practices, are described in the literature of the period.

On the "Witches' Sabbath", the night from the 30th of April to the 1st of May, the devils and witches would assemble in weird and lonely places. To this rendez vous they would come riding on brooms and sticks, on cart-wheels and hay-forks with their hair flying in the wind, and sometimes naked. Their feast would commence with dancing and with paying hommage to the devils, and would end up with a wild and voluptuous bacchanal. Such a night was the vision of Goethe, when he wrote the "Walpurgisnacht" ("The Witches' Sabbath") of his "Faust".

Similar descriptions remind us strongly of the feasts of the primitive peoples, from the grotesque costumes and masks which the witches wear, down to the killing of the sacred black goat for the feast, and the sexual excesses after the meal. These tribal memories are here presented in the form of fantasies and dreams, and as such are recorded in the legends, because, deeply buried in the subconscious, they must arise from time to time. Shakespeare gave us the most magnificent poetical expression of such a dance of the witches. He told us about it in "Macbeth". And countless ancient and modern poetic works develop the motive of the witches' dance. In the music of the Romantic period, these dances of witches, elves, sprites, and fire demons, play no small part.

While the medieval dances of the witches are, (as indicated before) frequently the expression and consequence of erotic and religious neuroses, we find another pathological dance form in the dance ecstasies of primitive peoples during periods of forcible suppression of their instinctive and natural impulses. In the Middle Ages a typical form of this dance neurosis is found in the dances of St. Vitus. We find this strange example of dancing frenzy spreading over Europe from the 11th- to the 14th century. It began with the appearance of men and women in the cemeteries, and their uncontrollable and wild dancing on the anniversary of the death of some person, or on a Saint's day. All over Germany, in Holland and in France such groups of frenzied dancers appeared preceded by musicians playing 14th century. It began with the appearance of men and women performed paroxysmic leaps and turns, and writhed as in epileptic fits. Behind them would follow the anxious relatives who tried in vain to bring the mad crowd to reason. Many of the dancers in their uncontrollable ecstasy of movement lost all notions of reality and became unconscious of their surroundings. Foaming at the mouth and emitting wild cries they danced until they sank to the ground, if they were not released from the magic obsession by the efforts of a high churchman, some bishop or archbishop. This madness was not confined to the Continent, for Giraldus Cambrensis in his travelogue of Wales, called the "Itinerarium Cambriae", speaks in detail of these dances. He describes at length how those, obsessed by the dancing frenzy, made gestures in their trance, uttering sounds as if they were busy at their own trades. They plow the earth, sit at the spinning wheel, make the gestures of a shoemaker or a tanner, — thus performing actions as in a dream during the dance neurosis. This epidemic form of dancing is a typical phenomenon of the Middle Ages. To us, in modern times, it is known only in medical science as St. Vitus' dance, and occurs in individual cases of persons afflicted with nervous disease.

In this connection we ought to mention the flagellation songs and dances performed by medieval groups originating within the churches from the 13th through the 15th century. From the point of view of Freudian psychology we may explain the dances of the witches as an erotic dream expression, the dances of the dead, as a pathological expression of suppressed necrophilism; in the dances of the flagellants we have a kind of masochism which has been transformed and transferred into the field of religion. The self-infliction of punishment, the scourging, performed as an act of atonement, was found to exist among the ascetic practices of Italy, as early as in the year 1000, and the use of the lash was referred to in one of Paul's Epistles to the Corinthians: "Thus do I tame my body as I make it unconscious of pain". But not until 1260 did the great popular movement of the flagellants spring up, first in Italy, later beyond the Alps. With bared trunk, these fanatics traveled the country while they sang songs of mourning and repentance, and lashed their bodies till the blood flowed. The climax of their influence was reached during the years of the black plague. The evil became so great that the popes found themselves forced to take steps against it.

We have an interesting record by the churchman, Hugo of

Reutlingen, in his "Weltchronik" where he describes the scourging songs of 1349. The ceremony was severely regulated and
reminds one, as far as its psychological background is concerned, of the songs and dances of the Eastern dervishes. When
entering a town the band of flagellants sang a song to the text:
"Mother Mary, purest maid, take pity thou on Christendom",
and added to this there was a chorus repeated ten times in the
form of a litany. "May the good Lord help us". This song

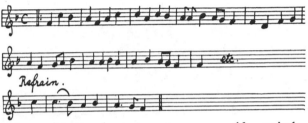

in F major, with its short monotonous motif reminds us of
the Arabian dance of the dervishes. The clap of the whip on
the body is apparent as the scourge descended during the singing and the fanatically short rhythm is definitely oriental in
feeling, with the tendency to limit consciousness by repetition.
There are fifteen verses to be sung to this melody and surely
at the end of it the singers were seized by a kind of spasm
which, like that of the Indian fakirs, made them insensible to
pain. As the scourged bodies of the flagellants writhed con-
vulsively in rhythmic gestures, the influence of Eastern mentality was all too apparent.

We have documents telling us about medieval dances in
Scandinavia where the dance was a form of movement close
to nature, reminding us of the dances of the primitive peoples,
in as much as the sex element is still of great importance in
spite of the fact that the social forms prevailing in these countries were already feudal, a culture of knights, singers and
heroes. Here is no trace of the refinement prevalent in the
social habits of the troubadours and minnesaenger. There is
no dancing of individual couples but only unmixed rounds,

that is, with men or women exclusively participating, accompanied by the singing of the old legends dealing with the heroes. During the round, there is walking, stepping and leaping. We never find a fiddle or other instrument. The old Song of Sigurd which Wagner used as the basis of his "Ring" was a favorite subject for the songs sung during these dances. Some of them have been preserved to our own day, particularly on the Faroe Islands between Iceland and the Shetland Islands, where the inhabitants had migrated from Norway in the Middle Ages. Here follows the song of Siegfried which was still sung in these islands as late as 1818 during the dance: The content

of this "Sigurd Snarenswend", (which means Siegfried, the nimble fellow), is as follows: Siegfried kills his father to relieve his mother's anguish, then goes to Gripir, mounts his steed, Grani, and with it jumps over a wall, whereat the horse breaks its backbone. This causes all to mourn. (Boehme).

A number of medieval pictures show dances accompanied by the music of a group of instrumentalists. We also have sculptures of such scenes, as for example the metal door of the Church of San Zeno at Verona. On this as well as on a picture of the Cathedral at Braunschweig in Germany, dating from the 13th century, we have the figure of Salome performing an acrobatic trick which is still practiced in gymnasiums and called "the back flip". We have various records of such acrobatic dances, performed by jugglers, buffoons and tumblers, who were the forerunners of our present circus as the professional entertainers of those times. Their tricks and move-

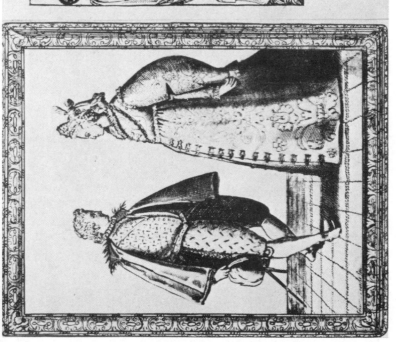

DANCE OF THE DEATH
(Hartmann Schedel, Weltchronik, 1493)

ARISTOCRATIC DANCE (PAVANA)
from the "Ballarino" (Fabritio Caroso) Venice 1581

MEDIAEVAL DANCE
(From an illuminated manuscript, Franco-Flemish, 15th century.)

ments must have been by far more uncontrolled and wilder than the images of the dance movements which were part of the courtly culture of medieval times. In the so-called "Manesse" manuscript, recording the songs of the Minnesaenger, we see miniatures portraying dance figures. The female dancer has her feet turned inwards, her elbows pressed back and swings sideways with one hip. We have here a most formal disciplined, regulated dance, and undoubtedly the difference between the juggler dance form and the dance of the courts must have had its counterpart in the music played to it.

In the Latin poem "Rudlieb", written about the year 1000, there has come down to us a most impressive and lively description of a dance. (It is interesting to note that this poem was written in Southern Germany, the home of the peasant dance, "Laendler" and of the Waltz). The hero Rudlieb, accompanied by his nephew, pays a visit to a widow who has a charming young daughter. In the course of the conversation, two harp players enter and perform so execrably on their instruments that Rudlieb begs the hostess to see whether she has not a harp in the house, on which he might play. She brings one which belonged to her husband, and which has "gladdened her soul" in times gone by. First he plays three beautiful melodies and then the ladies beg him to play a reel, so that the young man and the young lady may dance to it. And here follows the description of the dance: "Now the young man gets up, and then the maiden and then a chasing and hunting begins, sometimes with loud, then with soft music. They fly hither and thither, as when the falcon hunts the dove in the air. He has reached her, the hunt is finished, — but no, — she escapes again, and the game begins anew. Truly their art would fascinate the critics, so skillfully do the dancers master the dance, the leaping, the gesture of the hands".

We find in the above a transcription of a peasant dance as it may have been danced in Bavaria and in the Tyrol about a thousand years ago. Typical of this dance are the stamping and the turning, the seeking and the escaping of the female dancer and the encircling by the male. We find the same elements in the "Schuhplattler" (stamping dance) of these countries today. The play of the hands is particularly important, for it is most characteristic of the later Tyrolean dances and peasant rounds that the participants clapped their hands and beat their knees, as apparently did the young man and the maiden in the Latin poem, to the sound of the widow's harp!

But we must not forget a number of other dances of this early medieval period. We have in the first place, the round dance, or Reigen, called Chorea, Carole, derived either from Choreola, the dance, or perhaps from Corolla, the little wreath, the little crown. This dance was definitely distinguished from the dance of a couple as early as in the 14th century. Later the two concepts became interchangeable and the two words danzare (couple dance) and carolare (reel) were confused. The round dance was performed by a long chain of dancers, holding each other by the hand, moving in an open or closed circle, or in a long line. Sometimes such rounds stretched out for a long distance, and in a French fairy tale novel of the 13th century by Phelipe de Remi, called "La Manekine", there is a verse which says:

"Tel Carole ne fus pas veue
Pres d'une quart dure l'une lieue"

alleging, that the round stretched out for almost a quarter of a league. In most modern countries, such long rounds are still prevalent. The "Farandole" is that round from the Provençal country, where the dancers (in couples) form a long column, holding each other by the hand or by the ribbons of the women's costumes, and dance through the streets, making spirals and circles. Gounod has this dance in his "Mireille", and Bizet gives an example in the "Arlésienne". In Germany the last figure of the "Quadrille Americaine" was danced in an endless row of couples, and that Quadrille Americaine may have its origin in the "Virginia Reel". In present Southeastern Europe a favorite dance is still the ancient "Kolo", the "Wheel". The dance begins in the ballroom and is continued outside on the street, where new couples join the long line.

Such a "Kolo" stretches out for nearly a mile, and often lasts for more than an hour, and its hypnotising melody is as ancient as the following example:

In the City Hall at Siena in Italy we have the pictorial representation of such a medieval round dance in Pietro Lorenzetti's fresco, painted around 1340, which he called "The Good Regiment". In this picture a group of noble ladies hold each other by the hand and leave the circle to dance the "bower dance". One of them with castanets sings as they dance. What was the melody of her song? The dance suggests the children's game "The Golden Bridge". Two of the children form a bower with their hands, and the other children pass under this arch as they all sing:

> "Wir bau'n eine goldene Bruecke,
> Sie ist entzwei, sie ist entzwei - -
> Womit sollen wir sie flicken?
> Mit Edelstein, Granatenstein.
> Der Erste kommt, der Zweite kommt,
> Der Dritte soll gefangen sein".

> (We built a golden bridge,
> It broke in two, it broke in two - -
> And how will we repair it?
> With precious stones, with garnet stones.
> Here comes the first, the second there,
> The third will be our prisoner)"

According to Curt Sachs the basic difference between the round dance and the couple dance is the fact that the latter is pantomimic in character, while the former does not intend to portray any special dramatic action, but is mere procession, movement forward or in a circle. But, he adds, in the Middle Ages the limits of one form encroached upon those of the other, and the differentiation is therefore of little importance. Perhaps it is therefore preferable to retain the old classification of Boehme who distinguishes peasant dances, workingmen's dances, citizen's and clan dances, court and knightly dances.

The peasants, being closest to nature, are, in their dancing closest to the old pantomimic forms used by the primitive peoples. Though the participants walk about in the round dance, love of life, elemental impulses cannot be quelled and the disciplined form of the procession gives way to the couple dance, the goal of the rustic entertainment. The gestures and the movements of such a peasant dance were by no means measured or polite. The dancer swings his partner with all his might, and frequently all the couples turn in circles in wild confusion. Each couple dances a figure alone on the floor and not all simultaneously as is done in modern dances. The dancer kisses his girl partner and is not considerate of her coyness or prudishness. That the dance does not remain a mere symbolic form of his wooing is taken for granted and this custom has remained the same in many villages of the Alpine lands, as well as in Bohemia and in Hungary.

In the chronicle of Johann Koester, called Neocornus, the author writing in 1590 describes a dance of the North German province Dithmarschen in Holstein, which is still noted for its traditional forms of social culture. He says that these people had "two kinds of long dances" (reigen) in which all the dancers joined hands. The first was the Trimmeken dance, (derived from the word Trimmeke, a coy girl) "which consisted of many steps and was performed with gestures of the hands." This dance was already obsolete at the end of the 16th century. The other form of "the long dance" used only jumping and leaping and was called "hopping dance" — "Springeltanz", a wild dance in which the dancers (as the title says) hopped and leaped about. The German historian reports that in this dance: "the leader holds a cup in his hand and begins a song; when he has finished a verse, the dancers repeat it till they know it by heart. And so it goes until one of the crowd feels the urge to dance, leaves his companions, and — hat in hand — beckons the others to join him. Thereupon all join hands, one after the other, yet in such order that people of prominence have the 'upper hand'. Finally all are taking part in the dance, sometimes as many as 200 people". A melody for this dance has been preserved. It is sung to the words: "Ik weet mi eine schoen magt, ik nem se gern to wiwe", (I know a lovely maiden, whom I would like to wed). This old song, preserved in the form of a children's song, still heard in France and in Germany as well as in America and England, was recorded like this in the 16th century: Mozart used it partly

for his variations "Ah, vous dirai-je, maman".

The very names of the dances give some indication of the manner in which they were performed. The "Gimpel-Gampel" is a boisterous leaping dance. The "Firlefanz" or "Fulefranz" is connected either with the French "Virelais", a ballad, or has taken its name from the probable country of origin, Friulia, the province bordering the Northern lands of Italy. Then we have the "Hoppel-rei", of which the popular Minnesinger Neithardt of Reuenthal, living in the 13th century, says that it was danced so violently by the peasants that the girls' skirts whirled up high in the air. The whole body was in motion, the arms were swinging and the shoulders were thrown about. Another such dance is the "Houbetschotten", which was mentioned around 1230 by the Minnesinger Goli. It is a shrugging of shoulders, like in the dance "Rotten", only sliding along the floor, shaking the head. Probably it is an early form of the Tyrolean "Schuhplattler", according to Boehme. We may, however, look for a derivation of the expression "rotten". Does it come from "Rotta", the Italian designation which will be treated further on? Then there is the "Heierlei", a kind of shouting dance with "Hei, Hei" to accompany it; and the "Stampf", noted by Neithardt, which had a figure calling for vigorous stamping with both feet. The tune of the last mentioned dance does not appear so wild. Undoubtedly, when played for the dance itself, the fiddle would play the melody much faster than for the song. By itself the melody resembles rather a tune for singing, having a definitely churchlike diction

and is in the Phrygian mode. While the peasants may have been dancing with wild and uncontrolled leaps and bounds, the knights moved in measured and regulated steps in their dances. In place of the instinctive expression of sexuality and unbridled unsensuality, we find in these dances grace, tenderness and that quality of sublimated passion which the Germans called "Minne". Thus, the peasant forms remained the original, and were the inspiration of more cultivated and refined dances at the court: Instead of leaping, there was stepping. Burkhardt of Hohenfels, one of the poets of that time, describes such a dance. The couples advanced while walking or rather sliding along in the hall, while they held hands. The women carried their trains, "svanz" in their hands and smiled "Smiren" (smirk), and with their eyes signaled with love-sick and secret glances. Helmbrecht, another poet, describes how the knight walked between two ladies, holding each by the hand and the page walked between two maids. The fiddlers stood close at hand. The same picture occurs in the Manesse manuscript, (13th century) and in a fresco of the castle Runkelstein in South Tyrol. This is a "tour de mains", performed slowly with solemn steps, in long peaked shoes. All the dancers advance like this in a long row with dragging steps and two fiddlers play the music.

Some of the names of these courtly dances are partly preserved. There is the "Treialtrei" danced by twelve according to the poet Goli. Apparently four ladies and two gentlemen faced a similar group. Neithardt mentions the "Vanaldei" which I interpret as follows: "Unaldei", one against two, i.e. one gentleman and two ladies who face him. To find an explanation of this arrangement of two ladies with one man is not easy. Perhaps it was from marking the transition from the general round dance to the dance of the couple, or perhaps it harked back to hidden polygamous motives, certainly having their origin in the influence of the Eastern cultures observed during the crusades.

Among many others, we have the "Virlei", in France, reminding one of the metrical arrangements of the French ballad, virelais, the "Firgamdrey" and the "Trei", as well as the "Treiros". In all these dances the number Three plays an important part. We have besides the "Gofenanz", from the French word "convenance", signifying the demands of good manners, as well as the meeting of the knights. There is the "Ridewanz", derived from the old High German word "ridan" — "ridden", (English: ride) which means: to turn.

The two basic forms of medieval dancing, the round dance and the couple dance have corresponding differences in the music to which they were performed. As the expression of a collective unity of a group, the round dance is accompanied by the song of the participants. The round being more disciplined, and lacking in gestures, was characteristic of female, matriarchal cultures, while the pantomimic dances with wild movements belong to the male cultures. On all the representations of the period, we see that the courtly dances are performed by groups, and the peasant dances by pairs, whereby the couples leap and jump. And the round dance, whether accompanied by singing or by instruments, had a moderate melodic line, deriving from its vocal origin.

The song of the Middle Ages which accompanied the dance, was called the "cantilena", according to the writers of that time. It consisted of an alternation of verses, called "versus" or "pes", and a refrain called "responsorium", "refractorium", "ripresa", "volta". It is worth noting that "volta" means turn, and "pes" (versus) means turned foot, — thus showing that these modern concepts of poetics had their origin in the dance. We speak now of the "metrical feet". The refrain was left to the group of dancers, the "pedes" were the business of the leader of the song or the dance. The text dealt with spring, with love and beauty, with joy and the pangs of love. But there were also texts with themes of heroic deeds and historic happenings. One of the oldest folk songs of the Germanic cycle of legends is the song of Hildebrandt, which describes the battle between father and son Hadubrandt, neither recognizing the other, and the final return to wife and mother Ute. The melody, which appears for the first time in 1541 in Rhaw's "Bicinia" (which appeared at Wittenberg) is a typical medieval street singer's ballad, which was probably used to accompany dancing. In one of the verses at the beginning occurs the word "Ei ja" which indicates that at this point the chorus chimed in, while the preceding lines were sung by the leader, as he danced to them.

"Ich will zu Land ausreiten, sprach Meister Hildebrandt,
Wer tut den Weg mir weisen, zu Bern wohl in das Land?
Sie sind mir unkund worden, viel manchen lieben Tag,
Ei ja - in zwei und dreissig Jahren Frau Uten ich
        nit gesach"

(I want to ride my horse, said master Hildebrandt,
Who shows the way to Raven, in lovely Romanland?
I did not see dear Uta, I was not there for long,
Ei ja - - years passed - two and thirty, - I therefore
        might go wrong).

Another melody which was sung to the French novelette of the 13th century which dealt with "the two noble young children, Aucassin and Nicolette, tells of Aucassin's pain and sore anxiety for his sweetheart". The musician sings the poetical parts of the story to this simple tune:

And the chorus of his listeners ends each chapter with the refrain:

This novelette is a strange mixture of poetic song and prose and we may well imagine that the part of the text which was sung was also accompanied by a dance, in the manner of the itinerant ballad singers. Another story tells us of one of the most charming dance tunes of the Middle Ages. French jugglers arrived one day in the 12th century at the Castle of Montferat and delighted all their hearers with their performance of a new "Estampida" on their violas. Only one of the audience, Rambaut of Vaqueiras, the knightly lover of the beautiful Beatrice, sister of the Count of Montferat remained sad until Beatrice asked him to recover his gaiety while singing a song. Based on the melody of the estampida which he just heard, he composed the dance song "Kalenda Maya". The melody of the jugglers runs like this:

The Estampy, Italian's "istampita", Provençal's "estampida", is explained etymologically by the Frankish word, "stampon".

Originally it was danced with stamping of feet, but later in the 14th century it was transformed into a quiet, paced form of dance. Johannes Wolf dealing with these dances in an essay contained in the "Archiv fuer Musikwissenschaft", first volume, has given a detailed account of them. Such an estampita consists of five "points", that is, expressed in our language, five movements. Each one is developed broadly and is performed twice, at the first repetition with half an ending, at the second with a complete finale. All of them have special names: one of them is called: "tre Fontane", the other "Isabella", a third is "Cominciamo la Gioia". These may well be the kind of designations which were used for dances. If the "blue Danube" once served to inspire Johann Strauss, the same function might well have been performed by those "three fountains" of Rome. Another estampita is the following "Palamento":

We have here a fully developed dance movement which must have sounded very modern to the listeners of the 14th century. The instrument playing was probably the old Vielle, a string instrument having five strings, which was used at that time. It is possible that flutes and lutes of the period may have been used as well. But the Vielle, which was tuned in fifths, and fourths, was surely the one which was most often used, a fact, indicated by the numerous fifths of the just mentioned composition.

Dances much simpler than the one presented are recorded in the manuscript, called Harley 978, deposited in the British Museum. The dance music of the 13th century is fully described in a contemporary treatise by Johannes de Grocheo, called "Theoria", where the form and theory of the dances are explained.

We learn from this manuscript about the "Stantipes", about which there is endless discussion among musicologists concerning its name, origin and character. One of them, Robert Haas, believes that the word is merely a latinised form of "Stampenie", "Istampita". Others, taking their cue from H. J. Moser, believe that the word means "stante pede", that is a piece of music played but not danced. Some, joining Sachs, believe that the word has the same meaning as "stantia", used by Antonio da Tempo in his book on the art of poetry, where it simply means "verse" in vulgar Latin of medieval times. Since "pes" and "versus" have the same meaning at that period, "Stantipes" would be a pleonasm. In any case, the two middle parts of the four verses of the "Ballata" were called "Stantipes". And it appears that during the 13th century the stantipes was still used as a dance, while somewhat at the turn of the century it was merely an instrumental piece just like the later suite which came to be a number of the dance movements following one another, and constituting a new form of instrumental composition.

Boccaccio tells us of an Istampita and a Canzona, which were played on the viola between the telling of two stories, and does not mention that the company rose for dancing. (Decamerone VII -10). Istampita means here "Sonata".

Another record, Francesco Rondelli, tells us even in 1637 of the funeral of the German Emperor Ferdinand III.: "Giuntosi al Duomo, nell'entrare si fece una bella stampita su l'organo con la tromba". (Entering the Cathedral you heard a beautiful stampita, played by the organ and a trumpet.) According to this statement a stampita should be a church sonata.

A certain confusion results at the point: was the stampenie a round dance, or sometimes also some kind of a medieval sonata? It seems to me that both, stampenie and stantipes were originally one and the same, that is, dances, and later on lost this quality, becoming a mere instrumental form.

According to Johann de Grocheo the stantipes consists of six points, that is of six movements. Wolf records some of these pieces as he found them in the British Museum manuscript, (Harley 978). They are for two parts, and in contrast to the istampitas mentioned before, have a much more rigorous rhythmical arrangement.

3)

The above are the first three "points" of the stantipes. The other three have the same second part as the first three, only the first part is changed, so that the first and the fourth point, the second and the fifth point and the third and the sixth point have the same arrangement for the second voice, (tenors). I give the fourth point in notation for a clearer understanding.

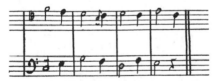

The whole piece has a very distinctive rhythm with its division into parts of four measures each, and is a proper piece for dancing. It is the first "variation suite", as the composers of the 16th and 17th centuries wrote for the dances, and in which they used the same thematic material for all parts of the suite. That these pieces originated from folk melodies is shown not only by the short, easily retained motive of the second voice, which is a real fiddler's melody in bright major. The piece illustrated here is neither a formal round dance of refined knights or ladies, but a real "Stampf", a stamped out folk dance. We must therefore distinguish between the complicated and artistic structure, and the more primitive "stantipes" of the 13th century, bearing the earmarks of a popular melodic line. The former, with their intricate melodic development show some resemblance to the musical art forms of the 19th and 20th centuries.

The manuscript in the British Museum (Add. 29987) which contains the istampite discussed above, shows also a number of other dances. One of them "Saltarello", is, as the name indicates, a leaped and jumped dance, but it is not certain whether it was really danced or only (like the gavotte and the passepied of Bach's time), for the entertainment of the listeners of the 14th century. The actual circumstances, namely the fact that music for dancing was played by fiddlers and pipe players who were unable to make any notation of it as they did not know how to write notes, make it likely that the only pieces that have come down to us were those written by trained musicians, in other words, we have records only of the complicated musical documents.

The next illustration (a saltarello), of which I shall give only two "points" is a special form of a medieval rondo and

is unquestionably a dance that reminds one of a Furlana melody (Venetian dance of the 18th century, recorded by Gretry in his memoirs, and of the English folk dances of the 17th and 18th centuries, Jigs, country dances).

Beside the record of saltarelli given in the British Museum manuscript, there is a Trotto. According to a medieval treatise which is quoted by Wolf, this form is in "tempus imperfectum", that is in two-beat time. We know nothing about the manner in which this dance was performed but that its name was derived from the Old High German "trotton", (Middle High German "treten", - step). Treten (trot) means to step heavily, to stamp down with lifted leg and foot like a high stepping horse. Musically there is little difference between this dance and the saltarello. There are records about this dance in the literature of the German Baroque, (there called "troeter") in the Chronicle of Erfurt, 1480, mentioning a "Trottart tanz", never seen previously as the story goes; and also in the satyric work of Sebastian Brant, "Das Narrenschiff", written in 1494.

Among the saltarelli recorded in the manuscript there are two pieces with programmatic captions. One of these is the "Lamento di Tristano":

In connection with this piece of instrumental music, divided into three parts, there is a dance movement, also divided into three parts, which was to be played fast. This is called a "rotta". "Rotta" signifies approximately refractorium, refrain, chorus. But it also means "interruptio", for the word "rotta" is derived from "rompere" - to break. This may indicate that the "rotta" serves the function of what was later known as the "ritornello" (Rondo). It is possible that the first part of the "rotta" was played after the first part of the "lamento" and so forth.

The word "rotta" occurs in later documents, for example in Caroso's manual of the dance, "Il Ballerino", 1581. The dance was played after the "Gagliarda", just as the old "Rotta" was to be played after the "Lamento". What is the significance of this three-beat Saltarello "Lamento di Tristano", which is followed by a fast two-beat Rotta? It may be derived from an old processional dance which was followed by a pantomimic figure, i.e. the Rotta. We may observe in this succession a root of the "variation-suite". The later music of the 16th century follows this pattern. The melody of the Rotta has been obtained from that of the Lamento by a special kind of technique which the musicologist Blume calls: "Suitenbildung durch Reduktion" - "formation of the suite by reduction". This matter will be discussed more fully in a later chapter.

On the whole, the tendency towards the formation of suites is a definite characteristic of medieval dance music. In this sense, therefore, "suite" here means the succession of two dances which are interrelated as variations of the same theme, and also related by the contrast they present.

Musically there is a certain correspondence between the round dance and the couple dance. The round dance is the conventionalized dance, taken over from the sung piece; the "dance", (rotta, ripresa, Hupfauf) is the wild leaping dance of the fiddlers and pipe players. Psychologically speaking: the succession of slow and fast, of stepped and leaped dancing corresponds with the gradual emotion of the dancers. In later times however the walked dance is in two-beat time, the leaped dance in three beats. (There are exceptions, of course.)

The manuscript Oxford Bodley Dance 139 shows us a typical English dance played by fiddlers in the 13th century. The short motive in major is developed in true fiddler's fashion, and in the repetition only the first note is changed. At the close the fiddlers or pipers play the dance in three parts, in the same fashion that we find in the polyphonic music of primitive peoples.

In these peasant dances we find the same natural exuberance which is present in our modern folk dances. Customs and traditions of the less cultured groups of society are less apt to change and this is particularly true not only in England, Italy and in Germany, but above all in those countries at the boundaries of Central Europe where folk-ways and folk-lore of by-gone days have been most vividly and actively handed down and preserved. The following dance melody of the 14th century was found by the Czech musicologist, Nejedly, in a Czech manuscript. In its general plan it reminds us of the saltarelli which were followed by a rotta. The word "Caldy valdy" which is placed at the beginning of this Czech "rotta" has not been explained to date, though Nejedly assumes that it was not meant to have any special sense, corresponding perhaps to our modern interjections like "Tra-lala", or like the "Aldi Daldi" which the Czech children still interpolate in their

songs. In this respect we should not forget that the songs of
primitive peoples are full of such apparently meaningless interjections, a kind of "baby talk", of the repetitions like the
childish "pa-pa" and "ma-ma". This Czech melody in common
with the above mentioned dance measures, is strictly in major,
and the "Nachtanz" (three beat dance) definitely and clearly
shows triad melodics. With "Nachtanz" we mean that part of
the dance which in German terminology represents the second
(hopping) part of a stepped dance. In the following we shall
frequently use these two expressions, namely stepper for the first
slower part, and hopper for the second faster part. This naturally recalls the statement made in the preceding chapter that
the leaping dances which are a part of the pantomimic dance
group are marked by wide intervals, as contrasted with the
paced and walked dances which have a melodic line marked
by small intervals like that of a song. All these brisk melodies
are characteristic of the peasant culture of the Middle Ages,
though in the following dance we may already recognise special
qualities of Czech rhythm and of Czech melodic style.

Comparing this with the dance melody of the Oxford manuscript we can imagine how the Czech fiddler with the rhythmic beat of the two eighth notes provides the accompaniment for the foot beat of the leaping dancer. And the Czech rhythm

♩ ♩|♩ ♩|♩

with its staccato emphasis gives us a foretaste of Dvořak's Slavonic Dances or of Smetana's "Dupak" in the "Vlatava". In countless pictures and miniatures of this period we have representations of rounds led by a fiddler. These dances are called "Ductia" (leading dances), and Johannnes de Grocheo distinguishes this dance from the estampida, different in time and rhythm. The purpose of the "Ductia" was to stimulate the dancers to move in graceful fashion according to the rules of the art of dancing. On another occasion Grocheo makes a distinction between the Ductias and the Choreas.

In a Veronese picture book dating from the 14th century, now preserved in the Museum of Art of the city of Vienna, we find a picture entitled "Sonare et Ballare". To the accompaniment of two shaws and a bag pipe, two ladies perform a graceful dance. In Trento, in an old Tyrol tower, there is a fresco picturing two couples pacing a courtly dance to the tune of two trumpets, two bombardons and a small tympanum. All such pictures show that the dances were accompanied by a number of instruments playing different parts and that the music which has come down to us in manuscript form is by no means a complete picture of the music actually accompanying medieval dances.

On the whole our knowledge of medieval dancing is relatively small. For example we know little or nothing at all of the "Danse Royale" which is mentioned in a number of French manuscripts, (Bibliothèque Nationale, fonds 844) in conjunction with the "estampie". What was the "estampie royale" which seemed to resemble the other estampies and saltarelli by its division into four movements, each beginning differently but all having the same refrain:

Apparently such a dance royale was a particularly dignified and solemn one, a royal form of stepped measure. Later in the fifteenth century, Guglielmo Hebreo describes a "Bassa Danza Reale" for two persons. In 1600 we hear that the dance theorist Cesare Negri discusses a "Bassa Imperiale", a dance created for a royal couple. He speaks of the melody in the "Dorian Mode" of such a dance, which is to be quite different from the simple major of the peasant dances. Another explanation of the designation is given by Cornazzano, the dance theorist of Renaissance times, who calls the "Basse Danse", the successor of the "Estampita", and designates it as the "Queen of all Dances".

CHAPTER V.

THE LATER MIDDLE AGES.

GRADUALLY the severity and the preoccupation with spiritual matters which characterized Gothic culture gave way to the more liberal, more worldly-minded spirit of the early Renaissance. The dances which had been banned by the church now were not definitely considered a part of a knightly education. The buffoons and the jesters, who were rather considered "undecent folk", in the early Middle Ages, became the interpreters of dancing and a special profession developed, that of the dancing master. He accompanied the prince or the count to whose court he was attached on all journeys, and, in fact, he occupied a position of trust and confidence in his patron's household. He was at the same time an arbiter of etiquette, where the instruction given the young men and women of noble family was considered an essential part of their education.

It is truly remarkable that looking through the lists of the known dancing masters of the Middle Ages and the early Renaissance, we find a large number of Jews. The first dancing master of medieval time of whom there is a record is the Jew Rabbi Hacen ben Salomo. He was commissioned in 1313 to teach a round dance to be performed around the altar to the Christian parishioners of the Church of St. Bartholomeo, at Tauste in the Spanish province of Saragossa. At the court of Urbino in Italy there were two Jews from Pesaro, Guglielmo Ebreo, and Ambrosio. Guglielmo, living in the 15th century, wrote a number of treatises about dancing. He is treated in detail in a study "A Jewish dancing master of the Renaissance", written by Kinkeldey, to be found in the memorial volume for A. S. Freidus, the New York librarian. We have also the Jew Giuseppe, a pupil of Guglielmo. Somewhat

71

later we hear of two Jews from Ancona, Grescion Azziz, and Emanuel de Rabbi Jalomacis, who were accorded the privilege of teaching dancing and singing by papal decree in 1575. And as late as the 17th century there were Jewish musicians at the Court of Mantua—the harpist Abramo dell' Arpa Ebreo, and his nephew, Abramino dell' Arpa, an actor and musician. Joachino Massarano, living in Mantua and later in Ferrara, was both lutenist and master of the ballet; and to complete the roster, we have the Jew, Simone Basilea, stage manager at the court.

We have records of theoretic studies on the art of dancing as early as the beginning of the 15th century. The first of these is a treatise by Domenico or Domenichino of Piacenza, who called his work "Da la arte di ballare et danzare". In the National Library of Paris we find an anonymous version of the same material dating from a later time. Guglielmo Ebreo wrote "De praticha seu arte tripudii vulghare opusculum", which was used by Ambrosio from Pesaro.

In the North, the art of this period is recorded in the famous manuscript "Basses danses", now in the Royal Library of Brussels, Belgium; and in England we have the directions for the execution of the "Basses Danses" in a work by Robert Coplande, entitled "The manner of dauncynge of bace daunces after the use of fraunce and other places translated out of frenche in englysshe". This volume was published in a new edition in London in 1871.

The choreographic literature just enumerated ignores the dancing of the "lower classes". What we know of this, is taken from pictorial representations, as for example from Mantegna's picture "Parnassus". The large movements and the wide-stepping figures of the peasant dances present a striking contrast to the strictly regulated, almost cramp-like contortionate gestures which accompanied the dances of the court and of high society. The same is true of the dancers in Giulio Romano's picture, "Apollo dances with the Muses". Though both these artists belong to a somewhat later time, we may assume that the dances of the people underwent little change in a short span of fifty years. - - In the City Hall of Munich, there are a number of carved figures made by the wood-carver Erasmus Grasser in 1480: Their grotesque twists and the wide movements of their limbs as well as their popular name "Maruschka Taenzer" designates them as dancers of moresques, that is, grotesque dancers.

Such gestures and figures were practiced in the folk dancing of the various districts, particularly in the Alps and the distant provinces. The mountain regions, so inaccessible because of road and travel conditions, played the same part in the dance culture of their day,* as do now the exotic lands lying beyond oceans and deserts. Just as in the early part of the 19th century, the Bohemian and Polish dances and the Spanish folk dances became the leaders on the polished floors of the Parisian ball rooms, and as the music of the Negroes and of oriental peoples was taken over by European and American dance composers in our own day, - in that same way, the later decades of the Middle Ages and of the time following this, saw the gradual usurpation of the courtly dances and music by peasant music and peasant steps. In this new environment, however, the robust art of the mountains became more refined and the steps narrower. It could not be otherwise! For who could expect the polite knight, dressed in tight-fitting hose, with long peaked shoes, to step out in lively dances, which were to be executed with feet turned in, knees bent, and high jumps? Nor could the noble lady, trailing yards of silken train, be ready to imitate the lightly leaping peasant girl, swung by her partner.

Here was the place for strictly regulated paces and gestures, and there arose a kind of letter tabulation which became international in all the lands of Europe.

b   signifies Branle
d   means double pace
R   is reverence (bow)
c   continenca or congé, leave-taking
r   ripresa, or demarche

s   simple, single pace
ss   two simples.

A branle is a step sideway with balancing of the body, or swaying. The Provençal dancing master Antonio de Arena who
died in 1544, and Arbeau, the French choreographic teacher, in
his work "Orchésographie", 1588, define "Branle" as the same
step as "congé", that is the swaying of the body with feet
together. The meaning of the word itself is to tremble, to
move. Later "branle" becomes an independent dance.

The double pace has the left foot advancing, and then the
right next to it. If two doubles are indicated, the order is
reversed, that is: the right precedes the left.

"Reverence" is the bow made by the gentleman to the lady.
"Congé" is the leave-taking from the lady, "wherein one must
bow before her, then take her by the hand and lead her back
to where the dance began". "Demarche" or "Ripresa" is the
stepping backward, the movement backward.

The simple, or single pace has the first foot advancing
slightly, and the second drawn up to it. Here are the first principles, the basic theoretical groundwork of the art of dancing
in the Early Renaissance.

Most important of all the dances was the "Basse danse",
the low dance, after which we might rightly call this whole
period from the 15th century till far into the 16th century,
the "Basse danse-period", just as we speak of the early nineteenth century as "the age of the waltz". The first mention
made of it is in the Spanish poem "La danza de la Muerta".
The "basse danse" is according to Cornazzano, the choreographer of the day, the "Queen of all dances". Slowly and
solemnly the dancer executes its figures with feet dragging
along and toes lifted from the ground. In the fifteenth century,
there was no given order for the bowing, the simple, double,
sideways, or backward paces. The dancing master was left
to his own devices in the matter of arranging the dance to fit
the space, the music and the special occasion at which it was
performed. And the execution of the dance was as indefinite

as the order of steps. Sometimes there are two, sometimes three or four who participate. Sometimes the dancers appear two by two, sometimes they form a long chain "alla fila". Everything is done delicately, the erotic element is only hinted at in the slightest way.

There were two kinds of basse dances, the large and the small. The latter consists of a "Basse danse majeure" followed by a "Saltarello", (a leaped step which was called "Pas de Breban" - Brabant step). This is the same dance pair which we have already heard of, the estampita which is followed by a high jump of the fast rotta. The large basse consists of a "Basse danse majeure" and a "saltarello" with another "Basse danse mineure", which later is called by Arbeau "Retour de la basse danse", and is half as long as the "Basse danse majeure". The one reported by Arbeau has 84 measures for the majeur, 48 for the mineure basse danse.

What is the significance of the name "Basse danse"? Is there any special reason why the word "basse", - low - should have been used to name this form of dancing? Is it a "low dance" without high leaps or hopping, as Sachs believes, or does the word "low" refer to the music to which it was executed? The pictorial sources of the period again enlighten us. The instruments used for the music of this dance were two, three, or even more. In a Veronese "Picture Book" of the 14th century we see two players on the shalm and bag-pipe accompanying the estampita. A cassone picture from Florence dating from 1420, the so-called "Wedding of the Adimari", shows us three couples pace a solemn and slow measure as two pipers on the shalm and one playing the trombone, make the music. An unknown artist of the time around 1430 gives us a picture of the Duke of Burgundy, Philip the Good, and his court. In groups of two and three the dancers pace slowly, and the round is accompanied by an alto- and a tenor bombardon. A magnificently illuminated Bible, belonging to the Count of Ferrara, Borso, (he died 1471) brings us a miniature of a dance in which three knights and three ladies form the figure of a circle to the music of a shalm, an alto bombard, and a trombone. The treatises on dancing, and the other documents mention other instruments in addition to these.

Even the organ is named as an accompaniment for dancing. Of course, this organ is merely a small portable one which is easily handled, the right hand manipulating the keys, while the left hand regulates the pipe. This kind of organ is seen on the famous triptych of Hans Memling painted in 1480, now in the Museum at Antwerp.

Again and again we find the dances described as "high" and "low", a reminder of the fact that the instrumental music of the time is also defined as "musique haute" and "musique basse". In the fourteenth century this meant that musique haute was played on high instruments, that is on those that had a loud, penetrating tone, (such as trumpets, horns, cornets, shalms, bag pipes), whereas musique basse was performed on the low instruments, (flutes, violas, lutes, harps). Music to be played at festivities was performed on the high instruments and this high orchestra was placed accordingly on a balcony, a platform or other raised locality. Low music, played softly, was apparently used for more intimate occasions; it was the chamber music of that day, and it did not require a special arrangement of the hall or room where it was performed. In a rhymed description of a banquet which was given by Cosimo de Medici in honor of Galeazzo Sforza at Careggi, (a country house of the Medici family) there is a verse:

"E come da mangiar quivi levorsi
Arpe e viuole e simili stormenti
Puliti giovani a danzar fur mossi".

(After the meal, harps, violas and similar instruments invited the valiant young people to join in a dance.) However, when a state celebration was arranged out of doors, in the "Mercato Nuovo" the music was played by:

"pifferi e 'l' trombone
cominciaro a sonare"

(shalms and trombones began to play).

If we should rely on these sources, we should have to assume that originally the "Basse danses" were performed to music played only by softly sounding instruments. The pictures however show us that "high" music was used for the dances. As we have noted already every basse dance differed choreographically from any other according to the arrangement planned by the dancing master. The musician accompanying the dance took a definite melody, a so-called "tenor" and expanded or shortened it to the requirements of the dance. That is the reason why in a Brussels manuscript the melodies are given in plain-song notation and not in mensural notation. The plain-song notes, which were derived from the old "neumes" did not designate any definite rhythmic values, and were used in the "Gregorian Chant" where the length of the notes was determined in unregulated chant by the words of the psalm or hymn. The manuscript which belonged to Princess Margaret of Austria, daughter of Emperor Maximilian, dates from the early days of the 15th century. For the most parts these "tenors" or main melodies were taken from vocal compositions, or from well-known folk songs. We find all kinds of names for these dances. For example, one is called "La Rochelle", another "La Belle", a third "La Margarite", apparently in honor of the princess, and one called the "Basse Danse du Roy d'Espagne".

From the Spanish peninsula we have the "Portingaloise", "Barcelonne", and "La Navaroise"; from France the "Engoulème", "La Francheose", "Avignon", "Lille a marier", "Bayonne", "La Potevine", (apparently the old form of the minuet); from Burgundy "Le Joieux de Brucelles" and "La Haute Bourgogne"; and from Italy the "Florentine" and the "Venise".

The rhythm of the basse danse was like that of the estampita: a measure with an even beat divided into triplets, - according to Sachs and Besseler. This gives us a 6/8 rhythm, which appears in the "Basse Danse du Roy d'Espagne", one of the dances of the famous Brussels manuscript.

An integral part of the "basse danse" was the "saltarello", called "alta danza" in Spain, "pas de Brebant" in France. The saltarello does not signify that it was executed with high jumping or leaping. It meant rather that this dance was one of these with double steps in quick time. The first part of the "basse danse" was just a kind of procession around the dance hall or the space reserved for dancing. This was followed by a number of dance figures which consisted of fast single steps backwards and forwards, a hop on the right foot, with the left leg advanced, a movement backward, (while the left leg strikes the right), and two hopping steps sideways. We have here a combination of dances, each of which has its origin in a different social strata, one of them coming from peasant tradition, the other definitely arisen within the higher level of society, among the nobles and knights. So closely are the two dances interwoven and joined, that the melody of the saltarello is not even noted down. The musicians would only have to read it in another time, "cum proportione tripla", as is inscribed in the old books of medieval mensural notation. From these directions, the three-beat measure was called in Germany: "Proporz", or "Tripla".

According to Cornazzano, the theoretician of the dance, the Germans danced the "Quaternaria" which was often called "Saltarello Tedesco". This dance consisted of two simple steps, each of them on two quarter notes, and then, on the last quarter notes of the measure, a leap, with a slight backwards movement. Such fast four-beat dances following on the main dance are already exemplified in the rotta of earlier medieval times, and we find them again in the 17th and 18th century in "Laendlers".

We should not forget to mention the "Piva", a dance performed to the sounds of a bag-pipe, "piva" being the name of that instrument. Such a dance occurs in the early 18th century in the ballets of the young Matteis. performed at the Austrian court. The "piva" is the "hornpipe" of the early Renaissance. Though originally a peasant dance, it was taken over later by the high society. Cornazzano says that the music for the "piva" was sometimes called "Cacciata", and Sachs hints that perhaps this word might be brought into relation

with the "caccias", the picturesque forms of the old Italian
Canzone, and that there surely is a connection of the word
with the Slavic term "Skakati", "Skakac", which means to
leap. The word "piva" itself sounds Slavic: "Piti" means
"to drink" in Czech, pivo means beer. Might it not be possible
that the "piva", like so many other dances, for example the
Furlana, originated in the Slavic borderlands of the Venetian
plain and had something to do with beer?

According to Cornazzano the music of the piva was a
three-beat measure and twice as fast as that of the basse
danse. The metrical scheme of this sixteenth century dance is

♩ ♩ ♩ ♩

As late as 1508, Ambrosio Dalza in his lute book publishes
"Pive" which were set to the music of lutes.

In the 15th century we also find a dance called "Calata".
The dance is mentioned in a poem by Simone di Golino Pru-
denziani in the second quarter of the century. Ambrozio Dalza
publishes two Calate, one which he calls "A la spagnuola", the
other, "alla italiana". In Florence, we have the dancing master
Santino Comesari arranging a ballet for the Tuscan Court, in
which there is a Calata, a Corrente, and a Canario, plus a Gail-
larda. The rhythm is in four-beat time, either four fourths,
or 12 eights, in very lively tempo. But we have no records,
neither of the dance itself, nor of the melody which accompanied it.

Basse danse, Saltarello, Piva, Saltarello Tedesco, and
Calata, are the usual dances of the aristocrats of the 15th
century. Unfortunately it was assumed by the dancing masters,
that everyone knew them, therefore they give little detail as
to their execution. Besides these, there is a number of other
dances which have special names and programs and are dramatic and pantomimic in character. These latter obtain more
attention in the treatises because they were instrumental for
the inventive faculty and the skill of the ballet masters. It is

quite natural that the courtship, the wooing of the lady, in its various forms and phases should become the subject of these "Balli", the generic name for all kinds of pantomimic dances. We have for example, "La Mercantina", the woman who listens to anyone's wooing. She is represented as a lady, followed by two gentlemen, one next to her, the other behind her. The dance prescribes eleven measures of saltarello, then a stop, the gentleman in back of the lady turns sideways with six ripresa steps, the lady turns around while the other gentleman advances in three steps. Now the first partner turns on his heel and joins her, and so the pantomime goes on.

We have in these dances the first traces of the ballet, which was originally, (as well as in the 17th and 18th centuries), danced preferably by nobility, although it actually had its beginnings in the lower ranks of society, as a popular dance.

In his article in the "Musical Quarterly" of July 1941, Gombossi has pointed to the difference between the basse danse and the ballo, and has defined it thus: in contrast to the basse danse the ballo is pantomimic in form. It consists of a number of separate parts, each of them called misura. During the dance itself the tempo is changed several times. The basse danse retains the same time throughout. The ballo has a melody in the treble which is often taken from a song and is not only slightly altered. In the basse danse the melody is a "tenor" which is expanded or shortened as the choreography of the dance requires it; while the melodies used in the ballo are called "canti", the basse danse melodies have the title "tenori". Therefore, says Gombossi, it is easy to understand that the favorite orchestra of the 15th century consisted of two or three shalms and a slide trumpet. There is no other combination of instruments that better answers the requirements of a polyphonic bassadanza. The slide trumpet obviously sounded the theme, the single tones of which were clearly audible, since the steps of the dance had to correspond to them. The rich figuration of the counterparts could not have been better performed than by the shalms which were able to play rapid passages and had a peculiar nasal timbre that contrasted sharply with the sound of the trumpet, so full of sonore dignity.

Cornazzano in discussing the ballet particularly mentions one which he calls "Giove". It consists of a group of three, one woman between two men. Permit me to quote Gombossi in his description of this dance:

"Giove" is a ballo for three persons. The lady is in the middle and one gentleman in front of her, another behind.

In this configuration they all dance together three measures of "saltarello tedesco" and a whole turn in the measure of the "bassadanza". This they do twice.

Then the man in front turns around and walks towards the lady and she towards him, each touching the other's hand, with a double step on the right foot. Then the lady stops. The man in the rear walks towards the first, who leaves the lady with a double step on the left foot, and this man who has left the lady turns towards the other while he, touching the hand of the lady takes the place of the first man and the lady takes the place of the second man with a double step on the right foot and, turning around, occupies the same position as before, without loss of time. Then, all together, they execute two single steps and a double step, beginning with the left foot.

Then they all do the same again.

Then together they immediately execute nine double steps, all with the left foot, turning themselves around so that the lady remains in the middle after the completion of the nine steps.

Then all perform two measures of "saltarello" together, and the lady stops while the men perform two more and change places.

Then the lady executes a whole turn in the measure of the "bassadanza".

This "saltarello" has to be performed twice, with the changing of places repeated and with a second turn of the lady in the measure of the "bassadanza".

They take hands, first the gentleman in front turning towards the lady, then the other gentleman in the back.

Then they begin anew.

Among the dances of the Early Renaissance two are mentioned in the Italian literature of the day: the "Brando" and the "Moresca". Count Baldassare Castiglione in his handbook of etiquette published in 1514, the "Corteggiano", mentions both of them, but states that neither of them is really fitted for courtly practice. Brando is the Italian form for branle which was a particular figure used in the Basse danse in the 15th century, but in the 16th century designated a round dance. I would like to attempt here to give the etymological derivation of the word "Brando" from the German "Brand", according to which the Brand-Branle (Brand meaning fire in German) may have been a torch or a sword dance (Littré). This may correspond to the practice followed in France where a "Danse des Brandons" was performed in certain districts during the festivities of the carnival and centered around a burning bonfire. This dance was very popular in the 17th century, and at this time retained its original semi-religious character. In the province called the "Limousin", this tradition was kept alive down to the 18th century and during the dance the participants sang these words:

Saint Marcian pregas per nous
Et nous espingares per vous.

Even as late as the French Revolution brandons were danced.

More important, however, is the moresca, in England called "Morris Dance". We find it mentioned most frequently in the 15th century. It was so popular and important that in the 16th century the terms "Moresca" and "Ballet" were practically synonymous. Boehme regards the Moresca as a sword dance which was practiced everywhere where "there existed traditions of the historic struggle between the Christians and the Mohammedans". Apparently this sword dance was a symbolic representation of the battle between the Moors and Christians and was probably of Moorish origin. The Czech nobleman Leo von Rozmital who traveled through Spain and Portugal from 1465 to 1467 reports that he saw "gar koestlich taenz auf die

REPRESENTATION OF THE "WIRTSCHAFT" PERFORMED 1698 IN VIENNA, IN THE PRESENCE OF THE CZAR. IT WAS FOLLOWED BY AN ELABORATE BANQUET IN THE IMPERIAL CASTLE.

17TH CENTURY OUTDOOR DANCE

Through the Courtesy of the Museum of Modern Art

heidnische Meinung" (delightful dances in heathen style). Like so many other exotic dances this, originally oriental, dance seems to have come to Europe by way of Spain. Here in the Western world it had a most important role to play.

Sandberger has dealt with this dance in his treatise: "Roland Lassus' Beziehungen zur italienischen Literatur", (Sammelbaende der internationalen Musikgesellschaft V.p.412.) Agreeing with Boehme, he declares that the dance was written in a fast 3/2 time and in its simplest form consisted of two parts of eight measures each. Gradually this simple form was developed and extended till it became a pantomime, in fact, a ballet, so that entire pieces which contained one Moresca, were called by that name exclusively. Besides this form, mention is made of pantomimic expansions and enlargements of the dance particularly in the form of interpolated figures, (intermezzi) ballet-like interludes which were made a part of the Italian dramatic performances so that, finally, the concept "Moresca" came to mean not merely a whole performance but also a special part of such a performance. In other words, the ballet "Moresca" also included a dance "Moresca". Count Castiglione describes a performance of Bibbiena's "Calandra", the first intermezzo was a Moresca danced by Jason, as a sword dance. In all the interludes of Calandra the dances were Moresche. It would lead too far afield to give descriptions of the countless Moresche which were part of the Masques in the early part of the 16th century and really belonged to the dramatic literature. Orlandus Lassus has composed a number of such vocal "Masques" (Mascherate) and it seems that these "Moresche" were the counterparts to other subspecies of the "Masques" as the "Bergamasche", "Tedesche", "Spagnuole", "Napoletane", "Toscanelle", "Ebraiche", in which typical popular genre scenes were played in the special native dialect. For example we find in the "Moresca" occasional interpolations of "Allah", and the Neapolitan Negro characters Lucia and Georgia, point to this fact. Here in Naples, where the tradition of the ancient struggle with the Moors was still alive, such dramatic "Moresche" were greatly favored. Sandberger in his preface to Lassus' work describes how the travelling comedians playing on the shore in front of the castles performed their realistic scenes. Clad in rags they followed a drummer and their only designation of what their stage was to represent, were the words which one of them wrote on the pavement with charcoal. In the evening the knights of Naples were their audience and took delight in the comedy which often verged on the burlesque.

Lassus' "Moresche" are written in the Neapolitan dialect in most lively and dramatically effective language, i.e. genuine Neapolitan art! The gibberish which he uses occasionally is also found in Vecchi's "Amfiparnasso". Here is a short illustration of the content of such a Moresca: The negress Georgia would like to serenade Lucia but is repudiated with the harsh words: "cula mia, cula caccata".

On another occasion Lucia is to be married off by her mistress and Georgia brings her the message. All colored people of Naples should be invited. No matter how fiercely Georgia screamed: "acqua madonna! al fuoco!" - - - Lucia refused to listen and let her scream till she was hoarse. In many instances the text is drastically realistic and unappetising that our modern more tender sensibility would be offended by a translation. And yet these compositions of Lassus' are a true picture of Neapolitan folk music. There is no doubt that these vocal Moresche were accompanied by dances. Their rhythm is homophonic and dance-like and they distinguish between step- and hop-dance - ("Nachtanz").

This last example is a shortened "hop-dance" of the same kind as we have noted in discussing the medieval rotta.

It goes without saying that Lassus' Moresche are highly

stylized. In the true Neapolitan comedy there were no madrigals but the hoarse and shrill-voiced negresses were represented by singers with hoarse voices screaming to the accompaniment of a primitive lute. Lassus, however, succeeded in giving a very realistic picture of the grotesque chatter of the black-a-moors.

At a later date Moresche came to be understood quite generally to mean an interpolation in ballet form within the comedy. It was quite usual at the court of Ferrara to introduce Moresche in every dramatic performance, and the above mentioned Moresca which was played in the "Calandra" had nothing whatever in common with Moors or Saracens. In 1638 Nicola Sabbatini in his treatise on the theatre speaks of Moresche, i.e. ballets "during which the musicians are to be placed on the balconies." Both in Cavalieri's "Rappresentazione di anima e di corpo" (1600) and in Monteverdi's "Orfeo" the term "moresca" means nothing more or less than the ballet.

In a previous chapter we have noticed that in the Moorish dances, the dances around a "black boy", an old primitive fertility dance was revived, and in this connection I should like to mention again the rattles which were regularly used during the harvest and fertility dances of the primitive peoples. In the same way, the "Moresche" were danced with bells, and Arbeau mentions them specifically. He says: "In my youth I had many occasions to witness the practice which prevailed in good society at the close of the meal. A boy with blackened face, his brow bound in white or yellow silk, wearing bells on his ankles, performed the Mauresque. He made a number of passages through the hall, returned back to the place from whence he had started, and again began new figures. This he repeated again and again, always changing his figures which was done to the great delight and amusement of the audience." Arbeau also gives us the music. On each quarter note there is a hop with one foot and on the half there is a jump with both feet. This Mauresque also had a hop dance which was danced in the same measure, but by having the notes divided into eights, was performed twice as fast. The sound of the bells is characteristic for the Mauresque. Here the melody:

These fertility motives which found their expression in the sword dances and bell dances resulted in strange combinations, for example in Spain, where the resurrection and the rebirth celebrated during the Easter festival harked back to themes of ancient days. We are told that in the cathedral at Toledo rounds are played at Easter time which contain the old Moorish battle theme. In place of the bells, castanets are used, and it is a remarkable fact that these dances are executed by six persons called "Seises", six, the same number performing the "Morris dances" in England.

In England dating from about the time of Edward III, the "Morris" was one of the popular forms of celebrating the first of May. We have no certainty that this Morris dance was in any way connected with the Moresca, but there is no doubt that it originated in old heathen practises in the same way as the "Furrey Dance". Frank Kidson tells in his "Old Century Dances and Morris Tunes": "In the Middle Ages the Morris dance was performed with the most elaborate ceremony. A hobby horse was a part of it and a jester contributed his share to the gaiety. The other dancers were men and youths whose garments were plentifully beribboned and with an infinity of bells sewn on them. The music was supplied by a pipe and tabor, or a bag-pipe, or both in conjunction. In Elizabeth's reign the Morris formed part of the Robin Hood games, and the outlaw himself, Maid Marian and other characters mentioned in the Robin Hood Ballads, were represented." Indeed, the horse seems to be a remnant from an old dance around a totem animal. The horse had a special role as a sacrificial animal in the England of pre-Christian time, (Hengist and Horsa), but it is true that we find dances with horse-masks in Spain and on the Balearic Islands, and also in Germany the "Schimmelreiter" (rider on a white horse) reappears at Whitsuntide. In North-Bohemia, this season brings us disguised men who ride about on white horses to the sound of bells and the cracking of whips through the fields outside the town, and they pass through the town in solemn procession. All these motives, disguise, blackening of face, the horse, the change of sex: man into woman and woman into man - are used all over the world and wherever they may appear they stand for the symbols of fertility.

The "Mauresques" which Arbeau has noted for us, are still being played in England and have been recorded by Kidson under the name of "Tabourot's Morris". My belief is that Arbeau's melody was originally English, and this because it was already printed in England in 1550. Sachs says: "The Morris dance is definitely a dance of wide steps, and depending on manly strength. We find in it no turns, no pointed toes, no gliding and no swaying. Its step is a vigorous advance with one leg, while the other hops up lightly". The analogy between these steps and the music of the "Mauresque" is obvious. We have measures with an even number of beats, march-like melodies in dotted eighths that mark the castanets, the bells and the down-beat of the foot. Down to the 17th century such "Mauresques" were used in the "Ballets". A later chapter will give us the descriptions of these in detail. Schmelzer, the "Kapellmeister" at the Court of Vienna, wrote one as follows:

In the Vienna of those days "Moresche" were of special significance, since this Austrian capital has been beleaguered by the Turks in the 16th and 17th centuries. The "Theatrum Europaeum", the political periodical of this time, tells us of a

"Moor Parade", "Mohrenaufzug" in 1652 as follows: "In the carnival there were so many Moor parades that almost only Moors and Turks were to be seen on the streets".

The following example is an English Morris dance melody of the 17th century which is still being played. It is interesting to compare it with the Schmelzer example.

Heckel's "Lute Book" of 1562 brings us a Moresca. Here in its South German form, called "Maruska Tanz", reminding us of the carvings of the "Maruschka Taenzer" of the City Hall in Munich:

All these genuine Mauresques, it must be remembered, are in no way related to the general meaning of the term which signifies "Ballet". Such were the ballets or moresques of "Orfeo" by Monteverdi, and "La Moresque" by Michael Praetorius, recorded in his "Terpsichore" and reprinted by Mersenne in 1636, and later in the collection "Amoenitatum hortulus" (little garden of delights). The last three are in 3/2 time, and they belong to the groups of ballets which we shall discuss in the following chapter.

CHAPTER VI.

THE RENAISSANCE.

WITH the turn of the 16th century we enter an age which is flooded by the light of a happier way of life. The social life of Gothic days always subservient to the all-dominant structures of the Church, is now imbued with a more liberal, varied and imaginative outlook which naturally has its counterpart in the colorfulness and fantastic display at all festivities and entertainments. Though the gap which existed between the classes persisted, peasant play and aristocratic entertainment had in common the folklore elements that could now be found in both of them. The discovery of America, and with it the greater broadening of views in a widened geographical world showed itself in the use of many exotic elements, both in the arrangement of the entertainment, in the locality chosen for the subject of dramatic pieces and in the forms of the dance.

The Renaissance is a time of self-expression, a time of the loosening of restraints. Man now is no longer merely interested in the development of spiritual values, but desires to become effective in the world that surrounds him. Printing, that most important of all discoveries for the release of the human spirit, is introduced and with it the veil is lifted which has hung over the dance music of previous centuries. At one stroke we have a flood of printed dance music for instruments such as lutes, guitars, organs, stringed and key-board instruments, and naturally the variety and the manifold forms of the dances which prevailed, appear in the musical field.

It has been emphasized that the peasant class, that group of society which in its cultural form is nearer to nature, favored

89

the sturdy dances with wide steps, dances that are pantomimic
as a whole or, at least, contain pantomimic elements of the
kind that we still see used in the play of children. Such an
influence coming from the peasant culture shows itself actively
in the Renaissance. Already in the former chapter, when we
discussed the Ballo as a "popular" dance, we saw that certain
dramatic elements could be found in it. The ballet such as we
see it developed in the Renaissance, is the most developed form
of pantomimic dancing, and embodies the new "folk" spirit,
the new "extrovert" culture of this period. We must, however,
not forget that its first beginnings occurred already in the
Middle Ages. One of the most popular motifs was that of the
Moresca, (also discussed in the previous chapter), with its
black man impersonating the Moor, the Saracen of history.
Such a dramatic representation was performed as early as in
1377 at the court of Charles V of France in honor of the
German Emperor Charles IV. During the banquet two pieces
were portrayed. Two topics: the one the city of Jerusalem
held by the Saracens, the other a galley manned by the soldiers
of the Crusader Godfrey of Bouillon. After a skillfully arranged mock battle the crusaders closed in on the city. Another
favorite subject for representations resembling ballets was the
reoccupation of Spain by the Christians, this indeed a true
"moresca". At the celebration of the conquest of Granada on
February 19th, 1493, a pantomimic pageant with triumphal
arches, a procession of Spanish royalty, Moorish dances, and
bullfights was performed. In 1571 a "Trionfo di Christo per
la vittoria contra i Turchi" was played before the Doges of
Venice, in honor of the victory of Lepanto. At the court of
Ferrara, in celebration of a marriage the interpolated ballets
played at a performance of Plautus' comedies in 1491, were
the most important part of the entertainment. Here the audience beheld a group dance performed by youths dressed in
garments of ivy, then Apollo appeared playing his lyra and
singing a paean in honor of the newly-weds, the House of
Este and the guests. Thereupon,—as "intermezzo" of an intermezzo—a peasant "Genre scene" took place with peasants

imitating in pantomime farm work. All this was followed by a mythological act with Venus, Apollo, Bacchus and their partisans.

To these ballet-like performances also belong the masqued processions and pageants which were held during the carnival and at the beginning of Spring. They were particularly popular in Florence. Such "Mascherate" are found again and again in the records of the 16th century. The text which accompanies them often is a direct allusion to the disguise used, "Zingari siamo" (we are gypsies) or "Nymphe siamo". It was the song of the passing groups and we may well imagine that the gypsy dances were accompanied by grotesque somersaults. Such scenes had, as we know, occurred already in Lassus' Moresche. Vasari tells us in detail of the celebrated "Masques" of Cosimo di Medici. His description of the scenes is so vivid that we imagine we see them enacted before us. At nightfall 22 to 30 pairs of horses, elaborately decorated, were led out by their riders, each of them differently dressed and accompanied by 6 to 8 servants swinging their torches. There followed a great chariot covered with exotic and fantastic pieces of precious booty. It is a matter of course that the music for such an extraordinary entertainment did not lag behind; but unfortunately none of the "entries" and flourishes of this time are recorded in the picturesque description of the painter-biographer.

The first Italian operas have their ballets and soon the ballet as an art-form standing by itself, is practised in Italy. Cesare Negri, the famous "il trombone", describes one of these which was presented in honor of the visit of the Archduke of Austria, Albert, and his consort, the Spanish princess Donna Isabella. Its subject was the pastoral poem "Armenia". Here we have the story of Orpheus and Euridice with the Argonauts appearing on the stage and with it the seductive dances and songs of the sirens. After all the items of mythology had been exhausted, a most beautiful "Bellissimo Brando" was danced, but there again are no records of musical notations from this performance.

During this period Italian art culture was the pattern for all other European court-life and the French court tried most anxiously to outdo the splendor of the entertainments that were performed in the House of the Medici. In 1582, when the wedding of Marguerite of Lorraine, the step-sister of Henry III with the Duke of Joyeuse was to be celebrated, a magnificent festival took place. Its climax was that famous "Ballet Comique de la Royne" which was directed by Balthazar, called Baltazarini, a violinist who had been recommended to Catherine of Medici, the consort of Henri III, by the Marshal of Brissac. Balthazar had been given the nickname "Beaujoyeul" because of the joyous plays that he had composed for the court. In reality this "joyous play" is a veritable monstrosity, a kind of endless variety-show in the style of the Renaissance; a lengthy succession of mythological scenes, dances, songs, in most elaborate scenic designs with the music of the royal musicians Beaulieu and Salmon, with the performance lasting from 10 in the evening till 4 in the morning. (Poor performers, poor spectators!) Truth be said, this ballet presents no comic elements, unless we may consider them involuntarily humorous, for the subject is the transformation wrought by Circe on her prisoners when she turns them into animals, a somewhat daring subject for a royal representation. Immediately after the notes of the famous "Air de Clochette" a gay piece, to the discussion of which we shall return when speaking of the Gavotte, the entire cast, nymphs, pages, even the ten accompanying. violinists are turned into immovable statues by the enchantress. She retires into a grove when Mercury suddenly descends to the earsplitting noise of thunderclaps from the ceiling of the hall. The prisoners are released by application of the magic herb, and the ballet and music accompanying all this, is on a scale as colossal as the number of the cast and the size of the scenic decorations used. In the cupola of the ball room were placed not less than ten bands of musicians with instruments of the most varied kinds to serve as an echo to the voices of the singers: oboes, cornets, trombones, violas da gamba, lutes, harps and flutes. It is quite natural that the music for this seems to us somewhat ponderous, as if wearing chains on its feet, quite unlike the music of the 18th century. The "delightful" Balthazar expanding French pathos and verbosity plus a kind of elaborate self-importance which seems to have been a personal characteristic of his, moves slowly and solemnly.

The dances themselves are rounds, long drawn-out. We have here the basic principle of the Suite, anticipated by the span of time of many generations. The first ballet consists of a long and solemn introductory movement, comparable to a basse danse in even beats, the composition of which shows that the composer was forced to follow the dictates of the choreographer. Following upon the lengthy development of a movement which begins like this:

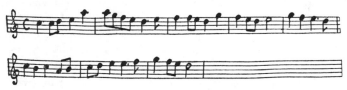

comes a "Tourdion", the successor of the Saltarello:

Thereupon after a short quotation of the first dance, we get that famous "clochette", later erroneously known as "Gavotte Louis XIII". But even ampler than this is the final ballet which in its plan and construction is already a forerunner of the Chaconnes of Lully's operas. A "branle" is succeeded by

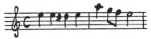

a dance in even beats, and so on and so forth. Though these dances do not in any way resemble social dances, being very loosely constructed, they have their part in a study of the history of the Suite.

In the history of the social dance a number of documents are most important. In 1536 Antonius de Arena published a little book in "Maccaroni verses", (Latin, with Provencal,

Italian and French elements), which he called "ad companiones qui sunt de persona friantes, basses dansas et branlos practicantes". Even more important is the "Orchesographie", 1588, written by Jehan Tabourot, who was a member of a religious order and whom we have quoted before under the name of Arbeau. Then there is the Italian Fabritio Caroso de Sermoneta, who published a text book for dancers in 1581, which he called "Il ballerino". This same book had a second edition in 1600, called "Nobilità di dame", and a third in 1630, having the title "Raccolta di balli". The book consists of two parts, the first of which contains a description of the steps and rules of dances, the second, a description of the dances customary in Italy, France and Spain, at that time. We have already mentioned Cesare Negri, called "Il Trombone", who was a lutenist of Upper Italy and came to Vienna as the dancing master of the later Austrian Emperor Rudolf II. In 1604, Negri published a book of instructions in Milan, which he called "Nuove Invenzioni di balli", containing many dance tunes as well as the short biographies of 37 famous dancing masters. Beccaria, who was active at the court of Rudolf II., used his methods, and these (under Santo and Domenico Ventura) prevailed until late into the 17th century. What do these various writers tell us about the dances of the time? Arena mentions only the "bassa danza" and the "brando". Arbeau, however, had a number of new dances. He, too, in his textbook which has the form of a dialogue between him and his pupil ("Capriol" - - "Somersault") speaks of the "basse danse" but says that it has not been performed frequently for 40 or even 50 years. But, says he, "I foretell that the sensible and honorable ladies will see to it that it will be taken up again". In order to prepare for this time, the dancing master tells his pupil just how the basse danse is to be performed somewhat like this: Capriol asks his teacher: "Master Arbeau, how should I do the basse dance?" And Arbeau answers: "Just as soon as you get to the place where the honorable company has assembled, choose a young lady, and while you take off your hat with the left hand, stretch out your right hand to lead her to the dance.

Now the teacher explains to his pupil all the three parts of the dance, the basse danse, proper: the "retour", and the "tourdillon". As a musical example he gives us a dance to the tune of the song "Jouyssance vous donneray" (to thee I grant delight) and under the various parts of the melody he designates the steps of the dance.

What a change we see here, what difference between this
and the primitive music of the basse danse in the 15th century!
We seem to have come upon a familiar ground after long and
strange wandering in a wilderness. But we must not forget
that between the dances of Marguerite of Austria and of Cornazzano and those of Arbeau a long period has elapsed, and
there are no documents of this time which might be a transition from this example of an old fashioned dance. Here we
breathe already the fresh air of the spirited and lively folksong,

but the musical example does not illustrate another important distinction set apart from previous ones. A remark of Arbeau's gives us a hint (though this was already true at the time of Arena) : no longer is the musician bound by the behests of the dancing master as was true in the 15th century; now the dancer must obey the music. Furthermore the time is shortened by half the value of the notes, a practice which was part of the developments of 16th century music. And lastly the former technique of a purely melodic flow without definite "measured" phrases, was replaced by a simple folk-like music with a period-icity, based on the phrase of four measures. The melody is embellished and arranged for instruments. We find it in the compositions for voices by Claudin de Sermisy and Rhaw's collections "Bicinia Gallica" of 1545, where he mentions it as a composition by Adrian Willeart.

The "hop-dance" of every "basse danse" was a "Tourdion". Arbeau says that the Tourdion was danced to the music as the "Gaillard", but low on the floor, fairly fast and brief, while the "Gaillard" was higher and slower. As an example he gives us this Tourdion:

Actually, the rhythm is exactly the same as that of the Gaillard, of which we shall speak later and in detail:

A number of prints which are published by the French printer Attaignant, and the Belgian composer and printer of music, Tilman Susato, "Het derde Muziekboecken", (1551) contain basse dances, set for four parts. He calls the dances "Bergerettes", doubtlessly deriving this name from the songs used.

The dances of this time are arranged for four or five parts

and the instruments playing them were viols or fiddles in the treble, alto, tenor and bass pitch. These old viols differed greatly from our old violins, not only in general shape but also in the manner in which the strings were attached and in the form of the sound holes. The body was almost pointed towards the neck, the openings on the side in the shape of half-moons, the upper part of the body was narrower than the lower; the side parts were higher than in our modern instruments, but the lower board of the body was quite flat without the smallest arch. The sound holes were shaped like sickles placed back to back and were so-called C holes in contrast to our F holes. All the different viols had six strings. Only the treble viol was set with five strings in France and was therefore called Quinton or Quinte. The strings were pretty close to another on the finger board divided by frets, the bridge was curved only slightly, and the playing on the middle strings was fairly difficult, though chords could be struck with ease. The sound of these viols was much deeper and darker, and compared with the brilliant tone of our violins seemed rather nasal. In addition to the viols, there were flutes, shalms, and cornets. The last-mentioned are wind instruments, no longer used now, similar in the manner of tone production to our horns, trumpets and trombones having a rounded mouthpiece into which the lips are pressed. It is however not of brass but of wood and has fingerholes. The mouthpiece of the cornet was of ivory or hard wood and its hole was only a few millimeters wide. The smaller cornets were for the most part straight "cornetti dritti" and were called "white cornets" in contrast to the larger "black" cornets with curved body. The "Cornetto dritto" sounded light, its mouthpiece was attached, the "Bass Cornet" had a harsher and more hornlike tone. Besides viols, flutes (recorders) and cornets, there were also lutes, organs and harpsichords; but apparently the lute, clavichord and organ arrangements of the dances seemed to have been intended for general music entertainment rather than as accompaniment for dancing.

For a long time the question was being discussed whether the "Basses Danses" had the tenor or the treble as main part.

In the 15th century, the tenor seems to have been used for the basses danses whereas the balli, as we have seen, had the treble. In the course of the 16th century, the melodic stress falls more and more on the treble. The tenor, however, continues to retain much of its former independence.

The "Basse Danse" as relic of a former time took refuge in the aristocratic circles in the same way as the minuet of the later period kept its place until the end of the 18th, even to the beginning of the 19th century, as the solemn dance of the upper classes. But its solemnity and stiffness, which expresses itself also in the music, was abandoned by the lower classes who took over a new, gay, lively and active dance figure, the Gaillard. Even though it is a "hop-dance", namely that of the Pavane, this latter dance disappeared more and more into the background in favor of the joyous Gaillard.

If we are to follow Arbeau, the renowned dancing master, we must place the Pavane at the head of all the dances of this time. It takes the place of the displaced Basse danse, is also in duple rhythm and may perhaps be regarded as its strictly regulated form, if we remember that this dance was in reality not at all prescribed in definite ways, but left to the invention and the taste of the dancing master. The name of the Pavane comes from "pavoneggiare", to strut, to blow up like a peacock. It was originally danced in Spain and the gesture as well as the music of this dance express "Spanish grandezza", a mixture of proud bearing and unapproachableness. It is written in four fourths time and danced with two single and double steps forwards, or forwards and backwards. When the Pavane reached Italy, it was somehow connected in the minds of musicians, particularly Germans, with the city of Padua, and we find that around 1600 it was called "Padovana". There are, however, genuine paduanas, which have nothing to do with the Spanish pavane and are written in 6/8 time, (sometimes combined in 2/8 and 3/8, as for example "Ein Anderer Paduan" taken from Noermiger's tablature of 1598. With proud bearing, and head held high, the gentlemen danced the pavane with sword at their hip, and cloak flung over their shoulder. Arbeau says of the pavane: "Let the noble gentleman dance it with sword and beret, the others in their long robes; the honorable merchant may follow its pace with serious mien. The ladies show a modest demeanour, lower their eyes and only from time to time glance up at the audience with maidenly coyness. For kings, princes and great dignitaries the pavane serves, that they may show themselves in their great cloaks and ceremonial robes as they lead forth the queen, the princesses and the ladies of the court, whose trains drag on the floor or are carried by their serving maids".

"The pavane is played by oboes and trombones, (this is called the great dance) and continues until all the performers have circled the hall two or three times, if they have not performed the dance by stepping forwards and backwards. At masques where gods and goddesses, emperors and kings appear on their triumphal chariots, the pavane is in order". Arbeau records a pavane in four parts. The tambourine gives the rhythms to the sounds of trombones and oboes as follows:

In 1604 Cesare Negri records a "Pavaniglia alla Romana" and a "Pavaniglia all'uso di Milano". These are prettified forms of the old pavane, similar to the dances which came from Spain around 1600 with the new name "Pavane d'Espagne" and spread all over Europe.

In Shakespeare's time, whenever a pavane was danced, it was followed without fail by a Gaillard, as surely as the Amen followed the prayer. Later, in the 17th century the Gaillard stood alone, but continued on its merry way. The Italian called it Gagliarda, the English Gaillard and the Spanish Gallarda. An allusion in Bojardo's "Orlando innamorato" points to the fact that the Gaillard was known already at the end of the 15th century. Attaignant prints Gaillards in Paris in 1529; in 1541, they appear in England, somewhat later in Germany. Meyer-Luebke gives us the etymology of the word. According to him its root is "galleus", a gall-apple, from which we get the Provençal galhart, French gaillard, Italian gagliarda, gay, full in bloom. It is erroneous to derive gaillard quasi vaillarde from validus as Taubert does in his "Rechtschaffener Tantzmeister", of 1717 and Walther does in his Dictionary, 1732. Michael Praetorius, one of the most reliable sources of instrumental music in the 17th century says in his "Syntagma Musicum" (Musical Treatise), "Weil demnach der Gaillard mit Geradigkeit und guter Disposition, mehr als andere Taenze verrichtet werden, hat er ohne Zweifel den Namen daher bekommen." (Because in truth, the Gaillard is executed with upright mind and good spirits even more than even other dances, therefore it has taken this name). "Er hat ein gar froeliches straffes Wesen" (Its spirit is gay and well-regulated).

The gaillard was danced in bold and exuberant fashion. Sachs says that it was the only dance of the period, which was performed with bare head, while the dancer carried his hat in his hand. This, however, contradicts a statement of Arbeau's who says that, after the bow made by the dancer to his partner during which he lifts his hat, he replaced the hat and goes on with the dance.

Each phrase consists of twice three half notes, but on this period five steps are to be taken, and for this reason the Gaillard is sometimes called "cinq pas" (cinque passa) - Shakespeare calls it the "sinkapas". First the left, then the right leg is lifted, then again the left and the right, and on the fifth note there is a leap into the air, while on the sixth the dancer resumes the first posture now on the left foot, so that he may begin again, this time with the right. The characteristic step of the Gaillard is the "grue" which means this: "that one foot is placed somewhat in front of the body as a support while the other is lifted as if wanted to kick somebody". In other words, the Gaillard, true to its peasant character and origin, is a "high" dance, a dance with wide steps; in accordance with this fact it was originally a pantomimic dance: the dancer traverses the hall two or three times with his lady and then performs a short solo-dance before her. She retreats, now dancing in her turn in the opposite direction, while the male dancer continues his choreographic pantomimic pursuit and his movements become brisker. And so the dance continues until the musicians stop playing. "Today," Arbeau complains, "the Gaillard is danced so violently and people are satisfied simply to make the five steps and quelques passages sans alcune disposition (figures without any planning). They dance it backwards to the side and across the hall." Arbeau's example of a Gaillard melody is as follows:

This rhythm is soon replaced by the following:

but in the Gaillards written around 1700 and later we find much uncertainty and ambiguity. Sometimes the rhythm goes like this:

sometimes divided like this:

and the interchange of rhythm is often indicated by an alternate use of these two rhythms in one and the same piece. Even the later rhythm of the Courante:

with its strange retarded syncopation is often found in the Gaillard. Note for example this Gaillard taken from Johann Hermann Schein's "Banchetto Musicale" of 1617:

We shall not deal at length with the tourdion almost identical with the Gaillard. This was a hop-dance of the basse danse, but became an independent dance in the 16th and 17th centuries. The one noted by Caroso resembles that of Arbeau closely:

The Courante is mentioned for the first time by Clement Marot in 1515 in his "Epitre des Dames de Paris". This dance was originally a pantomimic dance and one of the large group of courting dances. According to Arbeau's description it may have been quite an innocent affair at the beginning. This is what Arbeau says about it: "Six young people, three gentlemen and three ladies, place themselves in a row. The first dancer takes his lady to the farther end of the hall and lets her stand alone while he returns to the others. The second and third dancer repeat this so that the ladies stand alone at one end, the gentlemen at the other end of the hall. As soon as all three gentlemen are together, the first one, preening himself like a bird, returns again to his partner, with all kinds of leaps and loving gestures, adjusting his garments. She gently rebukes him and turns her back to him. Whereupon he retreats and with gesture indicates his disappointment. The other two do likewise. Following this, all three of them advance dancing towards the ladies, bend their knees, and with folded hands beg for mercy. The ladies permit their partners to hold them close and dance the courante to the end". Arbeau assures his pupils that "nowadays" the steps of the dance are the same, but that the young people no longer know the difference between a simple pace and a double pace, and dance as they please. "While they dance, they often make turns, let go the hand of their partner, then take it again and thus they go on. Just as soon as one dancer gets tired, the others elope with his lady". Arbeau's musical example is as simple as it can possibly be, but it is remarkable that it should be one with a duple beat.

The figure which constituted the characteristic movement of the courante consisted of an alternation of two simple and one double pace, first to the left and then to the right. In this way the couples zig-zagged across the hall. In accordance with the originally popular character of the dance, the tempo in the 16th and at the beginning of the 17th century was a fast one. Shakespeare in his "Henry V" calls the dance "Swift coranto". The changing rhythmical treatment of the Gaillard was also used in the courante. We find for example both these

$$\quad$$

as well as modifications of these two rhythms.

The parallel development of the French Courante and the Italian Corrente has been stressed. It seems that the Italian form had a swifter tempo and a more regular and steady rhythm.

Such Italian Correnti were written in 1620 by the Venetian composer Biagio Marini (1597-1665), who later became attached to the Court of the Count Palatine in Neuburg and

Duesseldorf and was the first violin virtuoso of importance. Both the French and Italian courante have the upbeat, but in the French one we find more frequently an inversion of the rhythm.

Thus Schein in the above mentioned "Banchetto" writes this "Courante à 5":

The development of the characteristic courante-rhythm—an alternation of the following rhythms

occurred in France and in Germany in the 17th century. Mersenne already in 1636 gives as an example of a courante with a typical French rhythm:

The French school of this century gradually transformed the fast courante into a slower, more solemn dance. It became the favorite of the aristocracy, the successor of the pavane, and the predecessor of the minuet. Its defamers called it the "doctor's" or "professor's" dance. There were courantes which bore the caption "largo" in which the couples circled the hall in regularly determined steps, holding each other by the hand or walking singly. There were different forms, the "Courante simple"—consisting of steps forwards only, the "Courante figurée" with forward, backward and side steps. There were the "Pas-de-coupé", a step with bent knee, which was followed by the "Pas-de-courante", a sliding step with knee bent and lifted heel which followed it. The figures were danced to these two rhythms:

The first of these had a step with bent knee, a certain syncopated dragging form and developed this rhythm:

while the paced step followed this rhythm:

Thousands of these dances were written and most of them had in common a combination of three different rhythms, the same combination which confronts us in Bach's Courantes. Take, for example, the first Courante in the First English Suite which I give here in one voice and without ornaments only.

The first three measures show the typical French courante steps, the fourth one the rhythm taken over from the old form of the Gaillard (3/2 beat). Bach gives us the Courante after the

Allemande, Arbeau does the opposite. The Frenchman tells us that the Allemande was a dance used by the Germans in moderate time, apparently one of the "oldest dances". The Allemande, too, seems to have been a pantomimic dance. A slight reminiscence of this is present in Arbeau's description. It was an open couple dance similar to the Basse Danse or the Pavane. With the difference that the steps in the Allemande were simple steps forwards and backwards and the couples followed each other as they traverse the hall. Arbeau says: "Occasionally the young man dancing the Allemande cut in and those deprived of their partners try to get others . . . but I cannot approve this practice because it must lead to quarrels and to discontent". Apparently the motive of jealous partners and of the kidnapped bride, a primitive Germanic theme was the pantomimic nucleus of the Allemande. This dance, too, had a lively hop-dance which was called in Germany "Hupfauf" or "Proporz". According to Arbeau the Allemande consisted of two parts followed by a third, danced in faster time and with shorter steps, accompanied by low hops just as in the Courante. The musical example given by Arbeau is the following:

Michael Praetorius characterises the Allemande as "not being arranged for definite steps and pas" and as "usually consisting of three repetitions, each of which consists customarily of four bars". Courantes from Schein's Banchetto show this clearly. This tripartite form of the dances, found in the compositions of Schein, and of the Austrians Paul Peurl and Isaac Posch is also usual in many flute and keyboard notations, where it is not confined to the allemande. But in some cases, forty years before and thirty years later, we find allemandes which are divided into two parts, as for example the "Allemande Bruyns-medelijn" (nut-brown maiden) in the collection of dances of the Belgian Pierre Phalèse, dating from 1571.

The following example is from the "Studenten-Musik" of Johann Rosenmueller, published in 1654.

This form of the allemande, a solemn and dignified round dance disappeared in the course of the 17th century. It should not be confused with the "Allemande", the German waltzed dance, which was the great vogue of the German ball rooms of the 18th century and played an important part in the compositions of the classical composers under the name of "Deutscher". We find the old form appearing in the works of Purcell, Bach, Handel, and many others.

At this point I should like to mention an interesting fact in connection with the Rosenmueller example: it shows (as many other dances of the same period, especially those of German origin) a rhythm which is completely different from both, the dances by Arbeau and those of the 18th century. It is a dry rhythm without impetus and vitality. Its weak accents are divided all over the whole musical phrase. I would indeed not blame any one not experienced in musical history who would say: these dances sound much more like church hymns than like dances. . . .

We must, however, leave Arbeau, our cleric dancing master

and deal for a short time with sources concerning the dance called "Passamezzo" which is mentioned so frequently in the Italian documents of the 16th century. Caroso writes "Passo e mezzo" which might justify us in taking the translation "step and half" dance. Praetorius, however, gives another explanation in his analysis. He says: "Just as the Gagliard (as he calls it) has five steps and is therefore called Cinque pas, so the passomezzo has scarcely half as many as the latter, that is to say "mezzopasso". In reality this dance was the Italian pavane, danced in a somewhat faster tempo. Sometimes we find the designation "Pass'e mezzo moderno" and "antico". These were no doubt the names for more ancient and more modern melodies. The lute and keyboard tablatures contain countless Passamezzi. But the musical line in these is often completely hidden by undecipherable figurations and elaborations, as is the case with the first bars of the passomezzo, (published in 1577), from the organ tablature of Bernhard Schmid the Elder, a citizen and organist of Strassburg.

Every passomezzo had "il suo saltarello", which at that time was a lively courante favoring a strongly dotted 3/4 rhythm but occasionally—especially in the later part of the 17th century—was in 2/4 time.

This is the place to speak of the English "Measure", the dance of Elizabethan times, performed as a solemnly paced dance. The same name was given to dances which were part of the "Masques". Old measures were the proper dances of the masques, while new measures were the unbridled dances of the "Antimasques". Reyher in "Les Masques Anglais 1512-1640" says that the measure sprung from the basse danse, a statement which is surely justified, as we frequently find that in the 16th century single steps lend their name to entire dances, so in the case of the branle and the volta. We also find the name "Maass Tanz" (measure dance), occurring frequently in Germany. In E. N. Ammerbach's Tablature of 1571 we find a "Bruder Conrad's Tanzmaass". We do not know much about "Bruder Conrad", except that he is also mentioned in the Tablature of the Elder Bernhard Schmid of 1577 in a "Bruder Conrad Dantzmaass", though there the melody is quite different. There is also a "Maass Tantz" in the lute book of Stefan Craus preserved in the Vienna State Library with the following beginning (a version without ornamentation).

An even older form is recorded by Hans von Constanz in Kotter's Tablature of 1513 as "Dantz maass Benzenauer".

The measure which was danced on festive occasions—even the philosopher Lord Bacon did not hesitate to join in it—is described by Shakespeare in "Much Ado about Nothing". Beatrice says to Leonato: "For, hear me, Hero: wooing, wedding and repenting is as Scotch Jig, a measure and a cinquepas: the first suite is hot and hasty, like a Scotch jig, and as full as fantastical, the wedding mannerly modest, a measure full of state and ancientry and then comes repentance, and with his bad legs falls into the cinquepas faster and faster, till he sinks into his grave". German writers and musicologists[1] have misinterpreted this passage translating jig, measure and cinquepas into the terms, courante, minuet and pavane, sometimes even sarabande and grave, ignoring the fact that at the time of Shakespeare the minuet and the sarabande were not danced in England. Shakespeare has quite correctly let the Gaillard, the cinque pas, follow the measure as a post dance.

In Shakespeare's "Henry the Fifth" Bourbon declares, "They bid us to the English dancing schools and teach lavoltas high and swift corantos". This is a mocking invitation to the beaten knights of the Battle of Azincourt to teach the French

---

[1] Compare Hans Scholz's dissertation on Joh. Sig. Kusser.

dances then in vogue at English dancing schools. Volta, which signifies turn about, revolving, was considered such a lascivious, immoral dance that contemporaries were full of invectives against it. Johannes von Muenster writes in 1594: "Ueber ungottseligen Tanz": "More particularly there is among these an important dance, called "la Volta" which has its name from the French word "voltiger", that is to fly about in a whirl". And Johannes Praetorius in his book on witches called "Blocksberg Verrichtungen" ("Practices of Witchcraft", 1668), speaks of the "gaillardische volta", "einem walschen Tanze, da man einander an schamigen orten fasset and wie ein getriebener Topf herunterhaspet und wirbelt", (this new gaillardic volta, an Italian dance, at which the partners touch each other in shameful parts and whirl each other about like a top spinning around). The volta was one of the first folk dances which penetrated high society coming from the peasant classes. The dancers embraced each other, turned about, and one of the figures was whirling the lady high up in the air. This was done while still hopping and turning and, to prevent falling during this confusion, the partner grasped his lady tightly by the wooden front board of her stays and kept his hold while lifting her over his head. The contemporary engraver Theodore Bry shows this in one of the pictures brought to us by Curt Sachs. Henry the Third was passionately fond of the Volta and the famous tale of the weddings at the French court in August 1572 tells how his predilection was shared by the noble ladies of the time. To return to Arbeau, who gives us the melody of the volta,

we may repeat his dictum that he considered it a matter of taste whether a young girl should throw herself about as much as the large steps of the volta required and run the risk of getting dizzy.

The last example shows us the rhythm of the Gaillard which Michael Praetorius noted in his voltas. It is entitled:

"La volta du roy" and may have been one which the French king danced so ardently that he was said to have been enchanted and bewitched by it. Five years after this, in 1577, Bernhard Schmid, the Elder, printed it in his organ tablature in 2/8 time. But we also know that both, the saltarello and the Gaillard, sometimes changed from triple to duple time, especially when a particularly fast tempo was desired. Schmid's "Volte des Koenig's" goes like this:

The two exotic dances which Arbeau mentions are the "Moresca" (which we already have discussed) and the "Canario", in French "Danse de Canaries", resembling the "Courante" in as much as it was a wooing dance, a pantomimic "Dance of the Coy Maiden". Arbeau describes it thus: "A young man chooses a lady and dances with her to the end of the hall, then he leaves her, dances backwards and forwards and his lady does likewise". The movements are gay and lively but also exotic and bizarre, accompanied by hops and beating of heels as in the peasant dance 'Schuhplattler", a figure of ancient popular origin. This heel and toe marking is at present found also in the dances of the Slavic peoples. But we also find it in the "Zapateado" of Spain which Cervantes called the "Shoe-sole beater", a true translation of "Schuhplattler". It is still danced in Spain as well as in Peru where it has the name of "Tapada".

Arbeau's "Canario" air is as follows:

The very same canario is recorded by Praetorius in the "Terpsichore", though it is in 6/4 time. We note that "exotic" dances in the 16th and 17th centuries use almost always stand-

ardized tunes, as in the case of the "Moresca", the "Folie
d'Espagne", and others. The dance of the "Canaries" has
another standard melody, for we find Caroso closing three of
his ballets with one and the same air for the canario:

It might almost appear that the canario took the place of
a kind of ecstatic whirling dance following the pavane, Gaillard
and saltarello, in the manner of the "cancan" of later days.
In the 18th century, the canario passes over into the jig. In the
"Neueroeffnetes Orchester" Mattheson says the following: "Canaries are very fast, short jigs, in three eighths time and the
first three notes in every bar are dotted and are then followed
by a sixteenth". In one of his ballets Schmelzer presents a
canario which was very popular in Vienna around 1670. It
is merely a transformation of the melody given by Arbeau.

Of all the dances which Arbeau has recorded, the greatest
space is devoted to the "Branles". As we understand the term
now, it refers to French folk dances, as they were executed
in the various provinces of France. They were round dances
in which the various couples following each other, moved sideways in a long file, or in a circle. The branle combined
absolute choreographic figures with pantomimic elements in
one and the same dance. The branle double was a solemn stepped
dance, with three paces forwards and two backwards according
to Arena. Arbeau has a double pace after the bow to the left,
and then a double pace to the right. He gives this melody:

The "Branle simple" used a single pace instead of double pace
toward the right side. The melody was therefore shorter and
simpler and like this:

This type and method of varying a melody shows quite plainly how the airs were adapted to the needs of the dancing master and uncovers for us the secret of the variation suite. But of this later. Then follows the "Branle gay", a wildly jumping dance. This is followed by the "Branle de Bourgogne", danced lightly and briskly. All these four branles were the foundation of the old French dance suite. They were adapted to the three different groups of participants at festivals. Arbeau says: "The old people dance with measured step the branle double and simple, the young married couples executed the branle gay, and the very youngest step lightly and gracefully the branle de Bourgogne". Besides these there were, however, a number of other branles. The "Haute Barrois", taking its name from a province in Lorraine, was danced like the double or the bourgogne, but faster, with arms and shoulders moving. The melody is that of the "Branle de Monstierandel", later called "Montirande" (apparently taking its name from some monastery).

Musically interesting is also the "Branle coupé" called "Cassandra" the melody of which is that of the hymn of Henry IV,

which became the French National Anthem in 1587, after the battle of Courtras. There is also the "Branle de Poitou", a triple measure, which is identical with the "Branle Amener". The six bars are characteristic of the most of the branles Poitous and Ameners as well as of the "Poitous" which Phalèse publishes around 1583.

This is Arbeau's Poitou:

This is Phalèse's:

On the other hand, the pantomimic form of the branles is shown in the "Branle de Malta". It is explained by Arbeau in the following manner: "A number of Maltese Knights arranged a ballet for a masked ball at court and appeared there with an equal number of ladies, all of them dressed as Turks". He adds that after every repetition of the melody a number of new gestures and expressions must be portrayed by the dancers, such as folding of hands, raising them to heaven, pantomimic expressions of surprise and worship. Apparently this branle was supposed to imitate a dance of dervishes:

The melody is in fact slightly exotic, as is shown by the repetition of the short motif in the second part. Among the pantomimic branles we must also count the "Branle of the washwomen", the "Branle of the peas", the "Branle of the hermits", and the "Branle de la torche", which was danced with torches or candles. Among them are also a number of branles bearing the names of localities. Arbeau mentions the Gavotte, taking its name from the Gavots, the inhabitants of the district Gapençais in the northern Dauphine. It was a suite in itself within the framework of the various branles doubles (which by themselves constituted a branle suite) and was danced to two-part time with small hops, double pace left, and double pace right, like the ordinary branle. All these doubles were, however, interrupted by figures made by the gentlemen independently, and ending with a figure like the Virginia Reel, but with the difference that instead of swinging her partner, the girl kissed him, a practice which was however in some instances reserved only to the couple arranging the festival.

Praetorius writes gavottes consisting of a branle simple and a "Gilotte" which are quite similar. "Gilotte" seems to be an error of hearing or recording. These gavottes lack the classic measure of the gavotte of the 18th century, the two fourths or the two eighths upbeat, which we find already in the works of Lully. The most famous gavotte dates from the 16th century, the "Air de Clochette" in the above mentioned "Ballet comique de la Reine" by Beaujoyeux of 1581. It was famous

in the time of Henry the Third, but not until the Parisian composer H. Ghys used the theme for his "Gavotte Louis XIII", which became a popular hit in 1868, was the melody awakened into new life.

CHAPTER VII.

THE BAROQUE PERIOD. I.

Arbeau speaks of the practice used by the musicians at entertainments to have a regular order in the arrangement of the branles. They began with a "branle double", followed by a "branle simple", succeeded by a "branle gay", and ended with the "branle de Bourgogne". And we may note that the same melody is used for the first two dances with a melodic variation, which is demanded by the change in pace of the second of the two dances. This adaptation of the melody to the requirements of the dancer is characteristically medieval but it led directly to the development of the "suite", a cyclic form of composition, and finally to the "sonata" with its different movements and to the "symphony".

Already in the 14th century we find that the stantipes retained the tenor-part, (called the "cantus inferior") on which the melodic variations of the "cantus superior" were based. The "Lamento di Tristano" and the "Manfredina" consisted of three parts related to one another as variations; these were followed by a "rotta" which was not only danced in much faster time, but also shortened as far as its melodic line is concerned. The tenor parts of the "basse danses" of the 15th century, though always adapted to the choreographic needs and desires of the dancers, nevertheless remained nucleus as they were, of the various portions of the whole dance. As an example let me quote the basse danse called "La Brosse" from the Attaignant collection dating from about 1530:

117

Blume called this piece the oldest suite for orchestra known to us. It is indeed the first recorded variation suite for instruments. We have here a main theme which is developed into a succession of three related but independent movements. This is an illustration of a very advanced development of the medieval principle of variations, but there is no intrinsic difference between this and the modern form. The same principle which prevailed in the church music of the Middle Ages and of the early years of the Renaissance, that is the retention of the

"Cantus firmus" taken from some hymn or some folk music to serve as a pattern, a kind of skeleton upon which the whole work was erected, now prevails for dance music. The theme is freely expanded and developed though the composer always follows a given pattern. And when the dancer performed his estampida, his basse danse, or his passamezzo, he asked for a definite melody and the player on the instrument had to abide by his wishes. The ancient custom of the minstrels to chant the heroic legends to a special melody and a special tune, harks back directly to the oriental custom using the maquams and ragas, mere melodic skeletons.

But let us return to the 16th century. We find at this time that the variation principle was used everywhere and in the most complicated and intricate ways. Phalèse's "Pass'emezzo d'Italie", dating from 1583, first exposes a theme in five different "modi", then continues with a "ripresa" (repetition), which has three "modi", and ends with a saltarello with four "modi" and a finale "ripresa". This practice is therefore definitely not of German origin; on the contrary it seems that the variation suites, as they were written by Schein, Peurl, Posch and others, at the beginning of the 17th century, were already examples of the declining vogue of this form. Nor is it possible to call the old primitive combination of "Tanz und Nachtanz", (step-dance and hop-dance) such as we find them in the lute and organ tablatures, the first variation suites. These lute and keyboard suites held up against the French instrumental suites, are extraordinarily primitive. In one of the oldest printed lute books, called the "Intabolatura de Lauto", dating from 1508, which was published by the famous printer of musical scores, Petrucci, in Venice, we have combinations of pavanas, saltarelli and pive. Antonio Rotta writes in 1546, coupling passamezzo, gagliarda and padovana; Jacopo de Gorzanis combines passamezzo, saltarello and padovana.

Dating from 1570 the combination : allemande, courante occurs more frequently. From 1620 on, the French lute books show a type which adds the newly introduced Spanish "Sarabande" to the paired dances allemande and courante. This new form, which I should like to call the "new French dance suite" is in contradiction to the former succession of branles. It appeared for the first time in a manuscript from the library at Copenhagen which bears the date 1626. This form was further developed by the Parisian lutenist Gaultier. In the famous Hamilton Codex, written in the years 1650-1655, we have the succession: prelude, allemande, courante (often repeated), jig, sarabande. The "Classic order": allemande, courante, sarabande, gigue, was taken up and developed by Froberger. We shall return to this in a later chapter.

Compared with the progressive Italian and French lutenists, the German composers of the 16th century appear relatively very conservative, for we find that they used only "Tanz und Nachtanz". It is interesting to note that Chapman in "Alphonsus, Emperor of Germany", says at that point:

"We Germans have no change in our dances,
An almain and an up-sprung that is all".

In one of the oldest tablatures, that of J. Kotter, 1513, there is for example a "Dancz" by Hans Weck, followed by a "Hopperdancz" (hop-dance). The bass of these dances and the harmonies are the same, but beat and tempo are different.

In the organ tablatures of Bernhard Schmid the Elder, 1577, a "saltarello" follows a "passamezzo", and an "Allemando novelle" precedes a "Proportz darauf", which signifies a dance related to its predecessor. The only exception to this practice is the "Pass'emezzo antico" in the tablature book of Jacob Paix, 1583, is an exact copy of the "Passo e mezzo d'Italie" from the collection of Phalèse. Both Paix and Phalèse appear to have taken their material from a former source.

A number of folk dances which were found in the German tablatures, should be enumerated at this point. There is for example an "Ungarescha", (Hungarian dance) which shows that the "Saltarello" is simplified in order to fit the needs of the "Ungarescha" with which it is combined.

We also find in these books the Venetian dance "Furlana", a "Ballo Milanese", a "Ballo Angelese" and a "Schirazula Marazula" which is apparently a linguistic corruption of the Italian "Scaramuccia", the comic character from the Italian "Comedia del'Arte". In other German records of the time, there are also Hungarian and Polish dances. Hans Neusiedler's lute book, 1536, brings us a "Beggar's Dance", a dance of nuns, and a "Zeuner Tanz" (dance of the fences). All these are pantomimic folk dances which have come down to us in the form of children's games. In the "Zeuner Tanz" the participants formed a chain crossing their arms and hands to make a kind of fence (Zaun). The solo dancer stood in the center of the circle and the others were to keep him from breaking through the hedge, a manoeuvre known well to those who direct children's play. We have already mentioned Neusiedler's grotesque "Judentanz"—"Dance of the Jews". It is a dramatic and pantomimic dance, resembling in this respect Stefan Craus' "Der trunkene Binder" (the drunken keg maker, the "Stiefel Dance" (boot dance) and the "Affen Tanz" (monkey dance). All of these dances consist of a step-dance and a hop-dance, the second of which is often called "Hupf-auf" or "Proportio".

The music which has been recorded in "Il ballarino" by Caroso, 1581, is definitely "Gebrauchsmusik" (for the practical use for dancers), quite different from the skillfully and artistically built up music of the French, German and English composers. At the same time it is a remarkable fact that in Italy one actually danced to genuine variation suites, as for example to the following ballet "Laura suave in lode della Serenissima Madama Christiana Lorena de Medici, Grandduchessa di Toscana":

Another Italian ballet constructed in the same fashion was published by myself in the "Zeitschrift fuer Musikwissenschaft" (Vol. 2). It was composed by Ant. Brunelli, a Tuscan musician, danced in Pisa in 1600, and printed in Venice in 1616. It is dedicated to the noble ladies of Pisa and is notable because of the fact that it may be both sung and played. At the beginning, the five-part chorus sings a "Grave", a "Gaillard" and a "Courante", and then the whole thing is played by a musician on his guitar, with the necessary changes demanded by the instrument. Such vocalised suites were prevalent in Italy around 1600, and Hugo Riemann has pointed to an interesting dance suite of Monteverdi of the year 1607 which appeared in that composer's "Scherzi Musicali" and bore the caption "Balletto". It is set for 2 violins, 2 sopranos and a vocal- and an instrumental bass. Though Monteverdi has not designated the various parts of the suite by name, Hugo Riemann recognized that it consists of an "Entrata" for instruments, and a "Pavana", a "Gagliarda", a "Corrente" and a "Volta", an "Allemanda" and a "Giga" for voices. I personally should call the last of these a "Canario" rather than a "Jig", as these dances closely resemble each other, and it was the practice of Caroso to close the suites with "Canarios". Though this is not a genuine suite with variations, the most important ballet of Monteverdi, "Ballo delle Ingrate" which he wrote for the all-too coy ladies of Mantua in 1608, is a genuine one. The libretto which was written by Rinuccini, the famous poet of the first operas, treats a favorite subject of the time in humerous fashion. To make a long story short, the ballet itself pictures the retribution which is meted out by the God of the Underworld, to those coy and prudish ladies of Mantua who have not listened to the wooings of their lovers, and the sufferings of the punished constitute the climax of the ballet. The following theme is used in it to form the main motif for the variations that follow:

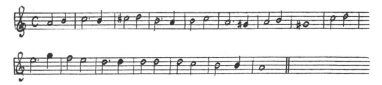

This "Pavane" is transformed into a "Gagliarda", then into an "Allemande" with a new melody. Then follows a "Courante" and thereupon the first "Pavane" is repeated. This repetition gives the suite a particular and interesting unity. The theme is not one of the common dance melodies; it is worthy of its great creator, who was one of the most outstanding musicians of all times. It expresses deep sorrow and pain, far more dignified and profound than the somewhat superficial subject of the "coy-ladies" demands,—it is the mourning for the elusiveness and the disappearance of beauty. We have here one of the examples of that strange intermingling of spiritual and grotesque motives which we find in other arts of the Baroque as well as in music. As the fury of the final dance scene dies down, the orchestra consisting of strings, winds, organs, harps, harpsichords and lutes breaks off and the dancers begin to sing in chorus, in four parts, apostrophizing the ladies in the audience "Aprendete pietà Donne e Donzelle", (Practice mercy, ye ladies and lasses).

We must, however, return to less impassioned ways and climes,—back to Germany. There we find a kind of suite much more intricate in its composition than the purely melodic variations of Italy. Mention has already been made of Johann Hermann Schein (1586-1630), one of the most important musicians of the German Baroque period and a predecessor of Bach at the "Thomaskirche" in Leipzig. We owe the development of the variation suite to him. His work "Banchetto Musicale" which appeared in 1617, has been made available to modern historians in the new edition by Professor Pruefer. There the order of dances is as follows: Paduane, Gagliarde, Courante, Allemande and Tripla. All of these are fully developed polyphonic movements, each of which consists of three repetitions. Paduane, Gagliarde and Courante are written in five parts, Allemande and Tripla in four parts. The divergence in parts points to a division intended by Schein and is not fortuitous. In fact, a good deal of the foreign dances were accepted by high society according to the well-regulated practices of the dancing masters, while the last two: Allemande and Tripla are the native dances, and the peasants and citizens performed them on the platforms of the inns and the boards of the barns. This partition expresses itself in the number of parts allotted to the various portions—the foreign dances are set in five parts, the native in four; and while the polyphonic Paduane is most skillfully arranged—the Tripla (the hop-dance of the Allemande) is most simple and primitive in its form. Here we have a phenomenon which we meet frequently in the musical history of the dance. Old-fashioned and demoded dances receive a more stylistic and artificial treatment, while the dances of the people, the newer and more popular dances appear in simpler garb. This also reminds us of the partition of the dances in the time of the "Basse danses", when cultural differences expressed themselves through differences of instrumentation. This is very clearly shown by Isaac Posch, an organist from Carinthia, who published his "Musikalische Tafelfreude" (Musical Delight) in a volume containing five-part Pavanes and Gaillards, and four-part Entrys and Courantes.

"Allhier hast Du, guenstiger Leser, den anderen Theil. . . . von allerley Neuen Paduanen, Gagliarden, Intraden und Courenten . . . . Auff jede Paduan (folgt ihr) Gagliarde, und auff jede Intrada ihr Zugehoerige Courante, doch auff eine andere Manier Denn fuer Erste sindt die Paduanen und Gagliarden als die ihr sonderliche gravitet haben wollen, mit 5 die Intraden und Couranten, aber die was frischer gemusicirt werden sollen, mit 4 Stimmen gesetzt, gebrauchen sich auch einer geschwinden mensur als jene. . . ."

Here the author definitely describes the contrast between the solemn and dignified Pavanes and Gaillards, and the brisk Entrys and Courantes. The dances that belong together are related to each other melodically and rhythmically in the manner of variations but each pair of dances is again a melodic entity. In spite of this one may place them in the category of variation suites, though they are already the declining phase of this particular form. For, the further we advance into the 17th century, the more do we find that the various dances are independent one of the other, and suite becomes merely a succession of more or less contrasted dances, inter-related only by the identity of the keys that are used. Around 1650 the principle of the variation movement with retention of one theme is replaced by that of rhythmic and melodic contrast, and the final climax of this development leading to the classical suite, is to be found in the suites by Bach and Handel.

There is no doubt that during this period the variation suite was especially popular in Austria. Eleven years before Posch, Paul Peurl (or Baewerl, as he also called himself), an organist in Steyr, (small town in Upper Austria) published "Newe Paduan, Intrada, Daentz and Galliarda, in four parts". His biography was for the first time published by myself in the "Bulletin d'Union Musicologique", in 1925. Here too, we note that two dances are always paired, though all of the dances may use the same melodic material.

In a manuscript of the "Museum Francisco Carolinum" in Linz (Upper Austria) a number of dances for organ or piano, written by Peurl, are recorded. Here we discover that to "Dantz 18" a "hop-dance" is appended, which has not appeared in the original version published by Peurl himself. It is interesting to note that in this instance the hop-dance is actually written down by the organist, though this was not usually the custom. The musicians were accustomed to improvise a "Proporz dance" on their own, and the result of this was that all kinds of abuses crept in, the kind of thing which Posch condemned so vigorously in the introduction to his book on the "Musical Delights of Banquets and Festivities". (Musikalische Ehrn-und Tafel Freudt), 1626. "At times", says he, "there is a great confusion in improvising of post-dances because musicians do act arbitrary, no matter whether the post dances are correct or not". This distortion of dance melody when it is transposed into the measures of the Triple, reminds one of the actual practice of band leaders to "jazz" well-known themes and melodies,—a practice, then as now, inviting the indignant criticism of more classically-minded musicians.

It would be quite erroneous to assume from the foregoing discussion of French, Italian and German examples, that at that time England had no part in the development of dance music. The contrary is the case; England's music was not only on a high level at home, but had the greatest influence on the continent as well. Indeed, it rivals Italy in this respect, for it played the leading part in the field of music as well as in that of philosophy, literature and dramatic art. Though it never brought forth a Michelangelo, or a Palestrina, there were Bacon, Shakespeare, Ben Jonson, and a host of others besides the musicians Byrd, Dowland, Morley and Wilbye, whose madrigals stand up well beside those of the Italian composers. And the playing of the harpsichord reached its climax in England from 1600 on.

Ever since medieval times, dances and festivals had flourished at the English court. The most important type was the masque, which was probably due to the influence of the French Court on English ways. Particularly in the reign of Henry VII, there was a lively exchange of intellectual and political values between the two countries. French actors performed in London, French musicians and dancers are spoken of in the documents of the time. We have, however, no authentic records of the many masques performed, except those of the masques composed by Thomas Campion and John Marston, which gave us some idea of what the improvised masques could have been, given in honor of the Virgin Queen on her many journeys through the kingdom. There was no festivity without its masque, whether it was a birthday, a wedding, or a formal reception of diplomats at the court, or the welcome of the Queen, at the castle of some faithful subject. Walter Scott's "Kenilworth" has a lively description of such a celebration. From the masques, later developed the play with music and the musical drama. Dancing was an integral part of these enter-tainments, and accompanying instrumental music was ordered by the managers of the shows. The masque "The Vision of Daniel" gives us some idea of the order and manner of the performance: on a mountain horns played at the entry and leave-taking of the goddesses. A second orchestra was played in the cupola of the temple which was situated on the op-posite side of the hall. That one accompanied the song of the three graces. A choir of lutes and violas played from the side of the hall.

For the "Masque at the Marriage of the Lord Hayes", the poet-composer Thomas Campion gives the following directions: on the stage and at the right side of the hall there were to be eleven musicians, (5 lutes, 1 bandara, guitar, 1 trombone, 1 harpsichord and 2 violas); on the other side, somewhat nearer the back of the hall 9 violas and 3 lutes. Six horns and six choristers of the Royal Chapel were to stand in the foreground on a raised platform "Because of the penetrating tone of the brass instruments". From the top of the mountain which was placed at the back of the hall, oboists played when the King entered.

This is quite a complicated and extensive apparatus for the playing of the Entries and Leave-takings, and we must regret that none of the music performed has been handed down to us. It is a singular fact that English music of this period is known to us principally from compositions printed and played in Germany. England continued to send its actors and groups of comedians to perform in Germany, just as Italy did with its singers. And just as the Italian stagione finally gave rise to the German opera, so did the English players influence and determine the development of German dramatic art. With these troupes of English comedians (called "Mummers") there naturally travelled musicians and composers. In Kassel they found a hearty welcome by Count Moritz of Hessen, the patron of Heinrich Schuetz. One of these friendly invasions of Germany occurred at Muenster in Westphalia, and the chron-icle of the municipality reports in 1599: "sie hatten bei sich viele verschiedene Instrumente, darauf sie spielten, als luten, zittern, fiolen, pipen and dergleichen. Sie dantzeden vielle neuwe dentze so hier zulande nicht gepruechlich am Anfang und Ende der Comedien" (they brought with them many different instruments, lutes, zithers, violas, pipes and such on which they played. At the beginning and the close of the comedies they danced many dances which were not practiced in this country).

Among the musicians of first rank who brought dance music for orchestral performances from England to the continent, was William Brade, born in 1560, and deceased in Hamburg in 1630. At various intervals he was a member of the Danish Court Orchestra in Copenhagen, also conductor of the City Council's orchestra in Hamburg and in Schleswig. Between 1609 and 1621 he published in Hamburg four books containing music for dancing, written for different parts. These volumes have been studied and discussed by the musicologist Oberst. We find in them branles, pavanes, Gaillards, and also entries with the queerest names, and many of these dances give the impression of having been originally written for English masques. There is for example "The Queen's Entry", "The Entry of the young Princesses", "The Entry of the young Princess". A "Pageant of Cornwall" is followed by "The Sacred Mountain", a ballet at that time very popular in England. This last ballet centred around a mountain erected in the background of the stage, and to the sound of certain instruments, the mountain opened to reveal the advancing group of dancers, male and female. For us the most interesting feature of these English dance suites is the fact that they too have a strong resemblance to the variation suite.

The "Schottische Tantz", taken from Brade's volume is most original.

Besides Brade, there is the Englishman Thomas Simpson who, in 1611 (Frankfort on the Main) published an extensive work dealing with dance music. Without observing any strict rules, he combined dances of the same key into suites. A work called "Opus neuer Pavanen, Gaillarden, Intraden, Canzonen, Ricercaren, Fantasien, Balletten, Allemanden, Couranten, Volten und Passamezzen" was followed in a kind of omnibus volume which appeared in Hamburg under the title "Taffel Consort, Erster Teil von allerhand newen lustigen musikalischen Sachen" (in four parts)—"nebst einem Generalbass, mit sonderlichem Fleiss zusammengetragen, verfertigt und publiciert von T. S. Engellaender, Hamburg, 1611". (Consort, first part of all kinds of new musical matters, in four parts —together with a thorough bass, collected, recorded and published by T. S. Englishman in Hamburg). In this collection we find pieces by Robert Bateman, John Dowland, Edward and Robert Johnson, and others. A "Pavane" signed by Dowland is remarkable for its solemn dignity, and surpassed by far many of the other pieces.

At home the English musicians were equally industrious and continued to make their mark in the field of the orchestral suite. Thomas Morley's "Consort lessons made by diverse exquisite authors for six instruments" started off the publication of musical suites, and for a long time English books were strong competitors of the Germans.

In addition to the publication of volumes containing series of dance suites, the composers of this period also published single dances. Valentin Haussmann, organist at Gerbstadt, published in 1604 a volume called "Neue Intraden", Melchior Franck in Koburg published in 1603 "Neue Paduanen und Gaillarden". It was left to the performers to select from the material given, what dances they would combine. There is H. L. Hasler who published "Lustgarten newer teutscher Gesaenge, Balletti, Gaillarden und Intraden", which were to be both sung and played, though, of course, the Entries were played only. In the same year, 1601, appeared a volume of Polish and Czech dances with and without text, in four and in five parts, by the Bohemian Christoph Demantius, who left his home under pressure of the Counter-Reformation in Bohemia. His Polish dances clearly show the influence of the Slavic background of his youth. We have Johannes Staden from Nuremberg who issued a collection "Neue teutsche Lieder byneben etlicher Balletti oder Taentz, Couranten, Gaillarden und Pavanen mit drei, vier und fuenf Stimmen" in 1606. Thanks to him the "Courante" was introduced into the German suite order.

The development of the suite continues, though the principle of the variation does not. Johann Rosenmueller, living from about 1620-1684, one of the most gifted musicians of the time (though of somewhat problematical character), had to leave Germany and fled to Italy. Scheibe, the well-known "Critische Musicus", who even did not spare J. S. Bach in his criticisms, calls him an equal of Lully. Rosenmueller made every effort to include in his dance suites new forms of dances. In 1645 he published his "Paduanen", "Allemanden", "Couranten", "Ballette" and "Sarabanden", and in 1654 "Studentenmusik mit drei und fuenf violen", as well as in 1667, his "Sonate da camera". The students of Germany are generally known to have drunk excessively and spent their time in fighting one another with rapier or fists. It is, however, a fact that they were no less assiduous in dancing, singing and playing. Those who were particularly gifted met in a "Collegium Musicum" (musical course), where there was a weekly performance for instrumental and also occasional singing. The famous "Gewandhaus Konzerte" of Leipzig grew out of this "Collegium Musicum" in Leipzig. We must conceive that the dance music of the 17th century in Germany, was for the greater part played by students. In his preface to the "Studentenmusik", Rosenmueller says that he wrote his work "meistenteils auf freundliches Begehren und Ansuchen deren Herren Studenten zu Dienst und Gefallen, wenn sie etwan vornehmen Herren und Standespersonen mit einer Nacht-Music beehren wollen, oftermals in groesster Eile aufgesezet" (This was written in haste at the friendly request and order of the honored students, for their service and pleasure when they feel inclined to honor noble ladies or gentlemen with music by night).

The "Studentenmusik" was lost for a long time and only

discovered by Professor Karl Nef, the Swiss musicologist.

Rosenmueller favors the following order of dances: Paduane, Courante, Ballo, Sarabande; and occasionally makes unimportant modifications as for example: having two Courantes following each other. There is no longer any mention of the Gaillard. He introduces a new element into these dances which he brought from Italy, although Paul Peurl used it already in his "Paduanes" in 1625. This novelty is the "Basso Continuo" which implies the use of a harpsichord or of some other thorough-bass instrument, whenever the dances are to be played in three parts instead of in five. The former German and French practice was to perform the dances in four or five parts which were fully developed and had no harmonic gaps. For this reason their performance in the open air was most appropriate with an orchestra of violes, sometimes replaced by flutes, cornets or other instruments. After the introduction of the "Basso Continuo" in Italy and later in the rest of Europe, the latter countries dropped their orthodoxy. It was now permitted to have instrumental music accompanied by a keyboard instrument, and one or more parts could be omitted. Thus Rosenmueller's "Studentenmusik" might be played either with five or with three violes plus a figured bass-instrument, and in order to make this clear, he so arranged the three-part Pavanes that they corresponded in key to the various five-part suites. In the choice of keys, Rosenmueller is guided by a strict rule, and following a consistent plan he creates a definite unity for each suite. The order of the suites, c major, - d minor, - e minor, - f major, - g major, - g minor, - a minor, - c minor, - d major, - is in conformity with the then prevailing system of keys, and points directly to the concept of the "Well-tempered Clavichord". In Italy the suites which were performed with a figured bass, were called "Sonate da camera", in contrast to the "Sonate da chiesa", because the latter (performed in church) did not contain any dance movements or at least no movements which were designated by the names of dances. In his "Sonate da camera" Rosenmueller takes another step forward, introducing movements which were not dance music, "Symphonies".

This musical form had already been used in the Venetian operas of Cavalli, Cesti, Draghi and others. Such a "Symphony" (related to the old form of the instrumental canzona) consists of a succession of short sections, contrasted in rhythm and character.

A great number of other composers could be enumerated here who tried their hands on the suite. Among these was Johann Petzel, who began as an Augustine monk in Prague and then became city-piper, first in Bautzen, later in Leipzig. Next to those of Peurl and of Schein, his suites were not only greatly favored by musicians, but popular all over Germany. "Leipziger Abendmusik" (1669), and "Fuenfstimmige Blasende Music" (1686), were the titles of his compositions. They are both music for out-of-doors.

During this period, more than before or later, out-of-door music was highly popular. The noises of our modern cities were not there to disturb the listener, and in the very center of the towns, in the market place, or in front of the City Hall, music was played in inauguration of a new official or to welcome the visit of some dignitary. This custom was also used for a birthday, a marriage, the entrance of the newly-weds into their new home, a serenade in honor of the new-born, and other ordinary occasions giving plenty of work to the municipal orchestra, the "Stadtmusik". Old and new dances, serenades and entries were played. And on the great feastdays: the day before Christmas or the night before the New Year, a "Blasende Musik"—a fanfare was played from the belfry of the church or the high tower of the City Hall. Sometimes such a fanfare was performed from a balcony to celebrate a victory, a treaty of peace, or the coming of a new functionary who would reward the players at the close of the festivities with an extra barrel of wine. Such "Turmsonaten" (tower sonatas) were written by Petzel (or Pezelius, as he also called himself). They are lively and ingratiating compositions, and their German character—which might be said to be of a stiff and formal simplicity, is as much a part of the style as of the melody. The conservativism of the German musicians, clinging to the spirit of the old variation suite is hard to overcome, and thus we find Petzel writing dance forms and variations on the same melodic theme.

These dances are set for two cornets and two trombones. A "Turm-Sonata" consisted of Intrade, Allemande, Courante, Allemande and Jig. Their rhythms recapture the half-solemn, half-melancholy spirit of the period, and one sees revived in them,—much better than in many pictorial representations—the spirit of the German Baroque as it existed in the town communities.

A later composer of orchestral suites was Hieronymous Kradenthaler, publishing "Deliciae musicales" in Nuremberg, consisting of Sonatina, Aria, Sarabanda, Aria and Jig. Jacob Scheiffelhut of Augsburg used another order in his "Lieblicher Fruehlingsanfang" which appeared in 1685, and had this succession: Praeludium, Courante, Ballo, Sarabande, Aria and Jig.

Let us now turn again to the "Ballet" of which we last spoke in connection with Monteverdi's "Ballo delle Ingrate". In addition to this ballet, Monteverdi composed a number of others, but the most important step in his career—as far as dancing was concerned—was his removal to Venice in 1613 and his connection with the leading men of Venetian opera, with Francesco Cavalli and Marc Antonio Cesti. His influence on the development of the Venetian opera was of signal importance. At that time opera in Venice was remarkable for the variety and wealth of topics treated, the use of sensational plots taken from history and from mythology, and the newly developed art and lavishness of the settings. In all these respects, the operas, such as they were performed in Venice, and—from the middle of the century on—also in Dresden, Munich and Vienna, were the result of the dramatic representations of the Renaissance period. It is therefore quite natural that dances played a fair part in all these performances, but unfortunately their true form is rarely preserved for us since the recorded scores of that time contained only the most essential parts of the music, and only the most important dances. The music, accompanying the ballet was not considered permanent, and both, ballet and dance music varied according to their different performances.

Venice was essentially a democratic commonwealth; the government was republican although there were a great many aristocratic families, on whose patronage the theatres and the opera were dependent since they received no grant from a royal treasury or a prince's major domo. To perform ballets was a costly affair, not only because of the large number of performers required, but no less because of the extravagance of decorations and costumes. At court this was never a problem and it is not surprising that one of the first courts to take up opera with ballets was that of the imperial house of the Habsburgs in Vienna. For almost a century close family bonds had joined this house to that of the Gonzagas of Mantua, with both Ferdinands, the Second and the Third married to princesses of Mantua. In 1622, Ferdinand the Second had married Eleanor of Gonzaga at Innsbruck, and it is most likely that this lady, a pupil of Monteverdi, introduced the opera in Vienna. The beginnings of the opera in Vienna are obscure, but the darkness is lifted around 1650 and from then we have records not only about the scores, the libretti and the personnel performing in the operas, but also of sources of the dances, the dancers and the music being part of the operas and constituting the ballets. And even though there is no printed record, but merely manuscript material, this is so plentiful that for the first time the historian of dance music is not at a loss for proper sources.

The famous musical department of the State Library in Vienna has a special division which is called the "Collectio Leopoldina". In these tomes, bound in white pig-skin we find the musical compendium of the Emperor Leopold the First (1658-1705), who not only made Austria a major power of Europe by successfully waging war against the Turks, but was himself a patron of all the fine arts. At his court with its lavish entertainments, his chapels with their enriched cult and ritual, his theatres, tournaments ·and great festivals,—he was himself, like his predecessor Ferdinand the Third, considerably more than a musical dilettante, practising assiduously the art of composition, writing sacred music, songs, "Singspiele", (musical plays) and dance music. In my book "Songs of the Vienna Baroque" (Das Wiener Barocklied), I published two of his songs which give proof of his extraordinary gifts. When his music teacher Schmelzer once remarked that he ought rather have become a composer instead of Emperor, he answered in his stiff and somewhat ironic way: "Never mind, I feel much better that way". (Macht nichts, es geht mir so besser).

This Austrian emperor has done more for the cause of Austrian music than can be enumerated here. Indeed, during his reign it flourished as never before. His predecessor, Ferdinand the Third, had already called famous Italian composers to his court, among them Pietro Andrea Ziani and Antonio Bertali. But under Leopold the First, there was no end to the operas and oratorios being performed in the magnificent festival halls of his castle in Vienna and at the summer palaces Favorita, Laxemburg and Schoenbrunn. Looking through the scores of the works performed here, we find no record whatever of any dances, only at the close of the acts, notes such as "here follows a ballet consisting of five parts" or "the ballet of the Planets executed by the archdukes" or "ballets of the ladies in waiting" or "ballet of the Prince of Schwarzenberg" or "ballet of the Prince of Kinsky". The dances, however, are in other volumes and these manuscripts of the ballets show clearly that the composers of the operas left the devising of the dance music to other musicians. For, while the operas were written by Italian composers, the dances and their music were written and planned by native Viennese talent.

What was the relation between the action of the opera and the dances performed therein? The opera was a matter pertaining directly to the court, often distinctly servile, that is worshipping and paying homage to the reigning family. The operas were performed on festival occasions and during the carnival, and more and more, the opera itself became the means of celebration where the person to be honored received the adulation of his subjects or his family. In 1667 the marriage of Leopold the First with the Spanish Infanta Margarita was celebrated, and in honor of this, a great musical festival was arranged during which a great opera by Cesti was performed. It was "Il pomo d'oro" (The Golden Apple), in which the well-known mythological story of the choice of Paris, which led to the Trojan War, became the subject of the opera. Before the opera, however, a number of allegorical characters representing the Austrian and the Spanish subjects of the imperial couple, paid homage to the pair, with one figure among them representing "America", the Spanish possessions in the New World. In the engraving which accompanies the libretto of this prelude, the person representing America is pictured as a Moor, an anthropological error which the creator of the drawing, Ludovico Burnacini, did not take too seriously. However, another drawing of that same theatrical designer shows another American in his work "Maschere" (Masks), this time "portrayed as a redskin with the traditional feather headdress" but wearing the little skirt of the Baroque dancer, which was better adapted to the polished parquet floor of the imperial castle of Schoenbrunn than to the primeval forest. His female partner is, strangely enough, portrayed as a white girl, whom you might easily take for an immigrant from Europe, to judge by her complexion and the shape of her head.

But to return to the prelude and the opera: the dark-skinned "America" sings the following pretty Barcarolle-melody:

"Si mira, s'ammira di gioie fecondo
Festoso, fastoso l'Americo mondo".

The dispute of the three goddesses about the golden apple as the prize of beauty is solved in a rather peculiar fashion, for the award is made by Paris to the Empress Margarita herself, although contemporary writers declare her to have been "ugly as a mole". After this the goddesses command their aides, the nymphs and the spirits of the air to form a beautiful ballet, while the stage is transformed into a great square with a magnificent view of the sea on which the actual dance takes place. At the close of the dance, the dancers range themselves to form a large "M"—"Vivat Margarita". This concentrated summary is given merely to indicate the interrelation of dance and plot of the opera.

Perhaps the Italian composers considered the composition of music for the dances as "inferior and beneath their dignity", — be that as it may, the custom in Vienna from 1650 on, till 1690 was to have the music for dancing made by Viennese musicians. To me it seems more likely that the court, in spite of its leanings to Italian art forms, found a kind of justification in allotting part of the entertainment to native talent, exercising a musical balance of power. That this is so, appears natural for psychological reasons as well. For in the dance, the man of the Baroque times, otherwise so restricted by rules and regulations, finds the way back to self-expression, to those old and time-honored symbolisations of spring, love, fertility and regeneration, of which the dance has been the most potent expression since times immemorial. This happened in an age when even the human voice was bereft of its inherent sexual significance for the sake of rarified beauty, as in the voices of the castrati; and it was not unnatural that man felt the desire to return to nature and to natural ways through the medium of the dance. And so, dance music was left to the musicians of the people and the consequence of this was, that even at this time of Baroque art, Viennese dance music, destined to overrun and conquer the world, first saw the light of the day and received its initial impulse.

Thus, opera and dance were considered to be two different kinds of musical activity. No. 18918 of the Viennese State Library contains the ballets performed in conjunction with Bertali's opera "Il Ciro Crescente". The composer was Wolfgang Ebner, who was the well-known organist at the court of

Ferdinand the Third, and famous for his keyboard and organ compositions. Interludes were introduced into the opera on the story of the Persian King Cyrus, and their special purpose was to celebrate the birthday of the Emperor Leopold. In these interludes Orpheus appears as the tamer of wild beasts. A ballet of various animals follows. (Hunt for Swans). The young Archduke Carl Joseph appeared in the ballet which consisted of an Intrada (Entry), an Allemande, a Trezza, a Sarabande and a Retirada (Leave-taking). While the prince performed his dance solo the remaining dancers marched in to the accompaniment of the "Entry". With the Retirada marking the leave-taking of the dancers, (with the same formality as their coming on the stage)—we have here another succession, a suite arrangement, which we may call the "pageant type" (Aufzugssuite). According to Praetorius the Retirada is the "Retrajecta"—the Latin translation of that word. In describing the ballets he says that they consist of the Entry and the Leave-taking, between which there are a number of "figures" which the masked persons perform in "stehen, tretten und umbwechslung der oerther und sonsten auf buchstaben in einem Ringe Crantze, Triangel, Vierecket, Sechsecket, oder andere Sachen formieren und sich durcheinander winden darauff, dann die gantze Invention und Essentia des Ballets bestehet und gerichtet ist". That is (the masked dancers stand, step and change their places so as to form rings, wreaths and circles, triangles and other shapes, wind in and out,—this is the intent and the essential purpose of the ballet).

We find in the Vienna State Library a manuscript bearing the title "Ariae ad ingressum et egressum suae Majestatis" (Airs for the entry and the exit of His Majesty). When the Emperor walks in to take part in a ceremony, the Entry is played from the platform, and when he leaves, the musicians blow the Leave-taking. In between, while he converses with the ambassadors, the archbishop and the other dignitaries, they play a number of dances. We have here a kind of politico-musical suite. Ebner died in 1665 and his successor was Johann Heinrich Schmelzer. He was born about 1623, and died at

Prague, in 1680. Schmelzer was the first "Kapellmeister" of German origin at the court of Vienna, where only Italians had hitherto been appointed. He was a vigorous and striking personality, and quite different from his predecessors. Called the best violin player of his time by contemporaries, his violin sonatas attest to his proficiency as a composer for this instrument. In addition he wrote masses, oratorios and operas, that have unfortunately partly been lost. However, we are fully informed about his dances which are recorded in two volumes of manuscripts in the Vienna State Library. This music has only the first violin part and the bass part, the so-called "Particello". This kind of notation was prevalent for a long time. The practice was to write the various parts each for itself, and so the score was a kind of partial piano score, the lower part serving also as figured bass for the harpsichord player. This practice has been retained to the present time and conductors of ballets use this partial score, with the so-called "Ballet-Geigenstimme" (Ballet violin part).

Schmelzer wrote hundreds of dances to be performed within operas, ballets, at court festivals, balls and other celebrations. In this quality he soon gained a European reputation, and his music was asked for everywhere. About 200 miles from Vienna, across the border of Moravia, the Prince-Bishop of Olmuetz had a summer palace at Kremsier, where he spent the warm months of the year and occasionally remained during the carnival. Everyone who is familiar with the biographies of Mozart and Beethoven knows of this place, but it is not generally known that in the 16th century already, a famous musician of the period, the composer of church music, Jacob Handl-Gallus, (1550-1591), lived there. The art-loving Prince-Bishop, Carl Liechtenstein Kastelkorn founded there an orchestra headed by the Bohemian composer and violinist Heinrich Franz von Biber. During my research work in Moravia I found in the library of the castle of Kremsier, hidden in an old chest, a large pile of music, numerous orchestral parts, and among them the ballets of Schmelzer. And while the Viennese manuscripts only contain them in particello, these here in

Kremsier were fully orchestrated, in four—occasionally in five parts,—most frequently for strings. And thus we finally obtained clear sight into the ways and methods of the dance music, prevalent in Vienna in the 17th century. Not only do we have in these manuscripts ballets to accompany operas and dances that were performed at masquerades and balls, but also dance music written purely for entertainment to be performed at festivals and during the meals. The Prince-Bishop carried on an extensive correspondence with Schmelzer, most of which I have published in my study on "Wiener Tanzkomposition in der zweiten Haelfte des 17. Jahrhunderts" (Viennese Dance Music in the Second Half of the 17th Century). Apparently the Bishop could not get enough of this musical material, for he continued to ask for new dances again and again. At the same time these charming letters give us a vivid picture of the musical practices at the Court of Vienna. On February 20th, 1676, Schmelzer gives us a description of a performance of a "Mascherata" (masque), in the bed-room of the Empress who was ill at the time. A Mademoiselle Fuerstenberg played the role of Cupid, and Schmelzer's daughter, one of the maids of the Empress, was dressed as a fiddler (she was an excellent violinist). On the following day Schmelzer was to play his new sonata for violin (in which the voices of various birds are imitated), called the "Animalien Sonata". But the high point of the evening was to be a satiric dialogue on the attempt of the newly arrived Italian prima donna Giulia Masotti, to capture Schmelzer's young son as a husband by pretending to be the possessor of a great fortune. The humorous dialogue invented by Schmelzer for this performance greatly amused the court and the Empress. This plot was part of the "Ballet der alten Jungfern" (Ballet of old Maidens), danced in the apartments of the Empress, and Schmelzer sent it to the Bishop at Kremsier with the words "Some old maidens still may be in Moravia —now the carnival is over—who would find pleasure in it".

The Bishop was equally thankful for the bit of theatrical gossip and the score. He did not hesitate to show his gratitude and forwarded the promised "checks" in payment together with six large cans of lard. Schmelzer reciprocates the attention of the churchman and sends him a large box of crullers ("Faschingskrapfen"), the traditional goodies of the Vienna carnival, baked in the imperial kitchens on the occasion of the performance of Draghi's opera "La Laterna di Diogene".

This gay and lively existence of Schmelzer's was typical for the Austrian musician of the time, who served their masters twenty-four hours a day. There were orders after orders from the imperial chapel, masses had to be composed, and to be written down, the parts copied in the copying plant which Schmelzer directed, and the music rehearsed and in the evening there were opera performances with new dances on request of the Italian court composers and of the powerful Imperial Master of the Ballet, Signor Santo Ventura. Occasionally a masquerade or a tournament took place, in winter time ceremonial sleighing parties of the court, and besides all this the management of the court orchestra had to be taken care of, and the instruction and supervision of the students and disciples who lived in Schmelzer's house and clamoured for his teaching.

Every time when the court went on a journey, the court orchestra had of course to accompany it, and whatever the destination was whether Augsburg, Graz, Prague or Frankfurt —the responsible manager was "Herr Kapellmeister Schmelzer". The various activities of Schmelzer's surely were comparable to the press of modern life, and the mixture of his occupations added to his real job as virtuoso and violinist sounds almost fantastic. Schmelzer did, by the way, not abjure the lesser pleasures of life, and when he died at Prague in 1680 of the plague (which the Vienna court had tried to escape by coming to Bohemia) he not only left his heirs a great collection of music and instruments, but in his cellar also a number of kegs of the best Austrian and Hungarian wines.

It was not without purpose that I have mentioned these apparently insignificant details in the life of Schmelzer. They mark and accentuate something of that exuberance, that joy of life which was characteristic for Austria already at that period, and culminated later in the development of the Viennese Waltz. One might indeed say that the Viennese Laendler and Waltz both have their origin in Schmelzer's dance compositions. We find amongst them "Intraden" and "Retiraden" (entries and leave-takings), "Gaillards", "Allemandes" "Courantes", "Sarabandes", "Jigs", "Balletti", "Canarii", "Trezze", "Tracanarii", "Saltarelli", "Menuets", "Gavottes", "Bourrées", "Chaconnes", "Branles" and "Moresche". These dances will be described later, except those which mainly belonged to the former period and which were already mentioned before. At this point I should like to turn to a special dance form, most intimately tied up with the place of its origin and, as it were, the ancestor of the Laendler and the Waltz.

The word "Aria" which I shall use here signifies "melody", sung or danced, and in this special instance the Austrian or Alpine dance in which the couples turn about as in the waltz.

Among the colorful varieties of French and Italian dances the Austrian "Laendler" (peasant dance) has no proper place. We see it represented in the etchings of the Westphalian artist Aldegrever, and the printer of Nuremberg, H. S. Beham. The French philosopher Montaigne has given us a description of it as he saw it performed in Augsburg at the home of the famous Fuggers, the South-German financiers, while on his journey to Italy in 1580. "Journal de Voyage de Michel de Montaigne". He says that the partners had their hands on each others backs and stood so close that their faces touched. On the picture one sees that they sometimes stepped back to back as it is done in the figure of the Virginia Reel, or that they skipped with raised hands. Another source quoted by Bolte, "Zur Geschichte des Tanzes", tells us that the mastersinger Kunz Has, hailing from Nuremberg, complains that:

"Itzund tanzt man den wuesten weller
Den spinner oler wie sie's nennen"

(Now they dance the godless "Weller", the "Spinner", or whatever they may call it). According to Curt Sachs, "Weller" means the same as "Walzer" - "Schleifer" (waltz-sliding dance). This dance was not always as wild,—"wuest"—as contemporaries describe it, for Hans Sachs says about it in his "Jost Amman, Eigentliche Beschreibung aller Staende", Frankfurt, 1568, that:

In a courtly dance, with light steps in polite fashion, does each man's sweetheart clasp her darling, that heart and mind may well rejoice, and dance with slight steps. Such a form of the "Weller" might well have been danced at the court, and, in fact, Rink, the biographer of Leopold the First tells how the Emperor often danced it with his consort. For never, he says, did the Emperor dance "according to French movements, but always in German figures". Such was the dance practiced in Austria, appropriately modified according to the age and dignity of the performers. Actually it was a kind of "Nachtanz" (hop-dance). The lady was conducted around the hall to the sounds of a two-beat measure, and when the tune of the "Nachtanz" sounded, the couple assumed the same position as in the "Weller" and waltzed around. The melody of these dances approached the one recorded in the Codex 16583 in Vienna, which Schmelzer composed for the "Balletto d'Amoretti e Trittoni", performed in connection with Cesti's opera "Le disgrazie d'Amore". It is a genuine "Laendler", accompanied

by a bag-pipe, and playing the "Nachtanz" in 3/4 time we get a true waltz. The name "Laendler" derived from "Landl" (little country)—by which is meant Upper Austria—occurs already in the 17th century, in a lute book, found and preserved in the monastery at Kremsmuenster. In this manuscript the piece called "Landerli" is written in two-beat time, but we know from previous documents that the "Nachtanz" was often not recorded by notation but merely improvised. Besides the "Landerli" there are also "Steyerische", called for the most part "Aria Styriaca" in the manuscripts. (One of these is included in one of my previous publications). There are many Laendler-like dances which have come down to us. The manuscripts which I found at Kremsier, contain such a melody from Styria with the dialect-title "Halter", meaning an alpine shepherd. The following "Aria"

is a typical alpine one, that of a shepherd playing on his curved horn, and was used as one of the sources for Schmelzer's Viennese dances. The following examples may serve to illustrate how such motives were used.

In February 1679 the opera "Baldracca" by Antonio Draghi was performed at the Viennese court. The solemn subject was an incident from the life of Otto the First, one of the German Emperors. In order to relieve the serious mood and to give a lighter touch, a dance of the serving maids and peasants who encircle a faun, and a "Ballo di Saltatori" were performed. This ballet of the maids was introduced after a quarrel between the traditional comic characters of the Italian comedy, Lumio and Delfira, super-imposed on the action of the opera. The grotesque dance of these maids is performed to the strains of the following aria, a genuine alpine dance. There is not the least doubt that this is a real "Schuhplattler", a tapped dance with the rhythm of the heel tapping the floor.

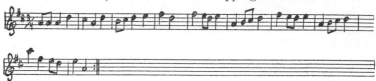

The melody gives us a vivid picture of the maids trying to sweep the frightened clowns from the stage with their brooms, and brandishing them in a kind of broom-sword dance.

In the next scene, the Swabian peasants appear, and their figures show them to be less violent. Here is no tapping or beating of heels but a mild and gentle "Weller" and the melody does not leave us in doubt about it:

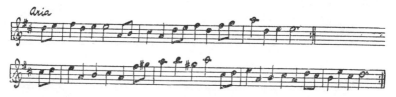

One of Schmelzer's characteristic traits is his use of the "Quodlibet" or "Potpourri" (medley) which became so popular in Vienna during the 19th century. In the opera "L'avidità di Mida" by Draghi, 1671, shepherds and nymphs dance such a "potpourri" which included a "Bergamasca", a "Canario", a "Gavotte" and a "Sarabande". The "Bergamasca" is an old Upper-Italian clown-dance, which appears in Shakespeare's "Midsummer Night's Dream". Its melody was sung in Germany during the 17th and 18th centuries to the words: "Kraut und Rueben":

"Sauerkraut and turnips were too much for me - - -
Had my mother cooked some meat - - -
Still with her I'd be",

and was used by Bach as a Quodlibet in his Goldberg Variations. This is not the only folkmelody used by Bach which appears in Schmelzer's Ballets. The "Grandfather Dance" of the "Peasant Cantata" was used by Schmelzer in 1680 in "Ballet of the Princesses". ("Balletto delle Serenissime"). It was later used by Schubert (in one of his dances) and by Schumann (in his Faschingsschwank). Schmelzer has a large number of such dances. The interesting feature of all of them is a mixture of Italian Baroque culture and Austrian peasant ways. At the court, conversation goes on in Spanish, Italian and French, mingled with bits of Austrian dialect, as spoken by the peasants and this is true of the music as well, which alternates Italian opera with Viennese servant's dance. At this time there originated popular folk ditties like that of the "Liebe Augustin". Corresponding to them were the highly popular and fervid sermons of the Court-Preacher, Abraham a Santa Clara, who thundered from his pulpit against the abuses of too luxurious living among the aristocracy.

Naturally it was part of Schmelzer's function to furnish the music for the balls and entertainments of the court. Among favored forms of these entertainments at the German courts and above all in Vienna, were the so-called "Wirtschaften" (inns), often called "Hoteleries". This latter title was also mentioned by Claude François Menestrier, a Jesuit priest who wrote two important volumes on the dance,—a strange subject indeed for a man of the church! In 1670, he saw in Munich the performance of such a "hotelerie" and was so charmed with it that he called it the "manière, la plus agréable et la plus spirituelle du monde". The "Wirtschaften" were dance-festivals at which the Emperor and the Empress acted as host and hostess for the remainder of the court and the invited guests. The guests appeared in native costumes decreed by the master of ceremonies on the cards of invitation and sent out in the name of the imperial hosts. The costumes came from different countries—there were Spaniards, Hungarian and Bohemian peasants, Dutch and Italians, even Americans, who probably wore the somewhat theatrical garb devised for them by the scenic painter Burnacini. When Peter the Great of Russia visited Vienna in 1698, he not only attended the performance of the opera "Arsace" by Draghi but was a guest at the "Wirt-schaft" given in his honor and arrived at the festival in the costume of a "Frisian peasant" "because he had already used this at a Dutch party in Holland". It is interesting to read a partial account of this feast. I found it among the documents of the Vienna Archives. It was hitherto unpublished.

"Both their Majesties, the Emperor and the Empress descended to the hall as inn-keeper and hostess and at the door of the hall—disguised as a garden—,they welcomed the Czar. Then the Czar with his partner, the Lady-in-Waiting, Fraeulein von Thurn and at the head of all the other couples each with his partner—led the dance. This continued until it was time for the banquet, laid in the gallery, at a great table for eighty persons. In the antichamber however, was a table laid for the servants and in order to go there one crossed the hall over the great spiral staircase. Their Majesties were seated way down at the end of the table with the Czar and his lady-partner next to them. As it is the custom of an innkeeper His Majesty repeatedly got up and drank to the Czar and to the other persons at the table. Then after the meal everybody left the table and returned to the hall where there was dancing until break of day. The service at the table was performed by 32 pages in costume. Two of them knew the Czech language and had been ordered particularly to attend the Czar".

Doubtlessly the composer of the dances forming part of the opera which the Czar had witnessed was Johann Joseph Hoffer who also wrote the music for the dances played at this "Wirt-schaft". What impression the Czar received from all this is, however, not known to us.

Similar arrangements in which the various dignitaries of the Court, beginning with the imperial couple played different roles, were the custom at the "Peasant Weddings". Here Royalty impersonated the parents of the bride while at the Landschaften and Königreiche, members of the court played the parts of King and Queen. The "Wirtschaften" and the "Peasant Weddings" were practised as late as in the 18th century and Casanova tells of one he attended in Cologne. It seems

quite understandable that the men and women at the courts
of the Baroque, governed by a stiff and rigid ceremonial
should have felt the desire to abandon from time to time these
ways of formal etiquette, to release their energy by imitating
the more natural and spontaneous forms of entertainment prevailing among the peasants and the simple servants. A similar
tendency was probably at the root of the delight taken by the
later French court in its effort to make a "return to Nature".

What was the mode of dancing at the "Peasant Weddings"?
Though we have no exact description of it, the dances which
have come down to us as "Gebrauchsmusik", tell us about it in
their own language. Schmelzer sent his patron, Bishop Liechtenstein, not only the ballets but also the music used at the
entertainments, for at the Bishop's court were also "Wirtschaften", "Weddings" and at times "Schaefereien" (pastoral entertainments) at which the lords and ladies appeared as shepherds
and shepherdesses. A short pastoral scene was performed accompanied by music highly popular in form. During my search
for old manuscripts in the Vienna State Library, I came upon
the original of such a pastoral play. Its contents are unimportant
but the finale which is sung to celebrate the reunion of a once
separated loving couple of shepherds is a genuine waltz, true to
form in every respect. The piece dates from the time between
1660 and 1670.

After such entertainments at the courts of Vienna and Olmuetz there was a general dancing, and the music which was played has come down to us. It is called the "Branle de Polion", the "Branle" or "Brawl" from Poland. The composer of that dance, Father Augustine Kertzinger, was the organist of the Prague Cathedral of St. Vitus in the year 1660. The "Branles de Polion" were performed with slow steps and followed by a "Nachtanz". The designation "Branle" marks these dances as rounds, followed by a highstepping Polish peasant dance, a real Mazurka. This is the seventh dance of the series:

In the time when Austria defended herself against the inroads of the Turks and stopped them in their march against Christian civilization, and when the national feeling expressed itself strongly by returning to national forms of music, there was the time of the "Laendler", the "Stampfer", the "Weller" (Waltzes), and the "Jodler" (Yodel). Later, when Austria became a world-power under Charles the Sixth,—this emphasis on native motives disappeared more and more. The "Laendler" and the "Jodler" were replaced by "Menuets" and by "Passepieds".

What documents do we have of these "Jodlers"? In my book on the songs of the Vienna Baroque Period, mentioned before, I have drawn attention to the first printed book of Viennese songs, "Ehrliche Gemuethserquickung" (Honest refreshment for souls), published in 1686. It is an amusing little book, showing us the background of the Viennese culture of Baroque times. All kinds of familiar and homely topics are the themes of the songs, of the idle and wasteful students, the insubordinate serving-maids, the cruel housewives who mal-treat them, or the "merry widows" who are on the look-out for another mate. Among the melodies are Hungarian tunes which might well be part of a modern Hungarian Czardas:

The climax of these songs is the so-called "Styrian Ruffian's Jodel" (Der Steyermaerkische Raufjodel), a song telling about a quarrelsome fellow from Styria who has the ambition to knock out every challenge to fight. In this song, "Jodel" is the abbreviated form of the name "Jodocus", and the "Jodel" —so designated—can really "yodel".

On the seemingly endless list of the duties of the court-musician we find also the winter-entertainments for which music had to be composed. The documents of the "Vienna Master of the Protocol" tell us of the sleigh rides which were arranged at that time. These were not spontaneously organized winter-sport practices, but minutely regulated affairs in which every detail was carefully planned and thought of. The order of succession of the various sleighs, which comes first and who is to sit in the leading vehicles,—all this is redetermined, ac-cording to the rules of the Spanish Court-Etiquette, the all-powerful arbiter of those days. First the procession was to circle the castle to the accompaniment of an Entry, then, the sleighs were arranged in the form of a wheel, while the music played a merry dance—a Gaillard or a Courante. Finally, to the tune of a sprightly Jig, the sleighs left the courtyard and rode through the gates out into the snow-covered landscape. Some of these airs for sleigh rides have been preserved and we may note here that the "Pageant Suite" as we may call it, was the musical model for this kind of composition.

As a rule, the long line of sleighs is accompanied by a choir of wind,—trumpet—, and cornet-players, who sit on the

"Wurst", a kind of bobsleigh—, and play flourishes and sleighing melodies. A "Canario" was composed by Schmelzer for a sleigh ride in 1678. One must not forget to imagine the sound of the accompanying jingles of the bells, which the horses wore around their necks . . . Outriders, grooms, rode alongside. The sleigh of the imperial participants had, besides two runners two body-guards and six pages who came along on horseback. The goal was one of the imperial summer-castles outside the city, where there was a stop for taking refreshments. When the sleigh-party had ended, the long column rode back to town where the younger members of the imperial family impatiently waited, for they knew that now it was their turn to make the circle of the courtyard in the sleigh of the Master of Ceremonies. In the evening a dance entertainment, a "Merenda" (afternoon entertainment) or a "Wirtschaft" took place.

These practices did not stop with the 17th century. We find them faithfully recorded in another "Schlittenfahrt", that of Mozart's father, Leopold. Perhaps he may have seen such a procession of sleighs passing the "Mirabell Garden" at Salzburg, and been so deeply impressed that he wrote the harpsichord piece. He used the "Intrada" to describe the beginning of the ride and introduced a number of effects: the champing of the horses, the shivering of the ladies in the cold winter air, etc. The close of the piece is the ball with Menuet and Allemande. In 1791, Wolfgang Amadeus Mozart, remembering this composition of his father's, called one of his famous "Deutschen": "Schlittenfahrt".

Besides balls, dances, masques and sleighs rides, there were the "Tournaments", where the aristocratic gentlemen showed their mettle, and their grace and bodily skill. After the introduction of firearms, the tournaments had become mere games of skill. During the Middle Ages, for the real tournaments, music had played an important part in the proceedings, and in the old description of these jousts the number of trumpeters is noted exactly. In the period of Baroque times, the tournament assumes a purely allegorical character, it is in reality a kind of dramatic show. Italy has a number of these tournaments in which almost military formations, consisting of many participants play against each other. In 1615, during the carnival, such a musical tourney, "La Guerra d'Amore" was enacted in honor of Duke Federico d'Urbino, the betrothed of Claudia, sister of Cosimo, the Second of the House of the Medici. The text was by A. Salvadori and Grazi, the music by Signorini, Turco and Jacopo Peri, (one of the founders of the opera). An engraving by Jacques Callot shows the choreographic positions of the participants.

In Solerti's book, "Musica, Ballo e Drammatica alla Corte Medicea dal 1600-1637", a large number of such tourney-ballets is mentioned. One of the most popular of these was the "Liberazione di Ruggiero" by Francesca Caccini, the gifted daughter of the co-founder of the opera, Giulio Caccini. The performance took place at the Villa Poggio Imperiale in Florence in the year 1625, in honor of the visiting Polish Prince Ladislav Sigismund. Special mention is made of those in charge of the scenery and of the machines, and likewise of the authors of the "ballo a piedi e a cavallo". The participants on foot and on horseback were carefully listed by name and are portrayed in a still extant engraving by Alfonso Parigi. In the castle courtyard a quadrangle is marked off, on which a semicircular vestibule is erected. In two not quite evenly matched squadrons (engravers of that period were not scrupulous about historical accuracy) the combatants face each other in open order. According to the libretto, twenty-four mounted men took part in the ballet at the close of the opera. We may assume that the ballet music, like that for the tournament, was not written by Francesca herself, but obtained elsewhere. On such occasions, the trumpet music already on hand, was frequently employed. In Italy as in Germany, trumpeters had a guild of their own, with special craft secrets and unusual musical terminology. Equestrian scenes, at which large groups of men on foot and on horseback were marshalled according to artistic principles, were customary during the Renaissance as well as in Baroque times. This delight in a kind of aesthetic military strategy went so far, that even in works on military tactics, aesthetic principles were instrumental. Choreography and strategy went hand in hand in the work of Della Valle, written at the beginning of the 16th century. He mentions not only the hollow square and the wedge, but enumerates all kinds of cross figures, ellipses, half-moons, scorpions and the like, all of which present military tacticians designate as mere outbursts of their fantastic imagination. It was an attempt to interpret even that least human of all sciences, namely military tactics, with aesthetic principles and the confusion of power and beauty dominating this period, found here another outlet.

These "Equestrian Ballets", as they were called, were a special form of the military ballets and we have a special theoretic treatise on them by Ph. Harsdorffer, 1607-1658, called "Schauspiele zu Ross". (Pageants on horseback). Squadrons of 52 men each, are led by four officers which are followed by twelve men on horseback. The music is to be exactly proportionate to the size of the squadrons, that is, consists of 52 notes, and is played by the trumpeters. Here is the piece:

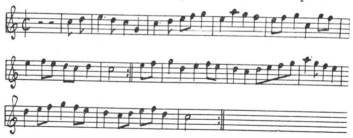

From Italy the horseballets came to Vienna and already Ferdinand the Third had them performed at his court. But the high tide of the Baroque period brought also the classical era of the Austrian "Rossballet" (Horse-ballet), during the reign of Leopold the First. Of the two grand equestrian ballets performed in 1666 and 1667, the first gained world-wide renown because numerous copies of a description were sent to all the important courts of Europe. It was entitled "La Contesa dell'aria e dell'acqua" (The Contest between Air and Water). The engravings adorning the description published in Vienna by Cosmerovius in 1667, show the performance in the Burghof, the yard of the castle. A towering structure of wood had been erected at the immense outlay of 600,000 Reichsthaler, almost as much as the cost of a military campaign, but the manager Francesco Sbarra had no scruples in the way of spending for these purposes.

The first engraving shows us a vessel upon which sits Fama, richly clad; the second one the Burghof encircled by tiers of seats. The other pictures give details such as the cloud-car, (an indispensable requisite in Venetian opera), the cave of Vulcan and various other particulars of the carousel. While the elements begin their contention with some of the gods espousing the cause of Water, while others take that of the Air, the altercation grows more violent and finally at the call "Battaglia"—battle is joined. The great machines are pushed aside and the real business of the whole, the equestrian ballet begins. Every art of horsemanship is displayed. While the choruses and the vocal music of Bertali have disappeared, the music for the movement of the men on horseback has come down to us. It was written by Schmelzer. The dances were a Courante, an Entry for His Majesty's arrival with his courtiers, played by trumpets and tympani, a Jig which sounded when the knights on foot came, a Follia that marked the coming and the manoeuvres of the equestrians, and a markedly slow Allemande which accompanied the evolutions of the Emperor on his white "Lippizaner Horse" solemnly moving about. A Sarabande closed the Leave-taking at the end of the ballet.

The harmonic accompaniment was played by cornets, perhaps by flutes or other winds, while two trumpets played the melody. For greater effect some of the trumpets were placed at some distance from the rest of the orchestra. When the Salzburg Festival of 1931 brought, maybe for a last time, a revival of these equestrian ballets with the still existing breed of Lippizaner horses from the Imperial stables, these old harmonies were played again, and sounded longingly and archaic to modern ears. They seemed to come from a world of long ago, a world of courtesy, brilliance and beauty.

How great an impression this ballet made is seen by the fact that in honor of her birthday, the Empress Margarita had another "Rossballet" performed, on July 12, 1667. This time the performance took place at the summer residence "Favorita". (I have described this ballet in detail in the "Musical Quarterly" of January 1933). For this occasion the music was composed by the famous Venetian composer Cesti, but the dances were of course by Schmelzer. The title was "La Germania esultante", and the subject of the ballet was the homage paid to the Spanish-born Empress by Germany, her new homeland. Here the ballet is combined with a "Corso de teste", a battle of the Emperor and his court with a number of wooden monsters, which are to be beheaded. Naturally the Emperor wins the fight, and then follows the equestrian ballet, accompanied by an Allemande, a Courante, a Jig and a Sarabande. Again the high trumpets, "Clarini", are placed at some distance to heighten the effect of their sound. Today the equestrian ballets are almost forgotten and the visitors of Coney Island and other amusement parks will hardly realize that these plain and simple merry-go-rounds are the only remains of the glamorous Baroque carousel.

This brings us to a discussion on the instrumentation of these compositions. The mostly used instruments were those with four or five strings, but there were all kinds of brass and woodwinds. As a favorite accompaniment of the strings the "Clarini" were used (high trumpets), particularly when the music to be played was intended for some great festival. Viennese musicians were conservative and had a predilection for old forms like old church-sonatas. It is therefore not surprising that we often find an instrumentation reminding us of old double choirs of Giovanni Gabrieli, the "chori spezzati", where two or more orchestras alternate with each other. This kind of instrumentation is frequently used for outdoor music, where two or more orchestras are placed in different parts of the square or courtyard, resulting in the most charming and interesting effects. Even down to Mozart's time this custom prevailed: we find it, for example, in the "Serenade" (Koechel 239), which, though it is a kind of "Concerto Grosso", has the atmosphere of the ancient serenades with two choirs.

In 1674, on August 13th, an outdoor ballet was given in the summer palace of Schoenbrunn, entitled "Il trionfator de Centauri". In the middle of a pond, a large platform and stage had been erected, and centaurs, nymphs, and satyrs performed to the music of Schmelzer, their exotic and strange leaps and dances. Perhaps the moon added its pale light to that of the more than a thousand torches which are said to have been the illumination of the three ballet groups, arriving on the stage from different sides. Each of these groups had its own instrumentation. The centaurs danced to a combination of strings, cornets and trombones, the graceful nymphs to the strings alone, but when the gods of the forest joined them in the dance, the shalms turned in, while the nymphs still danced to the sound of the violins. Every group is given its specific tonal color. In the "Aria di Tutti", in which all three groups dance together, all the three orchestras play at one and the same time. If we picture to ourselves that each of these instrumental groups was given a special position, we can see how the various lines of the dancers, moving in Baroque figures, have their counterpart in the acoustic interplay of sound coming from these "Chori spezzati" (divided choirs). Here we have an example of the over-meticulous delight with ordered and regulated artistic forms so characteristic of this period. The deeper meaning of tonal color is striking as we see that dances of the male deities of the forest were accompanied by shalms and those of the nymphs by string instruments.

Johann Heinrich Schmelzer, who might rightly be called the Johann Strauss of his day, was succeeded by his son Andreas Anton Schmelzer, (1653-1701), who occupied the rank of "Court Dance Composer" from 1680 until his death. But he was neither so gifted nor so popular as his father and we find little of the true "folkloristic element" of the elder Schmelzer in his dances. The same is true of Johann Joseph Hoffer, 1666-1729, his successor. Not until we come to the next composer of the court ballets, Nikolaus Matteis, who remained at the Viennese Court until about 1737, do we have a really interesting personality. Matteis was the son of an Italian, living in England, and had been raised there. He came to Vienna as a first violinist of the court orchestra and composed ballets. In the archives of the court he is called the "Engellaendische Geiger". A great number of dances for operas by Caldara, Ziani, Conti and others, which he wrote, are to be found in the scores of the operatic works in the Vienna State Library. Burney, the famous English historian of music, tells how he studied the violin with Matteis, after the latter had returned to England as an old man. (Compare my study on Matteis in the "Musical Quarterly" of July 1942).

Matteis was again one of the bearers of the old Austrian musical traditions like Schmelzer, and though his dances are not as deeply rooted in the folklore of the native population as those of Schmelzer's we find in his work a number of true Viennese "Laendler", though written by an Anglo-Italian. The following "Aria" which he wrote for Caldara's opera "La Verità nell'inganno" (Truth in Deceit) in 1717 is characteristic for Matteis:

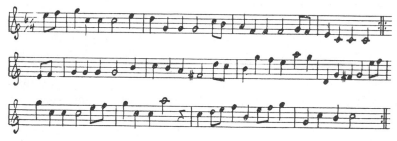

It shows that this "international" musician carried on the tradition of the alpine dance form, which the elder Schmelzer initiated. He carried it into the 18th century. There is no doubt that real waltz dances were written by this "Engellaender". But most of this dance music which might have been the link to our times has been lost, and we must look for its traces, left only on the symphonies, the menuets, the serenades and the divertimenti of the pre-classic and the classic music of the Viennese composers. This popular music was truly the basis for the later "Viennese Classic School", beginning with Haydn, but also of the "Viennese Waltz" of Lanner and Strauss.

CHAPTER VIII

THE BAROQUE PERIOD II

FRENCH BALLET, FRENCH DANCES, SUITES AND KEYBOARD-MUSIC.

The ballet is the true child of the Baroque period. The immensely heightened interest in all forms of display and magnificence, which first showed itself in the Renaissance in the triumphal processions (trionfi), the pageants, the street festivals and the aristocratic festivities, laid the seeds for the subsequent development of the opera and the ballet. Sachs rightly declares that in the 17th century a clear and strong cleavage occurred for the first time in the world's history between active and passive artistic expression, between the performer and his public. It is therefore not surprising that in this century the ballet reached its highest perfection. This did not, however, happen in Italy as we might have expected and, where we saw its first beginnings, rather in France shall we find its best examples.

We have already mentioned the "Ballet comique de la reine" of the Italian Baltazarini (1581). This is but a single instance, not important enough for further discussion. However, when Henry the Fourth (died 1610) married the daughter of Catherine de Medici, Marguerite, a Florentine princess, the relations between Italy and France were strengthened, and the Italians, Caccini and Rinucinni, the founders of the Florentine opera were invited to come to Paris. Rinuccini in his turn took back with him to Italy French ballet concepts, and these were revived in Monteverdi's ballet "Ballo delle Ingrate". Under

Louis the Thirteenth, (1610-1643) the French ballet flourished for a short time with the "Ballet de la délibération de Renault", (1617) and the "Tancred" (1619). The dances of the "Renault" are simple. They are, as was customary at that time, transcribed only for violin and bass, and are all fairly similar. There are intradas in duple time.

Occasionally there is a melodic relation between them, and in this respect they approach the "Variation Suite", as may be observed from this short example of two entries, one following upon the other:

The most famous ballet of the time was the "Ballet du roy", composed by Pierre Guedron, in which the King himself appeared as a "spirit of the fire", and the courtier, de Luynes, as Rinaldo.

The greater part of the festival and dance music of this period was transcribed by André Danican Philidor (d.1730), who was a cornetist of the "grand écurie", a composer of marches and dances, and assistant in the Royal Library at Versailles. He made a regular collection of all kinds of old instrumental music, pieces that had been performed at the court from the time of Francis I. in 1515: dances, so-called "carousels", (tournaments) hunting music, flourishes, fanfares and other various celebrations. Part of this collection has been lost, and the remainder has up to date not been published entirely.

In looking through the archives and annals of the French opera and ballet, we come upon a dramatic piece which was performed in 1645 in the Parisian theatre "du Petit Bourbon" on the occasion of a Venetian theatrical festival. This piece "La Finta Pazza" was composed by the Venetian Francesco Sacrati, and the dances were arranged by the Florentine choreographer, G. B. Balbi. Mazarin, the councillor and guide of the King, the confidant of the music-loving Anne of Austria, then dowager Queen, had arranged for the coming of the Italians. Though the piece was supposed to play in the harbor of Syracuse, the stage represented the familiar sites of Pont Neuf, with the statue of Henry the Fourth, the Notre Dame church and the spire of Saint Chapelle. In the ballet there were characters reminding one of a modern circus. The orchestra was disguised in the skins of animals and clowns performed their antics. All this was done to amuse the young Louis XIV, the later "Roy Soleil" who was but two years old at the time!

In vain did the masters of Italian opera exert themselves to win the French public. Luigi Rossi and Francesco Cavalli joined other less famous composers. Ballets were introduced to conform to the French taste and when Cavalli's opera "Serse" (Xerxes) was performed on the occasion of the wedding of the young Louis XIV, a former young scullery-boy, the Italian Giovanni Battista Lulli, who had shown his extraordinary musical gifts in the composition of ballets, was commissioned to write the dances for the performance. "Ercole amante" (Hercules in love) was the second of the operas given at the royal wedding. From this time dated his fame and his subsequent glory as the founder of French opera, now under the gallicised title, Jean Baptiste Lully. First, merely a composer of ballets as parts of Italian opera, Lully soon usurped the stage for himself and, composing music for both opera and ballet, threw the Italian product out of the French theatre.

Lully was born in Florence in 1632 and had come to Paris at the age of 14. He became the musical page at the house of a great lady, Mademoiselle de Montpensier and received a musical education as a violinist. He studied with the organist Metru and Roberday and his reputation soon was such that he was enrolled among the "24 violins du Roy" where he soon gained the favor and patronage of the King. Made the leader of this group, 1652, he created a special orchestra, the "16 petits violons" which reached an epoch-making high standard under his guidance. Lully possessed in a rare degree, far above his contemporaries, the gift of penetrating and adapting himself to the demands of dramatic dance performances, and of embodying in them the essential character of French musical culture. He was an excellent solo dancer himself, appeared on the stage repeatedly and created a sensation in the comedy ballets written by Molière, for which he had composed the music. This is not the place to discuss his activity and his importance on behalf of the French Grand Opera, the seed of which was planted by him. But he is all the more important for the history of dance music, because he, as no other, expressed in his dances the spirit of the time of "le Grand Roy". For he was able to mirror in them not only the spirit of the French language, but no less, the pride and grandeur of the court and of the King who was its symbol. "Gloire et Amour, grandeur et splendeur" mark the music, and in this respect it is a fitting companion to the classic dramas of Corneille and Racine with their exalted ideals of conduct and infinite emotional sensibility. It was not unusual that the King himself danced in the ballets in the role of one of the Gods or Kings, and his audience allowed itself to be carried away and to believe ever more in his "divinity". This climax of exhibitionism is quite in line with the trends of the Baroque. And this division, on one side the actor, on the other the audience is here carried to its highest point, where the top dignitary of the realm makes a show of himself to an adoring and servile audience.

It was natural that with the elevation of the dignity of the dance, the performers obtained new ideas of their importance and that in 1661, thirteen dancing masters of the "Communauté de Saint Julien des Menestriers" made themselves independent of the musicians, with whom they had been united in this group and formed an "Académie de la Danse". Thereby they raised the dance to the dignity of a special science and profession, in which movement, gestures, and pantomime were minutely defined and prescribed. Charles L. Beauchamps, (1636-1705), dancing master of Louis XIV, for over twenty years, determined once and for all, what the five positions and the steps of the dance were to be: the groundwork for the future of all the figures of the French court dances.

Only when all these "Ballances, Battements, Chassés, Jetés", and so forth, had obtained his sanction, could they be incorporated in the dances.

At first glance, all of them seem to have little connection with the music of the dances. But the dignified sobriety, the grace, and the occasional playful coquetry of these dances have their counterpart in the rhythms to which they were performed.

The queen of all the dances of this period was the "Minuet", the successor of the "Courante", which in its turn was originally derived from the "Branle de Poitou". Just as the "Branle" was at first a given figure of the "Basse Danse",—so the "Pas menu" was part of the Branle, a step, already mentioned in the account of a court festival at Nancy in 1445. Sachs says of the minuet that it was "unexcelled in its combination of dignity and charm, its restrained grace and its reserved galanterie" (courtly politeness towards the female sex). The "Minuet", like so many other dances of the time previous to this period, is originally a dance of wooing. With stately dignity the audience and the partner are greeted, then the dancer moves forwards and backwards with small steps and gliding pace. Then the lady and her partner both move hither and thither to escape and rejoin each other. Though hundreds of dancing masters invented hundreds of different minuets, the basic scheme always remained the same. Two steps with bent knees are followed by two steps with straight leg and each group of four steps is performed to two 3/4 beats. The right foot begins and as the left step with bent knee is taken to the note beyond the bar, there is often a kind of lilting rhythm. The prolongation of the "weak part" of the second measure may be explained in the same way, as for example in the following minuet from Rameau's "Zoroastre":

In the course of time, the tempo of the minuet has undergone important changes. The branle de Poitou was a dance performed in semi-quick time, but Lully's minuet is by no means a slow dance. Bach's minuets, as well, are rather fast than slow dances. (According to Quantz, two fourth notes are a pulse beat). Towards the year 1800 the minuet became the slow and solemn dance of the old-fashioned days, and in this tempo Mozart used it in his "Don Giovanni".

In its first form, the minuet was danced on a figure 8, later this figure 8 became a figure looking like an S, and finally like a Z. The gentleman was standing at one end of the S. or of the Z., and the lady at the other. Now they danced two steps to the side, then two or three steps forwards. "They danced away from each other, or met, they bowed to each other, made a 'tour de main' repeated this toward the left, and at the third meeting they joined both hands and finished the dance. Then they bowed down to the ground at the end as they did at the beginning".

In the transcription of his ballets, Lully rarely designated a definite dance by name but calls the dances simply "Airs". He includes under this title Minuets, Bourrées, Gavottes and all kinds of dance forms. To the music of such an air all kinds of skillfully performed intricate dance figures are performed but not the standardized ball-room dances. It is obvious that he chooses a somewhat exotic melody for a comedy ballet, called the "Marriage forcé", in which Louis XIV danced himself. The edition of Lully's ballets published by Prunières makes it possible for us to compare the French dances with those of the Austrian Baroque. The Austrian dances have a folk character, they are rustic in tone, the favorite dance is the "Laendler"; in their structure, they are simple and often primitive, while the French dances are highly cultured, sometimes full of pathos, and graceful. Even peasant dances, like the "Bourrée" and the "Paysanne" always show feeling for elegance and aristocratic demeanor.

When Lully, like his Austrian contemporary Schmelzer, wrote the ballets for the Italian operas given at Paris' theatres in order to make the foreign far more palatable to the native hearers, he went one step further: he wrote the overture in the typical French form. An introductory movement full of pathos to characterize the festive and solemn opening in the presence of the King was followed by a fast fugato movement to portray the chattering and lively court; the piece closed with a short slow movement. To please the lighthearted public, the melodic form of the "Xerxes" dances is extremely popular in tone, not unlike that of Schmelzer who wished to oppose his dances to the formal and stiff operatic style of Cesti. Frequently Lully's dances are in rondo form, giving a main theme, followed by a second one after which the principal thought is repeated, to be followed by a second accessory-theme after which the main motive returns. The close is always the main theme and the scheme is like this: a b a c a d a.

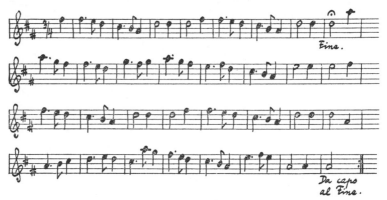

Such French rustic dances, probably derived from the branle de Poitou, are the seed from which popular dances, such as the "Gigue", the "Bourrée", the "Passepied" and others are derived; they are contrasting to the "Chaconnes", "Passacailles", "Courantes" and "Minuets".

In his instrumentation Lully differs greatly from Monteverdi and from the Italians and the Austrians by his quality of rich and full orchestration, already approaching that of the modern orchestra. Baroque traces are, however, still apparent in the use of lutes, harpsichords and different kinds of organs. Our present violin was indigenous in France, already designated by Monteverdi as "Violino piccolo alla Francese", when he used it in his "Orfeo". Already under Louis XIII there was a special group among the court musicians. which was called the "grande bande des violons", and consisted of 24 string players. They played at court, for all the balls, for the celebration of "New Year's Day", or the "First of May", or on the "Day of St. Louis", (August 25th) or whenever the King returned from a journey. Louis XIV added to this grande bande, another "petite bande" of 16 musicians, whose leader was Lully. Their function was to play for the more intimate occasions in the service of the King, and to accompany him on all his journeys. Just as for Schmelzer's dances we find the strings divided into five parts, which here are augmented by woodwinds. A French specialty was to have the full orchestra alternate with smaller groups of instruments, applying the principle of the "concerto grosso", contrasting the sonority of large groups to that of smaller bodies. Most frequently flutes and oboes with a bass supplied by the bassoon are contrasted with the strings, for their function is to play accessory and interpolated movements with three parts as "episodes" within the whole pieces. This form of French "trio" is one of the roots of the "minuet trios" within the classic form of the symphony. It seems to have been the tradition in France even long before Lully. We have a record in the State Library at Vienna of a "Serenata" by Don Remigio Cesti, (not the Cesti of the operas), set for six violins, four alto,- four tenor-, and four bass-violas, an orchestration called "uso di concerti di Francia". Two violins plus bass were to play the trio. Other transcriptions, as f. i of Monteverdi's brother Giulio, call the use of two high voices plus a bass contrast "canto alla francese". I also know a "Confitebor alla francese" from the State Library in Vienna, in which this type of contrast is used. The trios may therefore be assumed to be typically French. A specialty of these forms is the fully developed melodic structure of the middle voices, which was greatly neglected in the compositions of the Germans and Italians, wherever homophonic notation was used. In polyphonic dance movements—such as those of Hausmann and Schein, the middle parts were exaggerated and quite unfit for the rhythmic movement of the dance. Lully, however, not only gives us the leading part fully "apt" for dancing, but has light and freely formed middle parts, formed quite unlike those of the Germans. Schmelzer of all German composers, was the only one who approached him, in this respect.

Already as early as in 1660 and 1670, dances from Lully's operas were combined to form suites, preceded by an overture. To designate them as "ballet suites" was a happy choice of name. In 1690 such a collection appeared, called "Les trios des operas de M. de Lully, mis en ordre pour les concerts", and others soon followed. That the suite was preceded by a freely composed, not dance-like movement, is however not a French invention. Formerly Johann Rosenmueller was credited with having made this innovation, because he had his "Sonate da Camera" written in 1667, introduced by a Venetian "symphonie", that is an introductory movement. I have, however, in connection with my research work on Schmelzer, already found a suite of his, with a freely composed introductory movement,—one called "Serenata" of 1667, and another at Kremsier dated 1666. This new form started to be customary in Austria. These "Austrian" suites were not known beyond the small local circle of their performers, while the French suites circulated widely all over the continent. The manuscript transcriptions of French music began very early. I even found (among the Kremsier manuscripts) one with the title "Balletti francesi del Signor Ebner, A. 1667", which contained dances composed by Lully, the same dances that P. Colasse used (1695) in his ballet "Les Saisons". All these dances show traces of variation-suite structure. And surely they prove how early these French forms of dance music and dance practice arrived in distant countries. I assume that these dances were performed in the house of the French ambassador, Grenonville, in Vienna. There exists a letter of the Emperor Leopold I, to the Austrian Ambassador in Madrid, Poetting, dated September 27, 1666. In its strange form of "maccaroniprose", it is most amusing and characteristic of the intolerance and formal attitude of the

Austrian Emperor: "Past Sunday has, tandem aliquando, the wedding of Santillier with the Lady Drautitschin was celebrated. Post prandium, Grenonville had arranged for a ballet danced by divers Frenchmen. I write to you about it because Don Diego et alii have made a great ruido (to-do) about my having been an on-looker at a French ballet. Now I am of the mind that if one may watch a jester or buffon, one may well be permitted to watch a French fool and dancer, oltre che era una cosa si fredda, that it is really not worth while to make such a ruido about it. But the people that have little business in the world, they make ex mosca elephantem, id est, from a mere foolishness the greatest kind of negotium". At the time a Spanish-Austrian alliance pointed against France, was contemplated, and Leopold feared that his presence at the French ballet might be interpreted as a political faux pas!

However, such incidents had no influence on the triumphant course of French ballets and French dance music. How widely their popularity extended, is exemplified by another collection, published by Ecorcheville, preserved in the library at Kassel in Germany. Here we find mostly five-part suites for concert use, but also ballets, as for example the "ballet a 4", "zu Stockholm getanzt". Even in Sweden, French art of the ballet was known already in 1649. There is a textbook, printed by Janssonius in Stockholm, of "Les Passions Victorieuses et Vaincues, Dance en presence de leurs Majestés à Stockholm". The dances consist of numbers of slow and fast short movements joined together, in which the composer strictly follows the orders of the dancing master. To judge by the type of music, it must have been a grotesque ballet. This form of the ballet already resembles closely the "potpourri" form, which was called "quodlibet" (medley) in Germany. Such a combination of various dances, most of which are transcribed in shortened form, was particularly popular among the Viennese composers. Schmelzer has a "philosopher's" ballet, which is danced in Draghi's opera "La laterna di Diogene", followed by a potpourri movement, and introducing swift leaps and slow comical gestures of the dancers.

But to return to the manuscript of Kassel. It contains dances by French and German composers. Among the former are Mazuel, Verdier, and anonymous G. D.—in whom Écorcheville sees a pseudonym of Guillaume Dumanoir, the famous "Roy des violons". In fact he was the German-Englishman Gerhard Diesener at the time of the transcription in the service of the court at Kassel, later however, in England like so many other German composers. We have English records of his works. For example in the "Instrumental Ayres in 3 and 4 parts (overtures, allemands, branles, courants, sarabands, jigs and gavots) by Gerhard Diesener", as well as in Locke's "Melothesia", 1673, where there are four dances by Diesener, and a "Sonata a 4". Both these manuscripts are preserved in the British Museum. The Kassel document contains also a "Wiennisches Ballet" in incomplete form. A complete version of it, which I have shown in the "Koczirz Festschrift", contains also transcribed dances by Wolfgang Ebner. It can furthermore scarcely be claimed that the Kassel manuscript has French dances exclusively, as it was asserted by French musicologists. A predominance of French influence in all these recorded "Allemandes", "Courantes", "Sarabandes", "Bourrées" and "Branles", "Passepieds", "Minuets", and even occasional "Gigues", can however not be disputed.

At this point, the dances of this period, which have not been discussed in detail up to now, should be defined. It is customary to mention the "Passepied" in connection with the "Minuet". According to Arbeau this dance is identical with the "Branle de Triori", which Sachs calls the dance of the upper part of the Bretagne, that district speaking French, not Breton. Praetorius calls his "Passepieds", "de Bretagne" and describes them as dances in which one foot was passed across in front of the other. Arbeau, as well as many composers at the beginning of the 17th century, have the "Passepied" in duple beat rhythm. The dance, reported by Praetorius, is a pleasant French piece in two divisions, (without upbeat), which seems to have been the most popular "Passepied" in the early years of the century. The same melody is found in the collection Philidor (Tome I) and in the work of Mersenne (1636).

In the Kassel manuscript we also find a passepied (Les passepieds d'Artus) which consists of a movement of six bars similar to an entry in four fourths time with an upbeat, to which a slow movement in 3/4 time is added. In the course of the 17th century this Bretonic branle changed its form, and like the jig and the minuet became a dance with triple rhythm. Brossard, in his Dictionaire in comparing the minuet with the passepied, describes the latter as being a faster and livelier dance than the minuet. Mattheson in trying to give an analysis of the "affect" of this dance—the doctrine of affections being the esthetic foundation of that century—says the following:

"Its essence is near to that of lightmindedness - - - but it is the kind of lightmindedness that has nothing sinful or displeasing, like that of many a female, who, though she may be of somewhat shallow character, thereby loses none of her charm".

Like the courante and the minuet, which were used "en suite" at the close of the 17th century, that is, two or three of them in succession, the passepieds follow one another in many a suite. Their only distinction is the faster time, and if the minuet represents the stately and reserved lady of high degree, the passepied is like the more lightfooted and easygoing handmaid.

The bourrée takes its name from "bourrir", that is, to flap wings. It must have been a pantomimic dance, for such it is still danced in its native country, Auvergne, where the men dance it with arms lifted high in the air, while the women pick up their skirts daintily. In the province of Languedoc, the bourrée is set in 4/8 or 4/4 time. For a long time, the bourrée was considered a popular dance and was not taken up by society until the middle of the 17th century. Its fresh and earthy flavor is clearly apparent in the melody used for it. Praetorius transcribes this bourrée

Mattheson says about the bourrées in his "Neu eroeffnetes Orchester" (Chapter IV), that "the bourrées have dactylic measure in such a way that two eighths follow upon a quarter: the beginning is made with the last quarter of the upbeat, which thus becomes the last quarter of the first repetition". Such bourrées are more usual in the 18th than in the 17th century and Bach's Bourrée from the second English Suite

corresponds to the pattern described by Mattheson. The "Musical Dictionary of Chemnitz" published in 1749 enumerates the bourrée among the slow French dances and considers it as one of the three "basic dances", the other two being the minuet and the courante. The Austrian dance composers mention it in the Italianized form as "buora" and use this rhythm for it:

But the following rhythm is also used, with emphasis on the second beat:

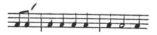

(Bach's Orchestra bourrées).

Such female endings are usually found in the bourrées of the 17th century. Bach's bourrées have the lively and original mood which is praised by the contemporary critics of the bourrée. That these dances had remained so, was largely due to the fact that they had been neglected by higher society and had been left to the common people. In 1676 Madame de Sevigné deplores the fact that nothing is known at Versaille of these rounds, the most charming of dances. "C'est la plus surprenante chose du monde: des paysans, des paysannes, une oreille aussi juste que vous, une legereté, une disposition, - - - deux filles et deux garçons qui sont ici avec le tambour de basque pour fair voir cette bourrée".

(It is the most surprising thing to see the countryfolk, men and women, with musical ear as good as yours, and with such grace and careful planning, I am quite crazy about it! How I would like to send you two of the girls, two of the boys to perform that bourrée for you at the wedding). Lully used the bourrée frequently in his ballets.

The "Rigaudon", (according to Rousseau so-called after the inventor Rigaud, though Mattheson says its name comes from rigo-river, and Sachs derives the title from rigolone, rigoletto,—a circular round dance), was the collective name for all the folk dances of the South-Eastern districts of France. (Georg Muffat in his "Florilegium II", names a "Rigaudon pour des Jeunes Paisannes Poitevines", that is, for the central province, Poitou). It was considered one of the liveliest dances of the time, though the choreographers differ greatly as to its execution. Even now, there still exists a rigaudon danced in certain parts of France, a couple dance, followed by a pantomime of the "coy" maiden. Mattheson says of it: "It is a gay dance in even beat, performed at festivities and in grotesque ballets. Its beat is 4/4, but it usually has three to four repetitions, of which the third is customarily short and humorous". This scheme is used already in a Da capo piece having the form ABCA written by Mersenne (1636).

For that matter, I have found few rigaudons written around 1700 which have the four divisions required by Mattheson. Only those of Muffat's "Florilegium", a "Rigaudon" in Fux's "Concentus", and some by Hoffer, have these four divisions. The main rhythm which forms the basis for most of the other rigaudons is:

$$C \quad \flat \; | \; \downarrow \downarrow \downarrow \; \flat$$

One of the most important dances of the Baroque is the "Sarabande" which came from Spain. Until a short time ago, it was assumed that the origin of the word, was the Persian "sar-band", the wreath used to fasten the female headdress. In fact, the name is indicative of this, for in Ousley's Oriental Collection II. there are no less than 159 Persian songs with the inscription "Ser-a-band" and the etymologist Diez derives the word from the Persian, where "Serbend" is a kind of song. But Sachs doubts that the dance came from Arabia, for about the 17th century when the Saraband became popular, the influence of Arabian culture in Spain was supposed to have died out. One must, however, reply to this that certain customs of old Arabian origin have persisted to this very day in Spain. Frequently they have taken on Christian garb, as the Easter processions in Granada and Sevilla, and the Andalusian Church dances etc. Why then, should not old Moorish dances have survived until the 17th century? The name is certainly indicative. Against this stands the testimony of many writers who consider the "Sarabande" and the "Chaconne" as the same, and give as the country of their origin "New Spain" by which was understood Yucatan in the 17th century. It is also symptomatic that in Guatemala there is a kind of flute called Zarabanda. I believe that the Sarabande was originally an Arabian dance, that it was introduced by the Spaniards of Conquistador time in the West Indies, and from there reimported with the Indian modifications into Spain. This recalls, incidentally, another American-Arabian connection, the laments of the Indian population of the Quechuas. The descendants of the Inca Indians of Peru belong to the most interesting musical products of this unusual musical tribe. Albert Friedenthal reports in his book on "Musik, Tanz und Dichtung bei den Kreolen Amerikas" that the music of the native Indians incited very little interest on the part of the Spaniards with the exception of these very Quechuas. The laments of the Quechuas are called "Yaravi", an Indian word that peculiarly enough has not the slightest similarity with any word in the language of the Quechuas or Aimaras. Friedenthal gives for this the following explanation. It is well known that the Spanish language in Moorish times borrowed many Arabian words. At this time the Spaniards probably heard often enough from the Moors a word that everyone knows who has travelled the northern coast of Africa, a word which daily thousands of throats call, sigh and sing: "Ya Rabi" ("O Lord"), an exclamation which expresses the whole melancholy and longing of the Oriental. To be sure the Spanish language has not retained this word, but is it not possible that the Spaniards of the Conquista period who must have still known it, were reminded of the "Ya Rabi" of the Moors when they heard the laments of the Inca Indians? Undoubtedly it was they who gave these songs the name Ya Rabi, a fact which was forgotten in the course of time when the word was lost in Spain. We find here the remarkable case that the Creoles consider the word Ya Rabi to be Indian,—the Indians, however, consider it to be possibly Spanish.

In spite of the later "Grandezza", the Sarabande, according to the testimony of the Jesuit-Historian Juan de Mariana (1536-1623) was originally supposed to have been a lascivious dance with indecent gestures.

An Italian writer on the dance of the 17th century, states that "sarabanda", "jacara", as well as "rastro" and "tarrago", all mean the same, and Sachs believes that the Portuguese "lundu" and "batuque" belong in the same category. All of these various forms have this in common that they are dances with sexual appeal, and are full of passion and fire. Cervantes says in his "Noble Kitchen-maid", "just go on playing your vulgar sarabandes, chaconnes and folias". We may therefore draw the conclusion that in the 17th century, the sarabande was a brisk and fiery dance: perhaps it was already so in the Parisian court ballet "La duoanière de Billebahaut", in which it was danced in Spanish costumes and to the accompaniment of guitars. The sarabande transcribed by Praetorius seems to have been a fast dance. (1612).

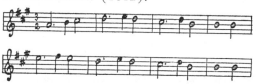

In the course of the century, however, the sarabande came to
personify the dignity and solemnity of the Spanish ceremonial
forms. In the ballet "Concorso dell' Alegrezza", which was
performed in Vienna (1666), to greet the arrival of the imperial bride, Margarita of Spain, a Spanish lady and her cava-
background of the sarabande when he calls it a slow and
stately sarabande. Lully's pupil, Johann S. Kusser, from Bra-
tislava in Slovakia, calls the sarabande "L'Espagnole" in his
collection of suites: "Composition de Musique". Mattheson
in his "Neu eroeffnetes Orchester" definitely establishes the
background of the sarabande when he calls it a slow and
solemn, somewhat short melody, very popular with the Spanish,
which always has a triple beat in very slow time, and two repetitions, and is most fit to be danced "à l'Espagnole", with castanets, and to an "Ariette" to be sung. According to the two
great choreographers of the century, Feuillet and Taubert,
the sarabande was a "heroic" dance, which was to be performed by a single dancer and his female partner, with
great dignity, and to the sound of castanets. In France and
in Germany, the tempo of the sarabande grew ever slower and
slower in the course of time while in Italy the original fast
measure was preserved. Lully's sarabandes are midway between,
as for example the sarabande from the "Ballet des Plaisirs",
(1655) which is inscribed "tendrement sans lanteur":

Like many other dances by Lully its periods consist of three
and four bars. One of the reasons why the time of the French
sarabandes grew ever slower was that the French lutenists
and clavecenists used it more and more as a contrasting
piece between the fast movements of the suite, the courante
and gigue (jig). Italy did not participate in this practice.
Lully's successors and imitators Rameau, Destouches and
Colasse wrote them even slower and more "languishing",
whereas the German "Lullyists", whom we shall discuss later,
made them solemn and majestic. As such Mattheson describes

them. He divides them into sarabandes "to be sung, played, or danced". But all of them are built on the emotions of stateliness and of pride, though "the dance sarabande is even of prouder mien than her cousins; so much so that no running notes are permitted for stateliness' sake, but that seriousness might be maintained and adhered to". The prevailing rhythm of the sarabande in the 17th century, namely that used by Feuillet and Taubert, gives way to the standard rhythm of the 18th century.

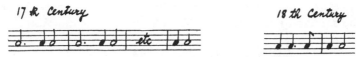

Of all the dances of the Baroque, the sarabande has the most consistently regular structure. For the most part it consists of two divisions, each of them having four or eight bars. This is what Mattheson designates as the "short melody". This regular construction is its Spanish heritage, for both, in popular and in art music; these themes, used later as "bassi ostinati" were made the basis of variations, called "differencias". We have here, perhaps, remnants of the old forms of Moorish melodies, with the short variable motives of the Orient, or old Mexican ones.

Although the standard rhythm of the sarabande often undergoes changes, the "classic" form is that which Handel used in the aria "Lascia ch'io pianga" in "Rinaldo".

The renowned "Folies d'Espagne", best known to us through Corelli's "Variations", have a typical sarabande rhythm, and their popularity may have had something to do with the musical development of the sarabande. "Folia" means madness, and this dance was a Portuguese dance for the carnival, a form of fertility magic. Covarrubias describes this dance in his "Tesoro de la lingua castellana", as "a noisy performance with many paced figures, to the music of castanets and other instruments; some of the dancers carry masked figures on their backs, while others in girls' garments with pointed sleeves, turn on their heels, play their castanets, while the noise is so great as if they were all out of their minds". In Spain the "Folia" was danced as a wooing dance, performed by a male and a female dancer, who went through the pantomime with impassioned and fiery gestures. The manner of performance was left to the invention of the dancers.*

With the exception of certain folias which have nothing to do with the famous "Folie d'Espagne" as for example the folia from Schmelzer's Equestrian ballet "La contesa dell'aria e dell'acqua", or Zelenka's "Ouverture à 7" or the one in Fux's "Concentus", the many folias of which we know are all based on the motive of the Spanish "folia" which is as follows:

The use of the tetrachord motive points to its Oriental origin. It is found already in the 16th century in the Spanish lute tablatures as I have pointed out in my article on "Zwei spanische Ostinato Themen" in the "Zeitschrift fuer Musikwissenschaft" (I). Besides Corelli many others have used it, Milanutio, Michele Farinelli, Vivaldi, D'Anglebert, R. Keiser in his opera "Der laecherliche Jodelet", and Bach in his "Bauernkantate". (Peasant Cantata). In this last piece the "Treffliche Kammerherr" is given the motive to characterize his person. Cherubini has used it in the overture to the "Hotellerie portuguaise" and Liszt incorporates it in his "Rhapsodie espagnole".

Indeed this "folie" had a mad career lasting over more than two hundred years and occasionally one still runs across it in Spain, South America, in Sweden and in Russia. In the province of Brandenburg in Prussia, it was considered for a long time to be a kind of dirge, a death dance.

The third of the Spanish dances is the "Chaconne". Lope de Vega says: "De las Indias a Sevilla ha venida por la posta".

---

* Gombosi's excellent paper was handed to me while this book was in print.

It probably came from Mexico to Sevilla. Sachs says that it is still being danced in Portugal and gives other proofs of its American origin. As an originally erotic dance it was at first performed swiftly and passionately. Cervantes says of it in the "Noble Kitchen-maid":

> Surely the bright crown of love
> In the chaconne's notes you'll find.
> As, with movement glad and light,
> All your earthiness takes flight.

Like the sarabande and the "Folia" the chaconne, i. e. "every-body's dance", a popular street-ditty, always has only a short melodic motive. It seems to have the descending tetrachord of the old Spanish folk songs "O guardame las vacas" which later became the basic chaconne tune. In the course of the 17th century this tetrachord melody which is still very popular in Spain became a bass theme, and in the form here indicated

became the basso ostinato of numerous chaconne tunes. In a volume of the Public Library in New York I found a copy of a description of a journey to America published by the German engraver Merian in Frankfort in 1634 and called "Historia Americae . . . pars tertia". There are references to the native dances of the Caribbean section. The etching shows us an Indian dance. Of greatest interest to us is the music which peculiarly enough displays that melodic characteristic of the early Spanish chaconnes—namely the descending fourth. Is it then going too far to imagine that there is some connection between the music of the chaconne and this old Indian dance?

A second chaconne basso ostinato is the other very popu-lar theme

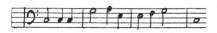

which underwent all kinds of modifications, principally that of the two descending fourths, transformed in the bell motive in "Parsifal". How typical it was of the chaconne is proved by a title from Negri's "Cantate" (1635), where he calls it specifically "Aria della ciaconna". Riemann considers it improbable that the chaconne was ever really used as the music for a dance, but Spanish writers as well as the chaconnes incorporated in Lully's and Schmelzer's ballets contradict this point of view. In most of the ballets the chaconne was used as the lengthy final portion with the dancers lined up in two long columns extending towards the back of the stage, the ladies facing the gentlemen, each individually dancing their figures. At the courts of Louis XIV and Louis XV, solo dancers performed a solo figure between the two files: Beauchamps, Pecour and Dupré are mentioned as the soloists.

In his dictionary Walther defines the chaconne as a dance and instrumental composition "of which the basso ostinato usually consists of four bars in 3/4 time: a theme which remains the basso ostinato as long as the variations and phrases last". It is not surprising, that chaconne and passacaglia are being confused, though, as Walther believes, the latter was more languid and not as fast as the former, neither was it as lively as the other, which mostly is written in the minor key. Mattheson on the other hand says that the chaconne is slower and more contained, but mostly in the major key leaving the minor to the passacaglia. These distinctions are however unimportant, the main thing is that the forms of the two dances are practically identical because of the similarity of their original significance. Both passacaglia and chaconne were originally "passacalle" (street ditties), far removed from the chaconnes and passacaglie of Buxtehude and of Bach, who borrowed from Spain only the stateliness and the dignified movement.

A weighty German volume by Werner Danckert gives us in detail the formal, melodic and rhythmic analysis of the "Gigue", called "jig" in English. Based on an erroneous etymological explanation propounded by Mattheson, who derived the name from gigue, giga, Geige—(the German violin), the English origin of this dance was not recognised for a long time and even the author of the article on "gigue" in Grove's Musical Dictionary (1906) looks for its beginning in Italy, asserting that the oldest records of the gigue came from that country. Some authors even went to Spain, identifying the gigue with the old Spanish dance "chica". L. C. Elson writing about "Shakespeare in Music" (Boston 1912) goes so far as to claim that the gigue was carried over to Ireland from Spain. His mistake is, that he considers the "Loure" the same as the "Gigue", imitating an error made by Mattheson which I discussed in my study on the "Viennese Dance compositions in the second half of the 17th century".

There is no doubt that name and antecedents of this dance are English for "to jig" means "to dance". Originally this jig was a popular dance which graduated from its lowly place as a couple dance of the people and came to court during the reign of Queen Elizabeth. But at the same time the word jig was used to designate an English dance tune to which a number of different dances were performed. Like the Ukrainian "Hopak", the Hungarian "Czardas", and the French "Rigaudon", the jig was danced with the trunk held erect stiffly, the heels beating the floor and the toes pointed now right,—now left, as it was done in Scottish dances.

From a musical viewpoint the form of the jig varies infinitely, as does even the measure. The most popular form of it seems to have been the "Nobodyes Gigge", recorded in "Fitzwilliams Virginal-book" in a version current around 1600, composed by Farnaby. It seems that this jig was used frequently in Germany in the 18th century as was the theme accompanying the appearance of the English comic character, the clown, called "Pickled herring".

The melody is also found in the "Dancing Master", of 1686. Its last version occurs in the opera the "Roland von Berlin" composed by Leoncavallo for William the Second.

Another gigue, also of English origin and equally popular on the continent, was the one known as "Song of Mars". Appearing in Scheidt's "Tablatura Nova" as "Est-ce Mars", it was then considered a French song, but a manuscript of the University Library at Breslau in which the same melody is called "English March", confirms its English antecedents.

The song won tremendous popularity and as late as the 18th century, the German students sang it to the words: "Lustig seid Ihr lieben Brueder". ("Musikalische Ruestkammer").

Other forms of the gigue show three-beat time with the characteristic syncopation and the phrase in thirds, as f. i. in the second part of "Nobodyes Gigge" in the version of the "Dancing Master of 1716":

with the frequent use of an upbeat and the standardized rhythm

others exhibit a peculiar form of periodicity consisting of three bars, like the following example from Robinson's "School of Musicke" published in 1603.

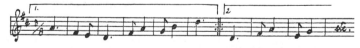

All these peculiarities are qualities of English folk music.

In the 18th century the jig takes on a restless whirling and twirling rhythm. The rhythmic movement is primitively simple; "The Beggar's Dance" from an 18th century manuscript is a good example of this.

All the English, as well as later the American folk dances, with the Virginia Reel as the most telling example, are illustrations of this "Jig" melodic line and movement.

These are usually dances originating in a special Italian province. The development of the suite shows that the great European nations contributed the four pillars to that musical form: the Germans contributed the Allemande, the French the Courante, the Spaniards the Sarabande and the English the Jig. These are the fundamental dances as developed by J. S. Bach in the "classical" form of the Suite. The Italians contributed only less important, non fundamental dance forms, as f. i. the Saltarello, the Tarantella, the Romanesca, the Furlana, and the Bergamask.

When Shakespeare has Bottom in the "Midsummer Night's Dream" dance a bergamask, he was choosing this dance because the men of Bergamo were known for their clumsy and rude manners and he thought it a fitting dance for his character. Still, Bergamo also was the home of Arlecchino, the lively comic character of the Italian comedy. To a melody in duple meter the gentleman and his partner parade in a circle, make a turn while dancing, and parade again. In my essay in the "Zeitschrift fuer Musikwissenschaft" (V.) I tried to trace the musical development of this dance form. The "bergamask" melody is based an a short motive, from which the "bergamask" theme is gradually developed:

The dance seems to have been very popular in Italy as well as in England. Scheidt has a "Bergamasca Anglica" recorded in 1621. Apparently English comedians had imported the originally Italian melody to the continent. In a Viennese manuscript the dance appears under the title "Bergamasque".

In the form here given, the dance is transcribed in many lute - clavichord tablatures, and is used in Germany as the melody of a popular folksong.

In 1733 we find the tune in the "Augsburger Tafelkonfekt", and when Bach wrote the famous "Goldberg Variations" for the harpsichord, he sensed the slight resemblance between the motive of the sarabande and the tune of the folksong, and used the latter in the quodlibet of the final variation. Here too this melody is to stand for the grotesque element, for the comical indifference of the clown. After the serious and learned counterpoint, Bach offers the bergamask as sort of humorous, topsy-turvy relief.

But this old fool's dance has come down to us in various forms. In Serbia it is danced as Kolo (Bojino Kole).

In the Valle di Reno in the province of Bologna a bergamask is danced to the following melody which is but a transparent disguise for the old form:

Besides the Northern Italian bergamask we have the "Trezza" presumably of Venetian origin. The etymology of its name is hidden. Perhaps it has some connection with the "Tresca", which was an old round dance executed by a long chain of dancers, mentioned by Adam de la Hale, and still alive under the name of "Trescone" or "Ntrezzata" as an Italian folk dance.* It seems likely that "Trezza" is the dialectal form of the word treccia, which means a braid consisting of three parts. According to this last interpretation, the trezza would be a dance of three rows of dancers, with figures, weaving in and out. The dance appears exclusively in South German and Viennese manuscripts, and is expressively given the adjective "Viennese" in a Swedish manuscript. It was probably a Viennese dance, was written in duple and triple time, and seems to have been the favorite dance of the musical Emperor, Leopold I. All his "trezze" have the following rhythm:

Schmelzer records a very strange form of "trezza". It is an exotic popular melody, without repetitions, apparently of Slavonic or Venetian origin.

The interesting fact about it is that it resembles closely the "Furlana" of the 18th century. This was a folk dance of the region controlled by Venice, a wild, wooing dance in 6/8 time.

---

* This dance was also known to G. B. Basile (brother of "La bella Adriana", the famous Monteverdi singer in Mantua) whose "Pentameron", written in Neapolitan dialect contains interesting references to music and dance.

Two or three couples approach, and then separate from each other, touch hands and feet, beat about with their arms, and turn in lively rhythms. Casanova reports that he danced it in Constantinople in 1744, after the performance of a pantomime with Sicilian dances, given by Neapolitan slaves. Originally coming from Friulia, a Slavic region controlled by the Venetian republic,—this dance, as Tuerk says in his "Klavierschule" "was very often performed by the 'man in the street' of Venice". This was its purpose in Campra's "Fêtes Venetiennes" (1710), where he used it to close a Venetian ball scene; it also occurs in Monsigny's "Aline". In 1742 William Corbett published a number of suites for strings and closed one of them, entitled "Alla Veneziana", with a forlana. A forlana composed by Hoffer for the Viennese Court also shows that this dance was used in the Viennese ballets. This forlana has the stereotyped repetition of one motive at the end of every reprise, a form similar to that of the trezza given above. A similar form of forlana is to be found in an English book of contredances. Melodies used for the forlana were also played for contre- dances and we even have an example where the melody is used for a Scottish military march:

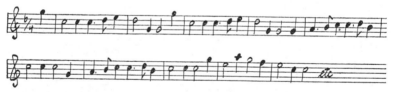

Bach in his C major Suite, Mouret in his ballet, "Les Amours des Dieux", and others, have contributed forlana melodies. Casanova seems to have been haunted by a special forlana melody and surely there must have been a particular and typical forlana air as there was a special tune for the folia, the bergamask and the chaconne. Gretry in his "Me- moirs", in discussing the "Vaudevilles", mentions a "Forlana" with specific Forlana phrases.

    Campra's forlana from the "Fêtes Venetiennes" differs from all the rest since it is in the minor key. Its second part with the diatonic scale dissolved into the harmonic elements, especially regarding the sequence of triads, has a definitely orgiastic character, corresponding to Casanova's opinion of this dance. Here too, we have the hypnotizing repetition of a short motive, reminding us of Oriental practice.

Bach's forlana is in C major. But even at the very beginning it moves to D minor for the duration of a bar, to mark its relation to the exotic character of the dance which is given here in stylized form. The former short treatment of motive characteristic for the forlana has disappeared, but its rhythm is retained. This motive repetition of the forlana harks back either to old cries in the barcarolle, or to exclamations and cries during the dance, — cries like those of the Spanish folk dances which underline the ecstatic erotic elements of the dance, the movements of which culminate in a trance. Gretry very keenly pointed out this fact by saying: "This last refrain has been used in a symphony by the very skillful artist Saint George: [who by the way was a mulatto] he has repeated it twenty times, but at the close of the piece one is regretting not to hear it any longer".

All the forlanas have rondo form and may be repeated ad infinitum. It is not surprising that Casanova continued to dance a whole long series of them to one and the same melody. At the Carnival in 1754, participating in a ball at the Nunnery of Murano near Venice, disguised as a Pierrot, he chose a charming Arlecchina and after a minuet danced with her in quick succession — twelve forlanas.

The dancing master Blasis tells us in his "Manuel complet de la danse" what he thought of the forlana: "It is a dance which tries to picture love and pleasure. Every movement, every gesture, is made with languishing grace. Inspired by the accompaniment of the mandolins, the tambourines and the castanets, the dancing lady tries to arouse the passion of her partner by her liveliness and graceful swiftness. The two partners join, then separate, and every one of their movements tries to imitate the gestures of love, of archness and of coquetry". Surely this was a fit dance for one of Casanova's kind!

And the music to which Casanova danced? Perhaps it was that "Polesana", a genuine forlana danced near Pola in the Slavic portion of the province Istria, which later became the favorite Venetian dance. The melody is printed under a charming sketch of the "Bridge of Sighs" and is taken from Lambranzi's "Neue und curieuse Theatralische Tantz Schul" (1716).

Polesana

While the forlana was the old Venetian national dance, the "Tarantella" became the Neapolitan dance of the 18th century. Ever since the 17th century this dance had been mentioned in connection with the disease called "tarantism", a kind of dance frenzy, like the Dance of St. Vitus, which had first appeared in the Middle Ages. It was believed that the cause of this disease was the sting of the Lycosa tarantula, the Apulian spider. Both dance and insect derive their name from the town of Taranto in Sicily and it seems likely that the feature which linked them together was the name and nothing else. It was believed that the great depression and lassitude brought about by the sting of the spider could be cured only by the dance and its melody. With the St. Vitus dance, the wild leaping Tarantella shared the quality of psychic infectiousness. The audience, as well as the patient, fell prey to the same manic dance frenzy when its melody resounded.

The Jesuit Father, Athanasius Kircher, a scholar and musicologist writing about 1673 in his "Phonurgia Nova", a collection of all kinds of musical and acoustic oddities, discusses the psychomagnetism of music and gives us a detailed description of the tarantella. An illustration shows us a "high stepping" couple, dancing to the music of a violinist and a second player, whose instrument is, however, not visible on the picture.

As "Antidotum Tarantulae" Kircher gives us this melody, also noting a tenor and bass part for it:

The melody as he has recorded it, is by no means exciting. It seems to have been played in binary and in ternary time. Nevertheless it already gives some hint of the wild and rolling rhythms of the tarantella as it was played in the 18th and 19th centuries. In the course of time, the "magic" powers of the dance, its magnetic influence were lost and it became a mere dance for entertainment, such as the authors of the day described it. Goethe in his "Italian Journey", 1788-1789, says: "In Naples the tarantella is popular among the girls of the poorer and middle classes. There must be at least three performers, one of them shakes the tambourine and lets it ring without beating it, the other two with castanets in their hands perform the steps of the dance. These are not actually distinguished and graceful dance steps, but, as in all these less refined dance forms, the dancers just beat out the rhythm of the dance, standing opposite each other and then changing places. Sometimes one of the castanet girls changes place with the tambourine beater, letting her dance and plays herself and thus they go on for hours, without caring about their audience. This kind of dance entertainment is only for girls, no boy would touch a tambourine".

Quite different is the description given by the writer of travel books, Rossmann, author of a volume entitled "Vom Gestade der Zyklopen und Sirenen" (From the shores of the cyclops and the sirens), published in 1880. He says: "Though the dance may go on for over two hours to the same rhythm, within that framework, the tarantella has such a variety of figures and gives the individuality of the dancer so much leeway for self expression, that it is truly pleasurable to watch it and even more so to take part in it. Like the greater part of the national dances this dance portrays the hunt and the escape, the playful teasing of a love-game and is with this rich and fruitful dramatic theme full of vividness and suspense. As every couple acts out its own little romance according to its temperament and mood, it is ever new and interesting. The fiery lover may rush forward to conquer and win over the object of his desires. But the object of his wooing, as cool as an iceberg, dances past him like an automaton, without giving him a glance. But finally, she may yield to his imploring, take his hands and twirl about wildly with him. The tambourine beats grow more and more insistent, the song of the tarantella begins and wildly joyous, the couple rushes onward . . ."

The instruments used for the tarantella were tambourines, castanets, flute, a rattle made of two wooden hammers, beating one on the other, a small drum-like instrument with a rotating stick in the center, a kind of clanging instrument.

In this description we see the ancient primitive themes of a wooing dance and as such even moderns have felt it. The poet Rainer Maria Rilke writes in a letter of February 11, 1907, addressed to his wife from the island of Capri: "What a dance is this tarantella! As if invented by nymphs and satyrs, old but newly discovered, covered with memories of times immemorial! Full of ruse, wildness and the intoxication of wine, men who move as if they had goats' feet, and girls coming from the court of Artemis!"

While, according to Goethe, the tarantella was said to be danced exclusively by women, others, even as early as Kircher, described it as a dance of a couple. All, however, agree that it is "endless", continuous, like the forlana, or the dances of the Orient. Coinciding with this "endlessness" is its musical line, a short characteristic whirling 6/8 theme, having hypnotic power, like the motives of the medieval saltarelli and of the forlana. This hypnotic motion of the rhythm reappears in the tarantella composed for dancing, as for example in that of Auber in the "Mute of Portici".

This descending and ascending rolling group of eights is the basic motive of the tarantella, which was also used by Stephen Heller, Liszt, Chopin and others. The ecstatic character of the phrase is brought out by the introduction and chromatic elements. Chopin in fact used this motive to create a dramatic, pictorial dance in which the primitive erotic element is raised to the height of ecstatic jubilation. It is strange, however, that this dance was not included in the suites of the composers of the 17th and 18th centuries. Though it has many characteristics in common with the jig, (gigue) the latter overshadowed it entirely. We find many suites of the 17th and 18th centuries containing a "Traquenard" or "Traccanar". Among these are Johann Kaspar Ferdinand Fischer's "Journal du Printemps", Muffat's "Florilegium", and some of Schmelzer's suites. Emperor Leopold I. was a great friend of the "Traquenar". The name is an equestrian term, for traquenard is a certain kind of pace, a horse-pace. Trac, according to Meyer-Luebke, is the trace left by the game in the forest. This was presumably a dance with steps imitating the pace of the horse. The music for it has a very definite, peculiar rhythm. The first part consists of two — , the second of four bars. There are female endings. The rhythm is illustrated here in an example taken from the "Ariae favoritae" by Schmelzer, (the favorite tunes of the Emperor). It is typical of the traquenards.

One of the most characteristic instrumental forms of the 17th century however, was the ballet-suite, introduced by the great Lully developed by his followers, especially by his

German disciples, the so-called "Lullyists". There were the Slovakian J. S. Kusser, the Austrian Georg Muffat (1645-1704), and Johann Fischer from Augsburg (1646-1721), who came to Paris as a young man and copied music for Lully. Others, like the Bavarian B. A. Aufschnaiter (d. 1742), Ph. H. Erlebach (1657-1714), Johann Kaspar Ferdinand Fischer (1650-1746), J. A. Schmiecorer (about 1700), J. Ph. Krieger (1649-1725), and so on. The usual practice was to put a French overture at the beginning of the suite of dances and to give them names which would lead the public to believe that they were taken from ballets. Frequently such ballet suites were called overtures in their entirety, as in Kusser's opus "La cicala della cetra d'Eunomio" of 1700, in which the suites are called "Overtures de Theatre", in order to give expression to the current popularity of dramatic musical presentations. In Kusser's suites called "Compositions de musique", 1682, we find a number of charming dances but, besides these, also a number of airs which are not at all suitable for dancing, or have rhythms not taken from dance music. On the other hand, later works contain pieces with poetic titles, or those pointing to a ballet idea, as for example "Air de vole des demons", "Les Paysans", "les Chasseurs", etc. In another suite we find that old Provençal theme in march time, which Bizet used for his "Arlesienne Suite".

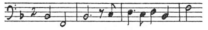

Even more interesting are the two collections of Georg Muffat, the "Florilegium primum" and the "Florilegium secundum". In the second of these, Muffat has written a preface giving a detailed account of the execution of this dance music. The fingering, the bowing, the time and the rhythm, such as they were practiced under Lully are discussed at length: "Let there be no noisy tuning at the beginning of the overture! When ballet and opera are being played the strings should be a whole tone lower, at least one and a half tone lower than was the custom in Germany. Let there be good violinists for all the parts, not merely excellent first violins and the other strings poor". And so forth. All these practical admonitions were given to bring out the French flavor. At the beginning the splendid overture, a mixture of pathos and grace, is a true picture of the French court and of its society. Weighty melodies with wide intervals give us a plastic picture of the Versailles company with the King as a divinity, charming the court in the turns of the ballet.

Every suite had its special name: "Eusebia", "Sperantis Gaudia", "Nobilis juventus", and is intended to conjure up the scenes of a ballet. All this, however, is no programmatic music. At any rate, it is not music in which the composer tries to illustrate actual happenings by musical means. But these "Entrees des Espagnoles", "Airs pour Hollandois", those "Gigues pour des Anglois", "Menuets pour des François", — had no need to have recourse to special means in order to portray the character of the dances, because the rhythms were sufficient for this. In one of these ballet-suites called "Laeta Poesis" ("Gladsome Poetry"), the composer had the court poets perform in their doctor's gown to a distichon rhythm and on this stately dance followed a gay skipping step danced to a triple rhythm.

Midway between the French and the popular Viennese suites, we have the work of the outstanding composer of the Austrian Baroque, the author of the "Gradus ad Parnassum", Johann Joseph Fux, court composer of Charles VI. His coronation opera "Costanza e Fortezza", written in 1724, may be known to some readers through its performance at Smith College. He wrote many suites of which the "Concentus Musico Instrumentalis" is most famous. He is not one of those who took much stock in the behest of the Lullyists.

His work is more colorful, more imaginative and grander in its whole line, than that of the disciples of the French master. He has, for instance, a serenade for outdoor performance, beginning with a march, which is played by three groups of instruments: 2 trumpets, 2 oboes, a bassoon, and a group of strings. Following, there are dances with a simpler form of instrumentation, a "jig", a "minuet", an "ayre", in the midst of all this, a French "overture", followed by a "minuet", containing a "trio", played by the oboes and the bassoon, as a matter of course. The piece continues with two "arias", two "bourrées" and a fully developed "entry", which is played by the high trumpet as a solo. There follows a "rigaudon", a "chaconne", another "jig", another "minuet" and finally, the lengthy composition closes with a "flourish", the former "retirada". The duration of such an elaborate out-of-doors piece made it unfit for other than the balmiest of summer evenings — at festivals in the Royal Park, where the nobility of the court promenaded to such music by moon light or by the gleam of torches.

Another occasion for such intricate and complicated dance music, were the regattas and water festivals. All these "Water Serenades" are suites with delicately stylized dance music. In order to really understand their background, one needs the help of imagination. They were an essential part of those wonderful Summer-night festivals under glittering stars, when the Austrian Emperor and his guests would honor Salzburg, or Linz, or one of the dreaming villages near Salzburg, when f. i. a race took place, or a regatta. The "Kaiserliche Hofkapelle" - - - "the orchestra of the Imperial court" - - - was then ordered to play the music, composed for this very occasion, and the inspired music would blend with the surroundings in perfect harmony.

The great time of the water serenades was in the 17th and 18th centuries.

One of the most appreciated water serenades is Handel's "Water Music". However, the account of the first time when this music was played, the famous trip up the Thames, which

resulted in the reconciliation of Handel with King George I.
is but a legend. George I. ascended the English throne in
1715,—Handel's "Water Music" was composed and performed
in 1717, and forms the subject of a recently discovered report
of the ambassador of Brandenburg to London which, however,
does not mention any such reconciliation between Handel and
the King. The report reads "Directly after the Royal barge,
came that of fifty musicians who played all kinds of instruments, trumpets, hunting horns, oboes, bassoons, German and
French flutes, violins, basses, but no singers. The music had
been specially composed for this occasion by the famous Handel
from Halle, the chief court composer of His Majesty. The
King was so delighted with it that he asked to have the music
repeated". It is easy to understand the King's satisfaction.
This music with its brilliant instrumentation, making sport of
all acoustic difficulties is genuine out-door music, not fearful
of being heard at a great distance, with its array of brass and
woodwinds added to an orchestra of strings. It was the most
delightful music for diversion. Following a miniature overture, there was a whole series of minuets, gigues, hornpipes,
pieces with divided orchestras and with the separate choirs of
instruments placed on different boats.

A second fine piece of out-door music is Handel's "Fire-
Music", for which the occasion was the celebration of the
Peace of Aix la Chapelle. A monster display of fireworks
prepared in advance during many months was set off, and
already the dress rehearsal brought an audience of 12,000
persons. Handel had marshalled a tremendous orchestra to
play his work, and there were not less than 56 brass and woodwinds.

Not even the noise of the rockets was able to impair the
acoustic effectiveness of the music. After the overture there
was a "Largo alla Siciliana", called "La Paix", several minuets,
and—of course—the "Rejouissance". All these glittering dance
movements, portraying so truly the waving of the flags, the
golden ceremonial coaches of the attendance, the lavish
decorations and dresses in the audience, — were the ex-

pression of the might and power of the England of that time, and yet, he who wrote that music was not an Englishman! He was as little English as Lully was French, although he also had the same talent for giving voice to French national characteristics most fittingly. He surely is an instance of the insignificance of racial antecedents, as far as musical expression is concerned.

At this point, I think, we must interrupt the historical order of our discussion anticipating a few points in connection with Handel and his contribution to ballet music. He has, of course, introduced such in all his Italian operas and it would go too far to deal with all of them. But we must not fail to mention one of his most beautiful operas, "Alcina", which just because of its dances — they were repeatedly arranged and performed in suite-form — has remained famous up to this day. In the above mentioned opera, which was written in 1735, and altogether one of the most imaginative and charming operas of all times, Handel comes very close to the French ballet-operas by Rameau because of the numerous pieces for dancing as well as because of its melodies — graceful as befit dance tunes, and yet so vigorous. This opera very obviously is one of the most impressive of Handel's works. Already, the overture, a composition in four sections: Pomposo, Allegro, Musette and Minuet, is a ballet. Were dances performed during the overture? The subject of this work, "Alcina" (from Ariost's "Orlando Furioso" — "Infuriated Orlando") is just the type of subject for a ballet as it was popular from Francesca Caccini's time on: Alcina, the sorceress, some sort of a Circe, derives a demoniac pleasure from transforming her different lovers into animals. Ruggiero, some sort of an Italian "Tannhaeuser", is most passionately infatuated with her and for her sake has left his fiancée Bradamante. Bradamante's freeing of her Ruggiero by faithful love from the bondage of enchanting Alcina constitutes the contents of the opera. There we have, of course, the most extraordinary incidents, adventures, fights and tricks of magic. The first scene almost reminds us of the scene in the "Venusberg" from

"Tannhaeuser". Thunder and lightning shell the "Alcina Mountain" and from the smoke emerge the contours, and then, more and more clearly, the structure of the Magic Palace itself, in which Alcina—making herself as beautiful as she can—sits next to Ruggiero who holds a magic mirror up in front of her. Pages and serving-maids bring gowns, young knights and ladies — adorned with flowers — form a choir whose music is itself a round dance in minuet rhythm and which is succeeded by a choral gavotte. But joined to this there follow the famous and wonderful "Alcina · Dances": gavotte, sarabande, minuet and again gavotte, so tender, so enamored, and so noble and dignified. How longing is the sound of the flutes in the sarabande, answering the violins like an echo! And when, in the second act, Alcina sees no other way to captivate Ruggiero than by her magic, and wants to rouse the ghosts from the Acheron river against the beloved man, her witchcraft fails because it lacks the power of wrath. Away she throws her magic wand. Thereupon appear all the "Ombres pallides" (pale shadows), the "Songes agréables, songes funestes" (agreeable and deadly dreams) in dream-visions, and dance their rounds to those wonderful dance airs which — partly by abundant melodies and partly by colorful illustrative passages — evoke these visions till they arrive at complete ecstasy. And then the end of the opera, filled with the expression of Alcina's sad resignation, features enchanting dancing pieces, which transport the melancholy of this unhappy love into celestial spheres.

The orchestra suites of both Handel and J. S. Bach have their roots in the ballet suite, created by Lully. They are expressing that most delicate and refined taste for recreation music which was cherished by the upper classes of German society, after the pattern given by the French. When Mendelssohn in 1830 played the overture to the first of his D major Suites for the ageing Goethe, the great poet seemed to see a long line of elaborately dressed people slowly and pompously descending a magnificent staircase. And it is a fact that all these pieces by Lully, Muffat, Fux, Telemann, Handel and

Bach are deeply bound up with the social habits and customs of the period. The stately, though at times somewhat chattering overtures, the dances of various kinds and emotional colors, reflecting special national types and characteristics, this sometimes unregulated and inorganic sequence of movements (quite unlike that of the suite for stringed keyboard instruments) — all this is a true mirror of its age and state of mind. It is indeed extrovert music, for entertainment of others, to picture and to serve them. This was the inner meaning of the kaleidoscopic succession of dances of various rhythms and types, the sequence of which had made a long course of development, from its roots in the variation suite of the Germans and the French. The ancient form of the variation suite with its parts based on the same thematic material was the image of the time of the "Early Baroque", when men felt themselves subject to some higher power. Not until the 17th century does the minuet become "freer", and the single movements of the suite more independent.

If we look for the basic quality of the rhythmic treatment in the works of the composers of the Early Baroque, of Franck and Schein, Hausmann and Peurl, Demantius and Hammerschmidt, — we shall find festive atmosphere, rich and full tone, and a sane but rather uninteresting melodic line. The single rhythmic changes are hidden by the regular course of the dynamic values of the piece. To illustrate this, you need only follow the movements of a conductor, directing the performance of such an old dance. All his gestures will come from the shoulder. The joints of the arm or of the hands will have no occasion to move flexibly and are held almost rigid. Though there is rhythmic movement, it is of a more general kind, — a lively motion, not a detailed to and fro, or up and down. Only one hundred years later the picture is quite different. The traditional stiffness has disappeared, and there is a greater variety and differentiation. Handel's rhythms are full of strength and power and of the consciousness of a forceful personality, backed by a self-reliant society. They arouse in the listeners a feeling of divine and superhuman quality of music itself.

While it still has maintained its intellectual trends dating from the days of the German Early Baroque, the music is now pervaded by the melodic and rhythmic details, their beauty and stylistic perfection (qualities which it possessed first in Italy). No longer will the conductor move merely from the shoulders, his beats will be rounder and freer, more graceful and supple. He too, must be a bearer and interpreter of this progress and expansion in musical expression.

Bach's and Handel's Suites for Orchestra are entirely different from the suites which they wrote for stringed keyboard instruments. The order of dances used in these two forms is not the same. The orchestral suites have an indefinite unregulated sequence, while the others adhere to a strict scheme. The former suites are brilliant colorful music for entertainment, while the latter are music for contemplation and meditation; introvert music. To establish the place of the latter suites, (the Germans call them "Klaviersuiten"), we must go back to the beginnings of dance compositions for keyboard instruments in the organ books of the 16th century. In the virginal books of Elizabethan times we find the first signs of highly developed music for a stringed keyboard instrument. Germany, however, was the land of the organ, the piped keyboard instrument, and the stringed instruments, harpsichord and claviers were more or less domestic substitutes for the organ used in halls and churches. In England virginal music was an every day matter, and exerted no small influence on Bach's and Handel's for stringed keyboard instruments, above all on their "Klaviersuiten". It is close to hand that the country where every man's "home is his castle" should have indulged in the individualistic forms of music while Germany favored the organ for the large gatherings, as for the church where the whole community assembled. Amongst recorded virginal music, we find no suites but pavanes, gaillards, courantes, jigs and voltas played as separate pieces. Now and then, however, we may come across certain pavanes and gaillards interrelated by variation.

Johann Jacob Froberger was the man who laid the foundation for Bach's "Klavier Suite". Though he took the order of the dances and the spirit and atmosphere from the French lutenists, he inclined toward a rich and compact way of composing, characteristic of the English. He was born in 1616 in Stuttgart, and died 1667 in France at the castle of the Duchess of Wurttemberg; he lived in Germany, Italy, France and Austria, but had likewise visited England and may well be called the most important master of the stringed keyboard instruments of pre-Bach times.

While the German variation suite in 1620 still clung to the forms of a practical dance music, the second third of the 17th century in France witnessed the development of a suite form which was a complete departure from dance music, and became pure music for edification. The "ballet suite" of Lully's became the pattern of the "lute suite" which first arose in the parlors of the French music lovers. Even their titles indicated a pantomime background. Like the dances, these movements for the lute had extravagant titles; a favorite one among these was the "Tombeau" (the tomb), during which the mournful music of the solemn allemande was effectively reinforced by the facial expression of the player, so that the listeners might be moved to tears. The death of a high born lady's pet, be it a parrot or a favorite small dog, was the occasion for the composition of a "Tombeau" and the famous Gaultier was not too renowned to undertake that kind of work. Occasionally this programmatic music depicted whole scenes, such as the "Tombeau of Monsieur Lenclos" which is followed by "la consolation des amis du S. L." and "Leur resolution sur la mort". We find a parallel to the "Pictorial Suites" in Bach's Capriccio "ueber die Abreise des geliebten Bruders" in which he laments with imaginative virtuosity over the possible dangers of traveling. The two Gaultiers, Denis and Jacques, (both died around 1670), developed a suite form, based on the allemande, the courante and the sarabande, adding the Spanish dance to the succession allemande—courante which had been customary before them. It was Froberger who added to these three dances the gigue he had come to know in England, a gigue in duple beat like the old English jigs. This, Froberger's form, laid the cornerstone for the later French suite, the type favored by Chambonnières and Couperin, an innovation and novelty in contrast to the old French branle suite. The introduction of the slow, stately sarabande between the fairly brisk courante and the fast gigue brought to the suite a principle of contrast in sequence, which was to have far-reaching effects on further developments of musical cycles. For the factor of solemn and contemplative mood which is exhibited in the symphonic and sonata adagio movements of the succeeding periods, has its seed here, in the sarabandes of the keyboard suites. That the jig was added at the close is a symbol of re-creation, optimism and new hope, which has its counterpart in the final movement of the symphonies.

No doubt, the origin of Froberger's suite was also the German variation suite. The following example from the second volume of the Froberger collection in the "Denkmaeler der Tonkunst in Oesterreich" is a good illustration:

Here the allemande is the dance which was planned first, and the other dances have been added to it according to the principle of diminution. As late as 1732, Walther calls the allemande of a suite "the proposition as it were" from which flow the other parts, the courante, sarabande and gigue, called "partes". The courante is closely related to the allemande, its beginning is identical in melodic line, but in the fifth bar it becomes quite independent. The structure has resemblance in measure too, in as much as the six-bar-period of the allemande becomes one of twelve-bars in the courante. The sarabande, characterized by the "short" (Mattheson's phrase) eight-bar period, has only the slightest superficial resemblance to the two previous dances. Like the courante it moves in the direction of a descending hexachord scale. The gigue, however, uses only the first phrase in its entry and then becomes free.

Froberger's suite type was expanded in the 18th century and interwoven with elements of the ballet suite. "Intermezzi" are introduced between sarabande and gigue as minuets, bourrées, gavottes, airs, fantasies, hornpipes, rigaudons, and many programmatic dances taken directly from the ballet suite such as "La Coquette", "La Badinerie", "La Chasse", "La Bataille".

All the facts marshalled here have shown us what the historical elements were which Bach's suites "for Klavier" contained. The various dance movements are, however, dissimilar in style, and we must recall at this point the theory enunciated when we are discussing the variation suite, namely that the old fashioned dances appear to be more stylized than those dance forms which are still extant. This is equally true of the suite of Bach. The highly stylized dances, as allemande, courante, sarabande, are mostly composed in the courtly, polite, baroque style of the French composers (derived from the arpeggiando lute style), and up to a certain point this is true also of the gigue. On the other hand, the intermezzi are written in a flowing and lively manner, practiced by Scarlatti and the Italians. They are simpler, more folk-like. This is not surprising, since these minuets, gavottes, polonaises, and bourrées were still being danced, while the other four had become the "old fashioned", obsolete forms which were only played but not danced anymore.

CHAPTER IX

THE AGE OF THE MINUET.

In a "History of the Dance" the time of Louis XIV, will usually be called the "age of the minuet"; this does not hold good in a book dealing with the *history of dance music.* For the minuet's strange fate consists in the fact that — as a form of music — it has not only outlived all dance forms of the Baroque but also received a rightful place in the first rank of musical forms, by victoriously joining the components of the classic symphony. The starting point of this "glamorous career" was, again, the suite within which the minuet, though not becoming one of the leading features among the prevalent forms (Allemande, Courante, Sarabande, Gigue), nevertheless played quite an important part among the "Intermezzi" interpolated between Sarabande and Gigue. The popularity of the minuet is clearly expressed by the fact that it often appears "en suite" within the suite, which implies that two or three or even more minuets are played in succession. And soon we find manuscripts of the 18th century, where six or even twelve minuets are noted one after the other without any allusion to the form of the suite, and this not only for orchestra, but also for stringed keyboard instruments.

Let us first cast a glance at the further development of the minuet, as well as at the development of the Baroque-dance at the time of Lully's successors in France. In full accordance with cultural and artistic trends during this period, the vigor and grandeur, the solemnity and pathos of Lully's musical language undergo a change towards daintiness, grace and playfulness. In dance music we also see most clearly the transition from French Baroque to Rococo. This is already expressed in the work of the great François Couperin (1668-1733), whose music is based on the magnificent art of Lully, but develops the ornamental elements, the embellishments in a most elegant, graceful and tender tonal language. And from this time on the pathetic and pompous style of Lully gradually was transformed into the refined and graceful manner expressing the spirit of the Rococo.

This period foreshadows the rationalism, already appearing in the course of the later 18th century and bound to be reflected as it were, in the melodic flow of the dances. A dance by Couperin is — as a contrast to the Baroque method of spinning a melody on and on — built up in periods and subperiods; groups are comprehended within symmetrical groups; accordingly, the interlocking chains of polyphony and the linear movement are transformed in their turn into the loosened forms of musical treatment where the chord is a distinctive feature.

Arpeggio chords ("Alberti basses" — after the Italian piano composer Domenico Alberti, who died in 1740) became more and more popular according to the new harmonic feeling.

Couperin's Rococo style also dominates the following epoch of Rameau, whose immortal melodies are unsurpassed. His dance music — whether written for harpsichord or for his operas (Zoroastre, Castor and Pollux, Platée, etc.), might even be considered as the climax of French dance music. The rhythm of his dances becomes, in a way, secondary; underneath the surface of the melody, the accent has dissolved into pure melos (melody). Now, that the "spinning melody" of the

Baroque is dissolved, one of the foundation stones for the new mode of treating themes in various contrasting ways is created. Exceedingly characteristic for this time, ante-dating that of the classical style, is the change of mood and feeling within one theme. A look at the "Contre Danse" from Rameau's "Zoroastre" will fully illustrate this phenomenon.

Meanwhile the cycle-form of the suite too undergoes a change. The great importance of the suite as music for entertainment in the open air, as serenade-, divertimento-, farewell-music has already been stressed in the previous chapter. This type of entertainment was kept alive in Austria for a very long time, — even up to the time of Franz Schubert, and when we take a look at the first "modern" symphonies as written by Haydn's immediate predecessors and by Haydn himself, we discover that basically they consist of the movements of suites, only no longer bearing the names of the respective dances as headings, — except the minuet. Even the good old French overture of the Lully type is not yet dethroned. What were the names of those predecessors of the Vienna Classicists? Among them we have, first of all, Georg Matthias Monn, (1717-1750), a Viennese organist and composer of numerous symphonies, divertimenti, piano sonatas and a cello concerto. In his works two ages meet: the old Baroque and the new Viennese pre-classic style. Here we find "Partitas" with French overtures and Italian intermediate movements, and "Piano Sonatas" with nine or ten movements (just as though they were suites), but also "Piano Sonatas" featuring the elements of the Scarlatti type of sonata, and those of the French suite, such as "Entrée", "Siciliana", "Minuetto", "Allegro", "Giga". The most important dance form, however, is the Minuet, which Monn was the first to use in a symphony. But it is extremely

characteristic of the new time as represented by Monn, that
this new minuet of the Vienna pre-classics is entirely different
from that of Bach or from the "courtly" (gallant) minuet of
Rameau. This difference may be illustrated by comparing
Rameau's minuet from "Castor and Pollux" (1737) with a
minuet by Monn (1740).

This last minuet with its wide intervals and its fanfare-like
melody is, so to speak "carved of different wood"; it comes
from the Austrian Alps and looks - - with its stamping rhythm
- - like a link to, or a continuation of Schmelzer's "Laendler"
(which Fux had put into a more stylized form). A glance
should also be given to the Ballet of the Swabian Peasants on
p. 146 — and perhaps to the Passepied "The Blacksmith"
by Fux.

Many of these minuets have those flourish-like melodies
and a rhythm becomes predominant, pointing to the old "stam-
per". The truth probably is that these minuets are not so
much minuets in the proper sense, but rather Austrian "Laendler" which only have received the name of "minuet". What
has such a minuet in common with the stilted Baroque and
Rococo? Monn's minuet of 1740 lacks the trio, (otherwise
characteristic of the minuet), though it can be found in a
rudimentary form since the second part of the second reprise
is started by the horns only, as a solo, so that this concluding
part fully makes the impression of a trio. As a matter of fact,
the trio is a second minuet, orchestrated for three instruments.
We have already mentioned that minuets "en suite" were very
much in favor within a suite. Preferably two minuets were
played one after the other, and in order to obtain a contrasting
effect, the second one was written in an orchestration for a

trio of instruments: two oboes, one bassoon.

In the "Concentus" (1701) by Fux we find a fully orchestrated "Rigaudon" followed by a "Trio Bourrée" (corresponding to minuet with a trio) and since Matteis wrote numerous minuets with trios for Viennese ballets, there is no doubt as to the sources of Monn's trio-minuets.

This rustic keynote is also struck by the symphony-minuets of Johann Wenzel Stamitz, Franz Xaver Richter and the other representatives of the so-called Mannheim-School, which Riemann calls the proper predecessors of the Vienna Classicists. While the minuets by Monn, Wagenseil and Starzer are strictly Austrian, those by Stamitz, Zach, Richter and Filtz—according to their Bohemian origin — show a distinctive Slavic folk character. While the former are derived from the Austrian "Weller", the latter originate from the old Czech folk dance, as it appears e. g. in the dances mentioned on p. 68, and later on, around 1800, in the "Rejdovak" dance.

Let us glance, for example, at the trio of Stamitz' minuet from the B major Trio, op. 1, No. 5

All such minuets, or at least most of them, based on Czech music, are tunes beginning with an accentuated note, without upbeat, thus corresponding to the trochaic rhythm of the Czech language which has no article. Its strong accent seems all the more emphatic being embedded in piles of consonants. The sharply stressed accents of that language contain in themselves an unmistakable suggestion of dance rhythm, thus again leading away from the Baroque principle of "Fortspinnungsmelodie" (spinning the melody), to a new melodic style.

We should not forget that it was Stamitz' minuet which was first performed in its new form in Paris, when Stamitz — in 1750 — scored his greatest triumphs there. At that time, in 1753, the pamphlet "Le petit Prophète de Boehmisch Broda" was printed and published in Paris, in which the encyclopedist Baron Melchior Grimm commemorates the Czech musician by the name of Waldstoerchel, a little student from Prague, who plays minuets on his violin. By magic he is transferred from his attic in Prague's "Jew's Lane" into the Paris Opera House, whose unnaturalness and queerness he experiences with horror. When back in his little attic in Prague, he realizes that he is no longer able to write minuets. The contact with the "culture" of Paris has destroyed his innate creative power. By letting the little musician play minuets, Grimm wants to symbolize the spiritual and ethnological basis of the new music which is rooted in the folk- and dance music of Austria and Bohemia.

The contrast between minuet and trio, originally only a contrast of colors, became later on—as a consequence—also a contrast of character and melody. In French harpsichord suites, and in Bach's work as well as that of others, we find — around 1700 — minuets (and also gavottes) which are followed by "musettes", movements of a rural character. The sequence: gavotte-musette - and reprisal of gavotte, was used for a long time and means, basically, only a revival of the old dual form: step- and hop dance. If we recall the contrast between the stylized dance with its decent walking steps, and the rural jumping and hopping dance, we find the old contrast reflected in the succession minuet (gavotte) plus musette on the one hand and the minuet plus trio on the other hand.

Even in the minuet of the classical symphony as well as in the scherzo of a symphony, melody and orchestration appear as "reduced" (to a simpler melodic flow and to a smaller group of instruments) in accordance with the principle of reduction in the old suite. In this *popular* spiritual and formal garb the minuet was used by Joseph Haydn in his symphonies, divertimenti, quartets and sonatas. He prefers like Monn and the rest of the early-Viennese composers (particularly in his earlier works) flourish-like melodies, thereby endowing his minuets with a certain solemnity well fitted for the aristocratic milieu for which his instrumental music was written.

The following minuet from the symphony No. 9 (of the new complete edition of his works) — written in 1762 — has much affinity with the yodeling character of the Styrian or

Upper-Austrian "Laendler" (typically wide-step melodics):

Such minuets of a genuine rustic character were collected and published by the Austrian folk-song collectors Max Schottky and Franz Ziska.

Those folk-songs were sung at Haydn's time and we may well assume that it were *those* "Laendler" which the "Vienna Classical Composers" had heard in their youth and by which their creative work was most profoundly influenced. A characteristic feature of this music is the "Dudeln" (playing on a "Dudelsack" which means bagpipe) and the "Yodeln", as an appendix to some of those songs. This part is mostly done in three-beat time, after the old fashion of the hop-dance. The words to this part of the song: "Scheni Krae, scheni Kaelm, scheni Buam af dr Alm", in its old Austrian dialect sometimes unintelligible even for people of German origin, means: "Schoene Kuehe, schoene Kaelber, schoene Buben auf der Alm" (handsome cows, handsome calves, handsome boys on the alps) and thus deals with the problem of the rustic dowry.

We are going to find these melodies built on triads also in

the "Classic" waltzes of Schubert, Strauss and Lanner, and they are most essential for the melodic flow of the Austrian dance. They are rooted not only in the construction of the rural instruments and in the melodic possibilities resulting from this construction, but also in the very special way of "yodel-singing" (the abrupt transition from one register of the human voice to another, which sounds very much like the Yodel-singing of the American cowboys). The alpine herdsman communicates with his companions on the neighboring alp by so-called "alp-cries". These are uttered so forcefully that the voice skips over into the octave, double-octave, seventh, fifth, fourth, and third, the direct consequence of which is the "yodel" itself. All inhabitants of mountainous countries seem to be talented and inclined to "yodel". I am giving an example of a Styrian "forest cry" ("Waldgschroa") taken from K. Mautner's "Collection of Styrian Folk Songs":

The reader should note that from the proper melodies of those yodel-tunes the accompaniment in chords, so characteristic of the 18th century, is evolved. The great importance of the "Uebersingen" ("oversinging") and "Ueber-blasen" ("over-blowing") — with regard to the development of polyphony, has been shown by Guido Adler in his study: "Repetition and Imitation, seen from the Viewpoint of Polyphony", in the "Vierteljahrschrift fuer Musikwissenschaft" (II). We have already pointed to the fact that the wide intervals in the melodies of the Austrian peasant dances express a husky and vigorous character. Indeed, the melodic flow of these laendlers and minuets of the Vienna Pre-Classicists, of Stamitz, Haydn, and the Vienna Classicists, indicate a new age of "masculine melodic character", contrasting sharply with the more feminine French melodies of the Baroque and Rococo.

And therefore it is no wonder that France took in this new art of Stamitz or the Mannheim School as though she

"FURLANA"

(Engraving by Giacomo Leonatiers (Leonardis), pupil of G. B. Tiepolo, made in Venice in 1765.)

Through the Courtesy of "Dance Index"

MENUET DE STRASBOURG.
Engraving from an almanac of 1682

would take in a breath of fresh air. A new age was in sight.

It cannot be our task to treat the further development of the minuet of the classic composers as an art form in itself. This would require a special musical treatise which would show how this dance form developed into a higher and more artistic form out of which, later on, Beethoven's scherzo was born.

Before dealing with Mozart's and Beethoven's dance music, it will be appropriate to take a look at the dances of their time. Mozart and Beethoven cultivated not only the minuet, but also the other dances in favor at that time: the "Contra Dance" and the "German" (Deutscher). The contradance, an English dance, originally a "country dance", was either a "round" or a "long way". The two forms of the round dance are mentioned in John Playford's compendium of the dance "The English Dancing Master or Directions for Country Dances" of 1651. The round dance is a branle, a dance in circles, whereas the long way is a sort of a longitudinal round dance where ladies and gentlemen are facing each other in a straight line. In both these forms we find subdivisions into different figures: groups of three, change of position, circling around, crossing over, chains, etc. The number of different figures is endless and every dancing master aimed at inventing new ones. What is particularly English in these contra dances which already in the 17th century were called "Anglaises"? As a matter of fact choral rounds existed at all times and with all peoples. The African Negroes knew them as well as the Spaniards and the Czechs, who have a "chain-round" in their "Chytava", their "Motak", and their "Motovidlo". Here again it is the old love-game, — advancing, retreating, parting, and re-joining, which forms the basic set-up of such a "chain-round". In the "Chytava" the couples, posted on two opposite fronts, catch each other, and in the Spanish wedding dances of the 17th century, chain-dances with the queerest figures are performed. Besides, in Paris as well as in Italy and Vienna, rounds are danced as part of a ballet, with groups of soloists, separating from the rest, especially during the closing chaconne. What was it in fact, which caused the English rounds to spread all over Europe in the course of the 18th century? Sachs sees the cause for this in one particular English feature, to be found nowhere else: in the gradual joining of the different couples, which is a most appealing combination between column dance and the dance of single couples. However, the scholar modifies his opinion by pointing to the fact that also in the Rhodesian "Baila", the couples step out of their lines and dance together. But in Europe only the English seem to have made this kind of dance an integral feature.

And, indeed, already the Spanish poet Augustin de Rojas, around 1600, in his play "El major amigo el muerto" speaks about this type of the "Branle" as about an English specialty; while in other Spanish sources of that time we find the same "Bran de Inglaterra". Particularly English is the idea that as many as may like to do so are allowed to participate in this dance. A simultaneous performance of certain figures presupposes a certain number of dancers. A round in which any number of dancers may participate, requires a "line-up" and much patience of the dancers to wait for their turn and this seems to indicate a sort of "democratic" principle which in itself was English. Already at the court of Queen Elizabeth this dance was said to be performed by "masters" and "servants" pell-mell. Around 1700 the victorious pageant of the "Contre" makes its start, and according to Chr. Haensel's "Anweisung zur aeusserlichen Moral oder Tanzkunst" (directions towards a decent way of performing the art of the dance), the so-called "Anstandslehre" (etiquette of the dance) (1755) the "Contre" was almost as popular as the minuet danced at courts and balls as well as at weddings. Dufort's "Trattato del Ballo nobile" (treatise of the noble dance) of 1728 describes only the minuet and the "Contre". Being a "professional" dance teacher, he was bound to be strongly prejudiced against it since there were no "Coupé's", no "Balancé's", nor tip-toe steps, but only a simple way of walking back and forth. The essential feature was the cooperation of the couples and the integration of the individual into the entity of the "dance concert". Here we have the inner sense of the "democratic" English Contre. It did not require any court-tutoring from French or Italian dancing teachers. Every human being with straight limbs and a normal amount of common-sense was able to dance it.

But the English dance shared the fate of the rest of the social dances of the 17th and 18th centuries: only in Paris was it made socially acceptable. This process is reflected directly in the dance's name. Because Paris made of the rustic, the "country's" dance a "contre", a counter-dance, whereby the emphasis was laid on the *counter*-position of the dancers. And step by step the "Contre" adapted this sense also in England proper and the original meaning of the "country dance" faded away.

Under the influence of the Contre the old English round was revived at the beginning of the 18th century in the form of the "round for eight", but was transformed to such a degree in Paris that it got the name "Contredanse française" (French counter-dance) and eventually became the French "Cotillon" (petticoat) — in allusion to the dance — song:

"Ma commère, quand je danse
Mon cotillon va-t-il bien?"

(My god-mother, when I dance
Is my petticoat becoming to me?)

The cotillon has an innumerable number of tours and eventually involves into a forfeit game the toure of which — as Robitschek hints in his psychoanalytical study on the "Cotillion" — approach quite often the realm of hidden sexuality. The name of the dance perhaps indicates that particular quality.

Finally, in the first half of the 19th century, a sequence developed out of the old Cotillion, which in its regularity once more recalls the old suite: "Quadrille", so called because the couples dancing in columns formed little squares of four dancers, (2 couples). It is danced up to this day, and consists of six tours (or figures). Originally it consisted of five tours, and the dancing master Trénitz added a sixth one to them, so that the form of the Quadrille as danced today, consists of the following tours: the "pantalon" (after the ditty: "Le pantalon de Toinon n'a pas de fond" — "The pants of Toinon have no bottom"), the "Été" (named after a song too), "La Poule" (allegedly because in the original music the cackle of a hen was imitated), "La Pastourelle", — 32 bars in six-eights, or in 2/4 rhythm, showing rustic character. The first 8 bars of each tour are not danced but paused. The melodies of the six parts of the Quadrille are preferably taken from popular pieces of music, from operettas and operas, and featured as a sort of medley. We shall come back to the music of the Quadrille. Now we want only to stress that it has one quality in common with the "Contre" from which it originated, namely its absolute detachment from any melody or rhythmical scheme. And thus, as a matter of fact, this dance again approaches the genre of the old "Basses Danses" which also allowed an already existing melody to be moulded and transformed according to the wishes of the dancers and the dancing masters, respectively, as was the case at the time of the "Variation Suite". However, these primitive rhythmical variations are by no means of a rank to compete with the elaborate technique of the Renaissance musicians.

To return to the old English country-dance: like the old "Jig" it was a two - or three-beat dance, and the most varied melodies were used for its music.

John Playford's "English Dancing Master" in the edition of 1651 (1654) brings the melodies of the different dances, and such old "Jigs" from Elizabethan times as "The Cherping of the Lark", a long-way for eight:

Some of these melodies are of French origin such as "Health" which is nothing else but the Bourrée from Praetorius' "Terpsychore". Some of them have kept alive even up to our day, right here in America, such as "Sedauny", or "Dargason", now called "Virginia reel".

Here we find this whirling and rotating movement which more and more takes the upper hand and finally becomes the proto-type of the 18th century Gigue.

Also on the European continent, the contra in the most varied forms is found. Already Georg Muffat, in his "Flori-legium Secundum" of 1698, features a "Contradanse" which he calls "Saltus a Giga non absimilis" (jumping dance not unlike to the jig) and which has the following rhythm:

Rameau in his "Zoroastre" features an entirely different contra dance; and as this dance in the second half of the 18th century came more and more into practical use, the classic composers also wrote contra dances besides their minuets and "Germans".

But let us first deal with the "German" or the "Allemande". We must not confuse it with the "Allemande" of around 1600 nor with the highly stylized Allemandes of Bach's time. It was already danced at the Court of Louis XIV. Therefore, in spite of its German origin, it became almost a French national dance. Thus the French dance teacher Guillaume says around 1760: "everybody knew that the Allemande came from Ger-many, but here — being the most popular French dance — it was danced quite differently". On the painting by Aug. de St. Aubin "Le Bal paré" of 1773 we see the couples perform their graceful "tours de mains". Soon the Allemande was included in the contra danced as one of the most popular figures and, for the reasons of social psychology achieved such popularity that it outgrew the general "Contra dance" — part of which it had been under various forms such as "Tyrolienne", "Stras-bourgeoise", "Alsacienne", — and became an independent dance. At first, these dances were performed in the meter of the "Bourrée". For an example let us take a look at the "Danse de Strassbourg" (around 1770), from La Borde's "Essay sur la musique" (1780):

The "Danse de Strassbourg" which Mozart used in the last part of his violin concerto in D major (Koechel 218), has some resemblance with the above example, and also with the "Ballo Strassburghese" or "Musette" from Dittersdorff's "Car-neval Symphony".

Not before the end of the 18th century was the 3/4 rhythm definitely and finally established, whereby the old Austrian peasant-dance was accepted for good, into high society too. It is significant that the 18th century writers in describing the new Allemandes, give consideration not only to the various steps, but also to the positions of the arms in their various characteristic details. The crossing of the arms, for example would indicate that these dances — while still exclusively folkdances and not yet assimilated and moulded into the Contra Dance — were, like the "Schuhplattler" (tap-dance), accompa-nied by a rhythmic clapping of hands. The crossed arms are to a certain extent, a sort of choreographic remnant.

The same idea was expressed in the music itself, in which, from now on, the accent on the first beat of the measure is characteristic and this is still further evidenced by the renuncia-tion of independent leading of the inner voices. This develop-ment was also promoted by the gradual transition from poly-phonic to homophonic style evolving in the course of the 18th century. Thus, as the "Courante" is typical of the Baroque, the "Minuet" of the Rococo, the "German dance" and the "Waltz" — are typical of the new era. The phenomenon that everybody was allowed to take part in those dances and that the partners were chosen freely corresponds with the newly developed style of homophonic music.

All of the great Classicists have written dance music, by which we mean not only the minuets of their symphonies, but dance music designed for dancing proper. Everybody will certainly recall the gay story about Haydn's "Oxen Minuet". In 1784 he also wrote "Germans" and, even while in London, he still wrote contra dances. Haydn's first dance pieces, (14 Minuets for 2 violins and bass, flute, oboe, bassoon and 2 horns) were published in 1767. Their original version for piano alone — as stated by Pohl in his biography of Haydn — still exists for our inspection and dates back to the 50th of the 18th century. The beginning of one of these oldest minuets by Haydn shows the usual flow in triad melodic line of Early Viennese style:

No doubt, even previously to these works Haydn had written a great deal of dance music, not only for the Esterhazy court, but also for the balls of Vienna which took place in the "Redoute", at "Trattner's", at the "Mehlgrube" (flour pit), and in aristocratic homes. Masked balls were still rare events in Haydn's youth, and had to be supervised by the police. This is not surprising when we recall the "Committee for the Preservation of Chastity" of Empress Maria Theresia. From January 6th on, such balls were permitted only during the so-called Carnival-time until the Tuesday preceding Ash Wednesday. The admission fee was one ducat of gold. The visitors arrived by car or by sedan-chair. But woe to anyone who showed up on the street, his face hidden by a mask! Without mercy he was instantly arrested. The orchestras of the great balls consisted of about 40 men united in their own fraternity. This fraternity was dissolved under Joseph II, and since then, those musicians who played for dancing assembled each Saturday morning behind a pillar on the "High Market" (Hoher

Markt) where they could be found by anyone who wanted to hire them: a real musicians' exchange!

About Mozart we know that he was a most passionate dancer, prefering the minuet. In Salzburg, once at a "peasant wedding" and another time at a masked ball, (in the disguise of a "barber boy") he entertained the whole party. In Vienna, as a newly-wed, he still liked to take part in the "Redoute-Balls" and when, in the Carnival of 1787, he arrived in Prague, the first thing he did was to attend together ·with Count Canal, the famous "Bretfeld Ball". In his letter of January 15th he reports to his friend Jaquin in Vienna: "I didn't dance and I didn't flirt — the former because I was too tired, the latter on account of my innate dumbness. But I was highly pleased to watch all those people dance to my music from the "Figaro", transformed into contra dances and Germans, and they hopped around with great pleasure . . ."

This passage of Mozart's letter shows, that not only for the contra dances, but also for the Germans the most popular melodies were adapted and in Prague at that time the most popular melodies were those of "Figaro". Mozart himself has adapted "Non piu andrai" for a contra dance and used this melody as the first of a selection of 5 contra-dances (Koechel No. 609) which he wrote in the year of his death (1791). But those "Germans" to the melodies of "Figaro", as played in the Carnival of 1787 in Prague, I found in a forgotten bundle of music in the National Museum of Prague and have, in part, published them in facsimile in my book, "Mozart in Bohemia". Connected with Mozart's sojourn in Prague is one more dance-tale about the great composer, reported by his biographer Nissen. Among the noblemen whose special protégé Mozart became in the course of his stay at the Bohemian capital, Count Johann Pachta is worth mentioning. Nissen reports that upon the Count's request Mozart composed the "Nine Contradances with Trios" (No. 510 of the Koechel catalogue). Often, and for a long time in vain, the music loving count, whose hospitable house welcomed Casanova quite often as a guest, had asked the composer for this favor. Only on the very day of the ball arranged by the Count, he succeeded in getting Mozart to write the dances, but only by using a trick. He invited Mozart for lunch but advised him that lunch-time should be one hour earlier than usual. When Mozart arrived at the given time, instead of a well-dressed table he found ink, pen, and music paper. Now he was bound to fall in with this practical joke and thus, it is said, the contra dances were written within an hour. These contra-dances, which are now in the Library of the Prague University, later turned out to be spurious. But this does not diminish our interest in them. They are "Nine Counterdances or Quadrilles" for full orchestra, consisting of 2 violins, bass, 2 oboes (flutes), 2 piccoli, 2 clarinets, 2 horns, 2 clarini, and kettledrum. The first dance is the "Quadrille or Seza", for 16 couples in 4 groups. The trio is, musically, a quotation from the music of the Austrian grenadiers, — the second dance, called "Contradance" has, as well as the subsequent "Quadrille", a trio which consists of three reprises. Another contradance is called "La Favorite", a third one "La Fuite" (the flight), and the closing quadrille is called "La Pyramide", — according to its pyramid-like figures. It is the "March of the Grenadiers".

Beethoven used its theme, arranged it to be played by a music-box, the mechanism of which conveyed the playing of a flute, and Carl Maria von Weber felt that he could not omit it, when he wrote his overture "Kampf und Sieg" (Fight and Victory).

The Czech folksong "Pepiku" (Joseph), whose melody — strangely enough — is known in Germany under the name "Manchester" is also used in the above mentioned collection. To repeat, those contradances are definitely not from Mozart's hand, and therefore Nissen's story can only refer to the "Prague German Dances", which were written in Prague on the 6th of February, during Carnival-time. At the end of his handwritten orchestral score Mozart wrote: Each "German" has its "Trio", or better "Alternative", after the "Alternative" the "German" is again repeated, then the "Alternative" comes again, and then, after the introduction, it goes into the next "German". The Prague dancers liked this succession.

In spite of the popular character of these dances a certain festive mood appears quite strikingly in them, and seems to indicate the destination of these dances as well as to point to the aristocratic milieu of Prague. This refers particularly to the first, third, and sixth dance. In the second one we find those characteristic "sliding-grace-notes" ("Vortragsschleifer") which may be found as late as in the "Allemande" of the ball-scene of "Don Giovanni", and which hint at the old Viennese tradition of the violinists who played portamenti when playing Laendlers. In these "Germans" also, Mozart features a quotation, namely the aria "Com' un' agnello" from the opera "Fra due litiganti" by Sarti, (at that time extremely popular in Prague). He also used it for a quotation in "Don Giovanni" and for the theme of one of his variations for piano solo. The single pieces are connected by transitional modulations and at the end we find a Coda, which uses — already quite in the style of our waltzes — the themes of the preceding dance-melodies. Those "Germans" written in 3/8 are highly stylized, their orchestration is expertly and carefully done, and also their rhythmic and melodic flow is substantially different from the popular "Laendler" melodies of the Vienna woods or those of the Upper-Austrian "Landl".

Mozart's activities as "Kaiserlicher Kammerkompositeur" (Imperial Composer) consisted for the major part in writing dances for the masked balls of the "Kaiserlichen Redouten-saele" (Imperial Ballrooms) at the "Hofburg" (Imperial Palace). Balls were held every Sunday during Carnival time. Joseph II encouraged them to a great extent as a means whereby the different classes of the population might take contact with each other. He himself appeared there quite often with his suite of courtiers and mingled with the dancers. There the minuet was danced and then the "German", but of course also contradances and Laendler. In the "German" and the "Laendler", however, only the dancers of the lower classes participated, the crowd being too great for those of the higher classes. Who would not recall the ballroom-scene in "Don Giovanni" where the noble guests line up for the minuet. The seducer himself dances the contradance as Zerline's partner, and Masetto is drawn by Leporello into the crowd and confusion of the "German". This reflects exactly the respective social positions of these three dances at the time of Mozart. If they did not mingle incognito among the people — as "Ochs von Lerchenau" does in Richard Strauss's opera "Der Rosenkavalier" — the aristocrats were those who danced the minuet; and the "Don Giovanni" minuet is more ceremonial and differs very distinctly from symphony-minuets by its slower tempo and its festival mood, as well as by its festive rhythm carried throughout the piece. The contradance, in its turn, is the dance of the burghers, in which all — but well and orderly in line! — were permitted to participate, whereas the "German" is the chaotic dance of the general public. The minuet, being the old-fashioned but noble dance, is as highly stylized, as was formerly the Paduane and, at Bach's time, the Allemande. It requires its own orchestra, just as the aristocrats in Vienna and Prague maintained their own house-orchestras. For Leporello and Masetto the primitive peasant "orchestras" — or better: the Viennese "suburban" orchestras, — were quite ample. For a long time this scene has been considered as one of the most appealing scenes of Mozart's master-opera. How splendidly, for example, is the successive beginning and joining in the different dances brought out: the amateur musicians of that suburban orchestra first get ready by tuning the chords in fifth, a little pizzicato is tried, a little trill played! Typical are the grace-notes of this "German", and its basic motive

which hints at the suburbs of Vienna or Prague with its primitive accompaniment. The melody of this "Contra" may also — in many variations and versions — be found in the concert music of that time.

Another feature — which, however, is not part of our discussion here, is the marvellous and subtle way in which the

three Don Giovanni dances with their entirely different rhythms
are melted and moulded into one whole.

Mozart showed the light of his genius also in his "minor"
works, the ball-room dances themselves. An almost inexhaust-
ible inventive power is revealed in all these dances. Within
those few bars allowed by the different forms of the dances,
a multitude of ever-changing ideas is met with. Just like the
minuet in "Don Giovanni", the rest of the minuets by Mozart
are also greater in style and art, and their orchestration reveals
all the charms of the Mozart-score. In comparison with these,
the "Germans" are simpler and more popular, throughout
homophonic, with chord-accompaniment, pointing back to the
former stamping rhythms of the old German dance, and this
accompaniment is from Schubert's time on henceforth obliga-
tory for the waltz.

The "Germans" which Mozart has written for Vienna, are
different from the more aristocratic "Germans" as written for
Prague. The Viennese "Germans" are more popular. On one
hand they are simpler, but on the other hand they feature quite
a few jokes appropriate to the taste of the middle-class people.
In No. 6 of the "Germans" of 1788 (Koechel catalogue No.
536), we again find the quotation from Sarti's "Fra due litiganti", for which Mozart seems to have had a special predilection, because he also features it in No. 6 of the dances listed
as No. 571 in the Koechel catalogue. In the trio of No. 6
(Koechel catalogue No. 536), he quotes the "letter duet" from
"Figaro" in the most humorous way. In the first Trio (Koechel
No. 571), after four bars of smooth violin playing, suddenly
the full orchestra breaks in fortissimo, and shocks all the
dancers. In the sixth dance, the chromatically plaintive Trio
forms the gayest contrast to the solemn "German". The plaintive mood quickly is driven away by a few energetic bars,
whereupon the solo violin starts "weeping" again. The Coda,
however, features as a special orchestral joke, the so-called
"Mannheim Crescendo", an orchestral mannerism which was
in vogue one generation before Mozart, and at which Mozart
apparently wants to make fun of. The most famous "Ger-

mans" are those of 1791, the year of his death. There is something very popular about those dances in which the gayety of the Carnival is tinged with a hint of melancholy, as though this music would say to us: "Under the surface of this crazy Carnival lurks Death". This is especially conveyed by the pathetic sixth in the fifth bar of the Trio of the first dance, as well as by the Trio of No. 3 of Koechel No. 600, but even more so by the "canary bird", the Trio to No. 5. Koechel No. 605 has as a Trio the already mentioned "sleighing party" in which Mozart features the sound of sleigh-bells blended into well-known Austrian folk-melody. In Schottky's folksong-collection of 1819 this melody is noted as "refrain" of the song "Weltlauf".

In 1791 the "6 laendlerische Taenze" (Koechel No. 606), originally written for orchestra, but preserved for our times only in adaptation for 2 violins and bass, were composed. The "Laendlers" differ from the "Germans" by the flow of eight-notes in third-, fifth-, fourth-, and seventh- intervals, originating from the yodel-tunes.

Just as in the "Contradance" also, melodies by other composers were adapted. As Sarti is quoted in the "Germans", in Koechel No. 607 Anfossi's "Trionfe delle Donne" (The Women's Triumphs), is quoted. And Koechel No. 535, — in the form of a "Contradance" in five parts and with the subtitle "La Bataille" (the battle), — depicts a whole battle, closing with a military march with fifes and drums, and with a Turkish march. Whereas the contradance "Der Sieg vom Helden Koburg" (the victory of the Hero of Koburg), (Koechel No. 587), has no subdivisions. This is rather a kind of symphonic picture of a battle. The victory over the Turks is depicted in the tone colors that Mozart used habitually to characterize anything Turkish. In the same manner the contra-dance "Les filles malicieuses" (Koechel 610) is conceived as program music, but we are not certain which one of the spiteful friends of Mozart was the model of the composition. All these dances deserve far greater popularity than they have received for, though small and not of great significance, they can charm us endlessly, and set our heart beating and our heels tapping . . .

And now about Mozart's contribution to ballet music. We have, in the first place, his youthful work "Ascanio in Alba", written in 1771 by order of the Empress Maria Theresia for the celebration of the wedding of one of the archdukes at Milan. Between the two acts of the piece a ballet was performed which consisted of eight different dances. Unfortunately only the bass part has come down to us, from which — as had been the custom in Schmelzer's time — the conductor had to conduct the entire music for the dances. A year later, Mozart wrote another opera, also for Milan, "Lucio Silla", and three ballets for which the choreographic arrangement was in the hands of Noverre. The first of these was the "Gelosie di serraglio", and Noverre has described it in his letters in detail, sometimes even giving the names of the dancers who were to take part in it: Casacci, Salomoni (a famous Viennese dancer)—(also called Giaspetto di Vienna), La Morelli, La Binetti, Pick, Clerico and Gabalata. (Casanova has also left us records of these dancers).

The ballet is Turkish and one of the Turkish melodies was later taken over into the Finale of the Rondo of the A major Violin Concerto. The other two ballets were "La scuola di Negromanzia" and "La Giaconna". But it was only in 1778 that Mozart really came into intimate personal contact with Noverre, when he hoped that the choreographer would help him to procure a commission for an opera for the "Grand Opera" of Paris. Though this plan was not realized, Mozart was able to write the music for one of Noverre's dance compositions, "Les petits riens", which were performed in Vienna in 1768, to music written by Aspelmayer. This new version of the ballet was intended to accompany the performance of Piccini's opera buffa "Le finte gemelle". We have, however, no journal or other record of Mozart's part in the performance, — a true indication how unimportant the composer of a ballet was regarded. This ballet was repeated for a performance of Anfossi's "Il curioso Indiscreto" but, after that dropped into oblivion until it was found in 1872 in the Library of the Grand Opera in Paris. Besides the overture and the ballet proper, the score contained an additional group of twenty dances, seven of which, however, were found to be spurious. The genuine part of the manuscript is the most delightful and amusing collection of dance music, a blending of French style with Austrian folklore elements. The overture used is that favored by the composers of ballets, in one movement, adhering only loosely to the sonata form, with a leaning to a definite type of rhythm. Mozart also follows his favorite practice to introduce some exotic color. The sixth gavotte, f. i. uses a Czech theme:

Compare this with the Czech folk song "Let us go to Bethlehem", recorded by the collector of Czech folk songs, Jaromir Erben:

Some of the other dances, as the passepieds or the "pantomime" are of French origin.

And then, we have the ballet music for Mozart's "Idomeneo", that opera still bound to the world of the Baroque though already imbued with the spirit and the fervor of Gluck's reforms. Its first performance occurred in Munich in 1781. It was revived by Richard Strauss and Lothar Wallerstein, and Strauss added to it from his own pen. Its ballet music, surely among the best of Mozart's compositions, should be heard more frequently. The introductory chaconne, identical in its beginning with that of Gluck from "Iphigenie en Aulide" approaches the sonata form by its treatment of two themes. It tries to picture that tragically heroic mood of Idomeneo, who is forced by his solemn oath to sacrifice his son to the angered god of the sea. Idomeneo would like to disobey the god, — a threatening interval:

he shakes with fear, and resolves to fulfill his pledge. A lyrical larghetto makes use of the old South-German folk song "Rejoice my heart" (Freu' dich, mein Herz), which we also know from Czech folk music.

The second act is filled with the conflict between Idomeneo's filial love and the revenge of the god, whom he has disobeyed. A dreadful storm arises and a sea monster appears. At this sight the remorseful king of the Cretians prepares to sacrifice himself. All these varied emotions and occurrences are expressed in the ballet.

The introductory chaconne gives us the parallelism found in Baroque compositions between choreographic and orchestral structure. When the whole ballet dances, the orchestra accompanies it: when the soloist appears at a point described by the words "pas de ..", we hear on a trio of winds, (flutes, oboes and horns). When the oboe plays a pizzicato solo, we may f.i. imagine that Madame Falgera, the solo ballerina, does her tiptoe dance. The storm is portrayed in a "Pas seul de M. Le Grand" with rolling figures, syncopated middle parts and booming basses, — giving us a wonderful piece of program music. Later, when Mlle Redwen dances the charming 18th century passepied with her partner, and the whole corps de ballet joins in a sentimental, melancholic gavotte (trio in minor), we get that mood of the period which we find in Gluck: a half-gay, half-sad evocation of that which was considered "classic antiquity" at that time. The third act brings us the pronouncement of the sacred oracle, demanding that Idomeneo renounce the throne in favor of his son and that his life be saved and that he be preserved to love Ilia, the daughter of Priam. The opera closes with a choreographically lavish passacaglia in the form of a rondo, which unites all the solo dancers and the entire personnel of the ballet on the stage.

As I mentioned already, Mozart himself was also active as a dancing master and ballet dancer. In a letter to his father, written from Salzburg on March 12, 1783, he wrote as follows: "On the Monday before Ash-Wednesday, we performed our masquerade at the ball. It consisted of a pantomime which took up half an hour during the intermission. My sister in law was the Columbine, I played the Harlequin, my brother in law was Pierrot, an old dancing master (Merk) had the role of Pantalon, a painter (Grassi) was 'Dottore Graziano'. Both the invention of the pantomime and the music were from my pen. The dancing master was kind enough to drill us and I may tell you that we played quite prettily (ganz artig). I enclose the announcement which was distributed by a masked person, disguised as a postman among the masked participants."

Unfortunately only the violin part of this ballet has been preserved. It was originally written for 2 violins, viola and bass. And of this violin part only a partial section, that for the scenes reminding one of the Italian Comedia dell'arte. While Pantalon and Columbine quarrel, their scolding is characterized by a number of short, pointed and chattering phrases in eighth notes. The appearance of the dottore is heralded by pathetic octaves and dotted notes in the style of the old French overture phases. The indispensable Turk accompanied by exotic minor phrasing appears. But the most satisfactory scene from a ballet point of view seems to be No. 7 in which the Harlequin "jumps from the box", as the manuscript has it and Mozart had the opportunity to exhibit his mimic talents against a more expanded musical background. As far as the short sketch which has been left to us shows, this was music written for practical purposes, without much thought for its pure musical content.

This, however, was not the only time when Mozart applied himself to providing entertainment for a ball. Another divertissement for which he wrote the music, if nothing else, was discovered by Ludwig Seitz in the Austrian city of Graz in

1928, and published by Roderich Mojsisovics in an arrangement for the piano and with an altered text. It is a peasant ballet called "Recruiting, or the Test of Love". The story tells of the forced impressment into military service of a young peasant and his subsequent release thanks to the efforts of his bride, who also appears in uniform and is ready to shoot him and herself. Intermingled with this fable there are all kinds of humorous scenes and dances between the soldiers and the peasant girls. The music is partly taken from well-known works of Mozart, partly consists of unknown pieces, and Alfred Einstein believes that these latter have nothing to do with Mozart. The writer of this ballet, however, refers explicitly to the "Coburger Ballet", meaning the "Coburg Contradance", written by Mozart, which fact may imply that the whole work was in some way connected with the circle around the master. It is likewise probable that this "Coburger Contradance" was part of such a ballet entertainment performed at a ball.

Also Beethoven, this giant among musicians, did not disdain to write real dance music for social entertainments, balls, and even more ordinary forms of jollifications. In the Seventh Symphony, he has raised the dance to a level unique in the history of music, but we do not wish to enter upon any interpretative attempts of this work. Professor Schering has made such in his book "Beethoven und die Dichtung", in which he tried to establish a definite connection between this symphony and the composer's reading of Goethe's "Wilhelm Meister". He takes it up, movement by movement: "First movement, Poco sostenuto — Solemn procession of the children into the festival hall crowded with the actors; Vivace — Mignon's wild dance to the music of the triangle and the tambourine. Second movement, Allegretto — Mignon's burial (Requiem for Mignon, sung by a chorus and the voices of boys), (Goethe, 8, 8,). Third movement, Presto — Philine cites from Faust: "the shepherds prepare for the dance", (2,11). Beethoven gives a description of the dance "Under the lindens" and (in the trio) the spirit of the pious pilgrimage during the "Easter walk" in the fields. Fourth movement: Allegro con brio. The boisterous and noisy party in Wilhelm's room as the whole troop of actors assemble there, (7, 10).

Such detailed and fantastic interpretation is far removed from Wagner's inspired designation of the Seventh, as a "great apotheosis of the dance". Every student of music knows the importance of dance rhythms in this work, and that the second movement is not a requiem, but a trance-like, dreamlike picture of the dance. With definite purpose and intention Beethoven in this and in the Eighth Symphony omitted the slow movement, thereby creating a new symphonic type.

He understood, as none other, the original primitive form of the dance, the low-on-the-ground, brisk dance of the people. This is made clear by his Pastorale Symphony. It is of little moment whether the third movement is considered a dance movement taking the place of a minuet, or a ballet scene, as Paul Bekker says. In any case, the dance is the "Deutscher", performed in a lively tempo, just as it was still being danced in the villages. This is the point where it may be interesting to listen to Schindler, Beethoven's first biographer, who tells us important facts about him as a composer of dances.

"What great importance Beethoven allotted to Austrian dance music is proved by facts. Prior to his arrival in Vienna, in 1792, he had not, as he says himself, become acquainted with any folk music except the 'Bergish' folk songs from his Rhineland home, with their strange rhythms. The list of his works shows how much he busied himself with dance music, notwithstanding the fact that the musicians in Austria were unwilling to acknowledge his compositions of Austrian dance music as Austrian. His last attempt in this direction dates from the year 1819, the year of the creation of the Missa Solemnis. In the inn 'Zu den drei Raben' at Moedling (a suburb of Vienna), there was a company of seven musicians who were the first to introduce to the young composer, coming from the Rhine country, the unadulterated real music of his new home. The friendship between Beethoven and these native musicians grew apace and a number of dances, Laendler and

others were composed for their use. I was present when in
the year mentioned above, (1819), Beethoven handed his new
opus to the leader of the band at Moedling. In a gay mood
the master mentioned he had so arranged the composition of
these dances, that from time to time one or the other of the
musicians could put down his instrument, take a rest, even go
to sleep. After the leader, having accepted the gift, had left,
Beethoven asked whether I had not noticed how the village
musicians often dropped off to sleep during their playing, and
then again, as they woke suddenly, would chime in with a
number of hearty loud notes, played at random, but for the
most part in the right key, and so would alternate between
napping and waking. In the Pastorale Symphony, said Beethoven, he had tried to imitate these poor fellows" . . .

And Schindler continues: "if you, dear Reader, will look
at the music on pages 106, 107, 108, and 109 (of the Breitkopf
and Haertel Edition) you will find the proof of it. You will see
the stereotyped accompanying phrase of the two violins on
page 105, you will see the sleepy second bassoon with the
repeatedly abruptly dropped notes, while the bass, the cello
and the viola have stopped altogether. Not until page 108, do
we see the viola waking up, arousing in its turn the neighboring cello, then the second horn begins, plays a few notes, but
ceases immediately. The last ones to be fully aroused to renewed activity are the bass and the two bassoons. The clarinet
too has its time and space for a period of rest. Turn to page
10, and the Allegro in 2/4 time shows in its form and character
the essence of the ancient Austrian dance music. For dances
existed in former times in which the duple rhythm changed
suddenly to 3/4 time. I, myself, watching the dances in the
woodland villages around the capital, have (in the decade from
1820-1830) seen such dances performed" . . .

The "Laendliche Tanz" of Beethoven's "Pastorale" does
indeed seem to be a highly stylized "Laendler". As a matter
of fact, we find that the laendler being played in Upper Austria
and Styria, down to our days, have this transition from 3/4
time to 2/4 time. One of the best experts on this type of

dance, Commenda, says in his book on "Laendla", what we may take to be a confirmation of Schindler's report: "Almost every fiddler or musician had his jealously guarded transcriptions of laendler tunes familiar to him, often handed down for generations of musicians. To read these notes was possible only for a learned and accomplished musician, and the usual practice was not to play from the music, but by heart, for the actual dancing. Most of the "laendla", transcriptions as well as those published from the old records, are in 3/4 time. The same musician will sometimes play the melody in 3/4 time, sometimes in 2/4 time according to the pace observed by the dancers".

May I recapitulate once more the old "Grandfather dance", beginning with a deliberate slow 3/4 laendler, and changing without transition into 2/4 time. In the Austrian province around Salzburg, such dances still are being used.

Schindler continues in his report that Beethoven wrote a number of waltzes, himself transcribing the parts, for the band at Moedling. To trace these lost dances seemed a vain task for Schindler, who simply said that the score was lost. It really seemed so for a long time.—Yet in 1907 Hugo Riemann found the parts of these "Moedling Dances" in the Archives of the "Thomas Schule" in Leipzig.

In all these waltzes, minuets and "Laendlers", the practice to which Schindler points, of the alternately sleeping and waking musicians shows itself in the changing roles of the various instruments. They are highly stylized in spite of this relation to folk style, and Riemann points out that in their composition the creator had left behind him folk-lore of Austrian music, and was in truth writing real "Beethoven" dances.

We know that Beethoven was fond of dancing, though Ries, the friend of the master, tells us that he never really learned to keep in step. (Even Johann Strauss, the "Waltz-King, did not know how to dance!) Perhaps this failing of the composer had some influence on the opinion of the Austrian dance composers of the time, who considered Beethoven's dance music unfit for dancing. While these severe critics of Bee-

thoven repose unread in music archives, the dance rhythms of
the master still delight the world. And yet, strange to say,
there are a great many of Beethoven's dances, which have not
been re-edited or re-printed, and, as far as the musicians of
today are concerned, are practically non-existent. In the "Complete Works", Series II, there are 12 "Minuets" and 12 "Deutsche Taenze", (probably dating from 1795); in Series XXV,
(Supplement), there are 6 "Laendrische Taenze" for 2 violins
and bass, 6 "Deutsche" for piano and violin, 6 "Deutsche
Taenze" for piano only, as well as 6 "Ecossaises", and some
other dances. In Series XVIII, (Short Pieces for Pianoforte),
there are 6 "Minuets" and 13 "Laendrische Taenze" (of these
No. 1-6, identical with those of Series II, No. 7-13 have
been preserved only for the piano). But we lack new practical
editions. Most of the Beethoven dances are arranged very
simply as far as their form is concerned, and in this respect
strongly resemble those of Mozart. Their structure shows a
division into eight parts, they are based on few themes, and
their harmonic plan is a simple one. Beethoven also likes to
use themes from his earlier works, for example, he used in
the "Moedling Dances" themes from his "Klavier Bagatellen",
or he quoted the accessory theme from the Larghetto of the
Second Symphony in another dance of the same series. On the
other hand, he used the seventh of his "12 Contra Dances" for
his "Eroica", such making it immortal. The most folk-like
and popular of the dances are the "Germans" and the "Laendler", where we find a melodic line with triad-chords, with
alpine strains, most obviously appearing in the trios. Like Mozart, Beethoven closes his "Deutsche" with a brilliantly developed long Coda, returning to one of the motives of the last
trio. The "Laendlerischen" go so far in realism and primitive
expression that they verge almost on caricature, as for example in the piano version of dance No. 3, when the bag
pipe accompaniment enunciates both tonic and dominant simultaneously and the impression resembles that made by the Eroica
tonic-dominant combination. In dance No. 7, the accentuation of the weak part of the beat gives us the syncopated step-

ping of the peasants in the "Landla" in true musical portraiture.

Beethoven's contribution to ballet music also is considerable. In his youth he wrote a "Ritterballet" (Court Ballet) which was performed on a Carnival Sunday in 1791, in Bonn. Its "invention", that is, its arrangement, was by his patron, the Count Waldstein. The dancing master Habich from Aix la Chapelle helped to produce it, but the music's creator was not mentioned, apparently because it was intended that the whole should be credited to the Count. He, indeed, may have contributed one or the other of the tunes. A report found in Bonn tells us that this ballet dealt with the favorite pastime of the ancestors, the hunt, the battle, carousing and love. It was, accordingly, a late descendant of the old ballet tournaments or perhaps a revival of one of those Renaissance "Trionfi" of former centuries. The music is extremely popular in form, adapted to the requirements of the aristocratic society. There is a march, a "Deutscher Gesang" (faintly reminding one of the melodies from Saint-Saën's "Carnival des Animaux"), a hunting song, a romance, a battle song, a drinking song, (resembling one of the German student songs), a "Deutscher Tanz" and a Coda which harks back to previously used melodies.

More important and significant than this court ballet is Beethoven's ballet, called "Die Geschoepfe des Prometheus", (The Creatures of Prometheus) which was performed on the 28th of March, 1801, at the Viennese Imperial Opera. This ballet, created by Salvatore Vigano, one of the most gifted choreographers of the time, has been so widely discussed that it may be superfluous to discuss it again. The program gives its contents as follows:

"The basis of this allegorical ballet is the legend of Prometheus. The philosophers of Greece describe him as a lofty leader, who, finding the men of his time in a state of ignorance, taught them science and art and the refinements of life. With this ideas as a basis, this ballet brings the representation of two inanimate statues, who are given life by the power of harmony and made sensitive to all the passions affecting men. Prometheus leads them to Mount Parnassus, so that Apollo may instruct them. The god orders Amphion, Orion and Orpheus to teach them the art of music. Melpomene and Thalia are to give instruction in the dramatic arts, Terpsichore and Pan will teach them the shepherds' dance invented by the latter, and Bacchus is to be their master in the heroic dance." The only part of this ballet which has become very well known is the overture, the other parts have fallen into oblivion, in spite of the fact that they contain much that is beautiful and would be well worth reviving. Riemann, writing about this work in an article in the magazine "Die Musik", has pointed out the variation elements found throughout this work and more particularly in the Finale. He speaks of two contra-dances, one of which is used in the Finale of the "Eroica" and in the Variations opus 35.—In the Finale of the ballet, which is to express the triumph of human culture over barbarism, Beethoven turns back to the material of overture. Riemann discussed the whole matter and showed how this famous E flat major theme provides the thematic foundation of the whole ballet. Be that as it may, we find here in the ballet by the great master, a revival of the old manner of the variation suite, a recurrence of a form of treatment, which is a red thread running through the History of dance music.

In the preceding chapter an attempt has been made to analyze the essence of the baroque dance rhythm by an illustration of the movements of the conductor, movements which represent the subservience of the Baroque Individual to a given rule and law. But what is the essence of the classical dance rhythms? Step by step and gradually the Baroque "Fortspinnungsmelodie", the "spinning melody", has given way to a new form, which reached its apogee in the minuet. The "spinning type" (according to Apel: "Continuation Type") was replaced by the "Lied Type" (Apel: "Repetition Type"). But the rhythm too, has changed. If we compare the rhythm of Haydn and Mozart with the one of Bach or that of the Pre-Classicists like Monn, or Wagenseil, we shall note the fundamental differences. Accentuations had become much more vigorous. They also followed each other in much shorter intervals. This music, naturally, changed the attitude of the dancers. Their bodies seemed to be shakened by the new rhythm in a — so far — unknown vivacious way. Also the movements of the conductors had changed entirely. The beat had become organically determined. It was no longer stiff as in the Baroque period but supple and freer.

Note in the now following example the first quarter notes, accentuated by the grace notes and the rest which follows. Finally the third quarter note. The rhythm plays with the melody and has full command over it.

One may say that around 1800 the principle of the "free will" passed over into the field of rhythm. This is even more apparent in Mozart's dances than in all others. Mozart's beat is characterized by a gentle soft beginning, followed by a more energetic, powerful urging accent, which in turn is relieved by a slight release of pressure. Just as the musician Mozart, also the man in him faces the problem of life with hesitation, but masters it with energy, until — in the end, he shakes it off with ease.

The curving line of Mozart's measure in reality mirrors the life and the attitude towards life of that great composer. How different on the other hand are Beethoven's measures! Take for example the beginning of the Fifth Symphony. The beats strike vigorously with an immeasurable force, in full consciousness of responsibility, impelling like a stroke of lightning. The crescendo of the beats, after a somewhat lighter beginning, is fast, furious and sudden, and the close equally rapid and strong. Such tempo, such measures, flow from a temperament, an individuality, prepared to go into battle and to struggle with fate. Beethoven once wrote: "Man muss dem Schicksal in den Rachen greifen" — "Man must rule his fate". This attitude is not confined to his great masterpieces only.

CHAPTER X.

STAGE DANCE, BALLET AND OPERA

DURING THE

CLASSICAL PERIOD.

WE have to refer to our previous chapter in which we mentioned the ballets of Lully and Rameau. It cannot be our task to follow up those traces in detail. Here we wish only to state that the French ballet exercised an extraordinarily strong influence upon Germany. True, the Austrian and Munich Court were under Italian influence for a considerable part of the 18th century, whereas the Middle- and Western-German courts, outdoing each other in taking over French customs, the French language and the French way of life, soon also took up the French ballet, though often in a rather provincial and bourgeois manner and form. In an article "Beitrag zur Geschichte des Sing-Ballets" ("Contribution to the History of the Sing-Ballet"), written for the "Zeitschrift fuer Musikwissenschaft" (Vol. 6), I have shown such a Southern German ballet from Noerdlingen. It is called "Die Frei gesinte Schaeferin Fillis" ("The Liberally Minded Shepherdess Phyllis"), and trees, fauns, monkeys, gypsies and shepherds are the characters of this primitive ballet. The steps are French and so is the music, whereas the simple songs point to the later German "Singspiel".

Soon the ballet was as popular in Germany as in France and one needs only to make a round-trip through the former South-, West-, and Middle-German court-residences and to pay a visit to their music libraries and archives, to find the proof. For example I saw in the Royal Library of Dresden the manuscript of a ballet "Von der Zusammenkunft und Wirkung der sieben Planeten" ("Of the Concourse and the Effects of the

Seven Planets") which an authority such as Hermann Kretz-schmar ascribes to the great master of German Baroque, Heinrich Schuetz. This ballet, which was still performed as late as 1878, has seven acts in the course of which the supporting characters — a doctor and a villain, a cavalier and a woman-matchmaker — have pantomimic conversations to the music of gaillards, courantes and sarabandes. Skipping a brief space of time, around 1700, the head of the famous Hamburg Opera, Reinhard Keiser (1674-1739), is considered to be one of the greatest masters of music. The weakness of his character, however, hindered the full development of his outstanding talent. He was one of the most gifted composers with melodic invention, often tenderly sentimental, often deeply religious. For the major part, however, he devoted his art to the low type of the Hamburg "popular" opera, which — by its desire to get rid of the ideas promoted by the Renaissance and the Baroque — became a style of utmost vulgarity. Kretzschmar himself vividly described one of Keiser's operas, entitled "Stoertebecker und Goedge Michaelis": "Stoertebecker was a captain of brigands who for a long time had been a threat to the land around Hamburg and who recently was decapitated. His story was dramatized in the opera. Throughout the whole play there was real bloodshed! (namely calf's blood poured from pork-bladders which the singers had tied underneath their dresses). The execution itself was also performed in the same way before the eyes of the spectators! So crude had art become . . . However, the opera from now on kept that pork-bladder as one of its most popular utensils. Decapitations on the stage were highly in favour, clysters were given, brutalized human beings ran around roaring . . ."

We have to admit that neither the Italian nor the French opera ever had produced such excrescenses of crudity, and purposedly relinquish drawing any conclusions as to what cultural developments might be based on this phenomenon of "Art".

In 1700 an opera was performed in Hamburg, entitled "The Leipsic Fair", in which merchants and students played, sang and danced to the delightful rhythms of French music.

Equally in the opera "The Hamburg Market", featuring pictures and intermezzi from Hamburg life, characters from the Low-German (Niederdeutsch) people, serving maids, market women, knife grinders, and others. We have a folk-opera and a corresponding folk-ballet. In the latter one, however, there are dances with — strangely enough — French tint. This is also the case in the ballet "Bauern und Bauernkinder" (Peasants and their Children) from the opera "Croesus". As a peculiarity of Keiser's music we have to note that the upper voice is written in the French Rococo style of dividing and sub-dividing the phrases, whereas the basses show the older way of the Baroque: the themes spinning on and on.

In the "opera seria" of the 18th century, the Italians make much scarcer use of the ballet than did the French opera with its wealth of intermediary ballets. Gluck in his reformed operas, following the French way, has given amplest space to the dance. True, some Italians did not lag behind the French in this respect, such a Traetta, whose "Ippolito ed Aricia" is a straight copy of French taste. But Gluck, who in his new-style-opera "Orfeo ed Euridice", written in 1762 for the "Theatre bey der Hofburg", the later "Burgtheatre" of Vienna, (in collaboration with the librettist Calzabigi) has given a new importance to the dance that was in closest connection with his idea of dramatic truthfulness and reality. He knew that both listener and spectator need lyric and colorful entre-acts and that the dance is a most welcome means for introducing them. Thus he consciously continued the tradition of the French opera. Compared to his later works written for Paris (up to "Iphigénie en Tauride"), he kept himself within moderate limits. At the end, with a sequence of four extensive movements, he went farther than before. From the dramatic viewpoint they have little importance, whereas the mourning pantomime and the short dance of the furies developed from dramatic situations. We know that Gluck later, in 1774, re-wrote "Orfeo" for Paris; he augmented the number of the dances, inserted among other pieces the great dance of the furies from his ballet "Don Juan" and closed with the great Chaconne. In accordance with the principle of dramatic truthfulness and reality, all of Gluck's ballet dances are unlike the formal dances of the French. The dance of the transfigured spirits in Elysium — a minuet — eliminates any reminiscense of the old dance. There we have perfect blissfulness, imbued with a halo of mild melancholy, just as from the Renaissance on, we are accustomed to visualize the Classical. A noteworthy detail of almost all of these dances is the uninterrupted movement carried through all the middle parts, as though the pace of tragic fate should be thereby indicated. Here the happenings on the scene are in closest connection with the music of the ballet. This music is expressive in the true sense of the word.

It is worth mentioning that Gluck wrote every note of dance-music for his great operas himself, unlike the habit of most opera-composers, way into Mozart's times! The great importance Gluck attributed to the ballet may also be gathered from the elaborate way he describes it in the introduction to his score. In the first ballet the mourning ceremonies are to be presented as performed in ancient times at the grave of the deceased, consisting in offerings and the burning of incense, furthermore in the strewing of flowers and the pouring of wine and milk around the grave (this is a direct continuation of the ancient and primitive fertility dances); the pantomime of the dance retains an expression of sorrow and grief, and eulogies to the deceased are sung. As a climax of the celebration, adolescents are led up to the grave, costumed as genii. They carry offerings with them and are selected according to the personality and the position of the deceased. Thus in this ballet guardian-spirits as cupids weep around Euridice's urn, one of them, Hymen, the god of matrimony, extinguishes his torch to symbolize the break of the marriage bond by death.

The new age, opposed to the spirit of the Baroque, is not only characterized by the emphasis upon the freedom of the will and value of personality, but by a yearning for truth. This is expressed not only by Gluck's reform of the opera, but altogether by the new style of dancing. The affected steps of the Baroque and Rococo, bare of any meaning for a long time, had to give room to more veracious and genuine dances, such as the "Laendler", the "Waltz", the "German" and the "Contradance". The same idea may be felt in the field of the spectacular dance. Just as the Laendler and its melodies — so strongly influencing the new symphony and the new music in general — originated in more extrovert cultural elements, thus also in the field of ballet which is the very essence of extrovert dancing, we may observe a trend towards greater intensity and a reformation in the direction of greater truth and enhanced expressiveness. The representative of this reformation was the French dancing master Jean-George Noverre (1727-1810), a disciple of Dupré. Early in life he came to Germany — Berlin and Dresden — where in 1747 he met Gluck. Garrick saw him in Paris and took him along to London. In 1758 he was again at Lyon, where he wrote his famous "Lettres sur la danse et les ballets" (1760). Then he went to Stuttgart, where at the court of Duke Karl Eugen he displayed abundant activity. He wrote numerous interpolated dances for Nicolo Jomelli's operas as well as for the Stuttgart ballet-composers Florian Deller and Joh. Joseph Rudolph. But the small court of Wurttemberg was not in a position to finance Noverre's costly ballets; therefore he turned to Vienna where he became Gluck's collaborator. His friendship with Gluck was still strong when — appointed by Marie Antoinette (1776) to work at the Great Opera — he had the opportunity to collaborate with the reformer of the opera, in Paris. Noverre died in 1810 as a "Knight of the Order of Christ".

Just as in the social sphere the field of the reform of the ballet seems to be based upon English influence, Noverre was called the "Shakespeare of the Dance", and it was, indeed, Garrick in London, from whom Noverre derived his inspirations. For it was only after he was in touch with the great actor, that he featured in his ballets that psychological truthfulness, which later on, he so strongly demanded, and which required the highest dramatic challenge of the performers. In his "Lettres" — dedicated to the Duke at Stuttgart, who in a way was sort of godfather to Noverre's ballet — he stresses as basic idea an old thesis, which Batteux in 1743 had featured as central idea of aesthetics, namely that art should be an imitation of nature. Even more than the art of painting, the dance is able to verify this idea, for the masterworks of painting give us but imitations of nature, whereas a good ballet is part of nature itself. Who does not recall the religious and philosophical background of the dance of the primitives, which in itself is art of their life and possesses deepest human and psychological reality? But the dance of that time was drifting towards degeneration, says Noverre, and should be in one rank with the other arts. Thus it could be led out of the "pit" into which it had fallen. It ought to keep close to the arts of painting, dramatic poetry and acting. How close to life were the paintings by Mme Lebrun, Rubens, Van Loo, Boucher and Teniers! And how senseless that automatic way of keeping the symmetric line-up and movements of the old-fashioned dancers! The overdoing of the principle of symmetry had for a long time robbed the performers of all individuality and abased them to the role of mere machines. Therefore symmetric planning should be limited and applied only at the beginning and the closing of the ballet, but there is no room for it in the "scenes d'action", in the action scenes proper, where the individual expression — "nature", as Noverre says — must dominate. Noverre's basic idea, however, is: the ballet should be a danced drama, corresponding to the sung or spoken drama. It has to follow Aristoteles' theory of poetry and has to have an exposition, a conflict and the solution thereof. Further requirements are: divisions into acts and scenes, clearcut characters and contrasting scenes. Each movement of the dance has to symbolize an emotional act — and yet, the dance-poem lacks the drama's most important requirement: the spoken dialogue which carries on the action. Consequently action should be condensed to feature the climaxes only supposed to impress the spectator with the suggestiveness of a painting. Music, however, is for Noverre but an auxiliary art, similar to Gluck's paradox saying that the composer of an opera should first forget that he is a musician. (He had, of course, the reform-opera in mind). The new dance-drama is a comprehensive work of art in which dancing, poetry, music and scenic design are linked together. The choreographer, in his turn, was expected to combine in his person the qualities of all those arts. Noverre also deals with the intermediary ballets of the opera which in spite of their independence of the drama proper — should nevertheless not lose connection with its basic idea. Their task consists in forming a transition from one act of the opera to the next, and they are indispensable for the whole work. Noverre's ideas created a new school of thought. Aside from his ballets there exist many others — partly by anonymous authors — in which his principles were adopted. The composers of music in their turn, were compelled to think in quite new terms: they had to clarify the nature of illustrative music, and therefore Noverre exercised not only the greatest influence upon ballet music proper, but also upon the development of program music as a whole. Such orchestra-pieces of program-music, in which the instruments depict scenic or emotional happenings, may be found in Rameau's and Destouche's operas, and also in the Italian operas of the 17th and 18th centuries. The Italians used to embellish the accompagnato scenes with instrumental illustrative music. When, for example, Orfeo in a recitativo invokes the gods of the underworld, then the accompanying instruments depicted all the horrors of the Inferno in psychological verisimilitude. "O ombra cara" ("O dear shadow"), is one of the best-known types of recitativo and air of Italian opera, when the hero bemoans the loss of his beloved while the orchestra depicts his grief in painful chromatic phrases. These are the sources from which too, Noverre derives the ideas and media for his dance-poems.

Among those who set his ballets to music, Noverre has given preference to the composer Florian Deller (1729-1773). He belonged to the group of Stuttgart composers, gathering around the Italian Nicolo Jomelli, who worked in Stuttgart as operatic composer and as "stellar"-conductor around 1760. Unfortu-

The Dancing-Master:

Or, Directions for Dancing Country Dances, with the *Tunes* to each *Dance* for the *Treble-Violin*.

The Tenth Edition *Corrected; with the Addition of several new Dances and Tunes never before Printed.*

THE DANCING SCHOOLE

Printed by *J. Heptinstall*, for *H. Playford* at his Shop in the *Temple-Change*, or at his House in *Arundel-street* in the Strand, 1698.

COURT and COUNTRY DANCES

COURT and COUNTRY DANCES.

Through the Courtesy of the Museum of Modern Art

Engraved for Wilson's "Companion to the Ball Room" (about 1820)

nately Deller's human qualities were in definite contrast to his talent, a circumstance which exercised a negative influence upon his artistic development. His "Orfeo" is the best example of the way a ballet by Noverre was set to music. The center of the whole work is the parting scene between Orpheus and Euridice in Hades. Its music portrays the story in the most suggestive way. In his other ballets, such as "Adelheid von Ponthieu" or "La schiava liberata" (the freed slave), he aims as best as he can to give a musical characterization of the leading characters. In his "Ballo polonais", he wishes to create a national dance-representation of Poland. Deller's colleague at Stuttgart was the virtuoso J. J. Rudolph (1730-1812). His "Rinaldo" featuring the old forms of the dance, was performed in 1761; a revival of this dance-poem by Milca Meyerova in Prague, a few years ago (under my assistance), showed that this type of ballet has a right of survival, even today. His "Medea" follows Deller's ideas with regard to dramatic requirements, but in a more external fashion. Rudolph depicts chiefly "outside stories", whereas Deller tends more for "inner stories", for psychological emotions. The older types of dancing are by no means missing in Deller's works. The opening scene f.i. of the second act of "Medea", featuring Jason declaring his love to Kreusa, then Medea interfering, and finally Jason giving preference to Kreusa, is carried out in the form of a passacaglia.

When Noverre in 1767 moved from Stuttgart to Vienna, he found the soil well prepared for his choreographic plans of reform. In their ballets and pantomimes, performed at the Kaernthner — and Burgtheatre, the German Franz Hilverding van Wewen (1710-1768) and his pupil Gasparo Angiolini (1723-1796) had featured similar ideas. Arteaga — in his well-known History of the Opera — even goes so far as to say that the insertion of the pantomimic dance into the structure of the opera has to be attributed to the Germans, and that the French had only taken over the cultivation of the dance. Erroneously, however, he gives Dresden as the place where Hilverding worked. Beside Hilverding, Antoine Phillibois, also a son of Alexander Phillibois, dancer at the court of Charles VI, lived and worked in Vienna.

Thus the stage was set in Vienna for the progress of the ballet. When Noverre came to the Austrian capital, he succeeded at once in winning a number of composers for his purposes; the most important among them were Johann Starzer, and Franz Aspelmayer, whom we mentioned previously on occasion of the history of the minuet. Starzer wrote the music to Noverre's ballets "Die Horatier und Curiatier" (a theme from ancient Roman history), "Diana and Endymion", "Roger and Bradamante", but he also used popular themes such as "Der Dorf-Eulenspiegel" ("Eulenspiegel of the Village"), "Der Englaender unter den Schaefern" ("The Englishman among the Shepherds"). Aspelmayer wrote "Iphigenie", "Acis and Galathea", "Flora" and — in collaboration with Starzer — some sort of an aviation ballet, in which the sensation of those days, Montgolfier's balloon, was represented in dances and pantomimes. The title was "Montgolfier oder die Luftkugel" ("Montgolfier, or the Balloon"). For the first time aeronautics entered the musical field!

Starzer's musical ways were always in accordance with the respective subjects. Those which Noverre called "tragic ballets" are very free in their construction and come nearest to the type of "program music". The rest of them are a number of pieces expressing lyrical moods and keep within the framework of the usual types of dance. The new original feature of Starzer's ballets is — in accordance with the tradition of Vienna — the use of Austrian folk- and suite-music. In this connection a report about Starzer-Noverre's "Don Quixote" — ballet written by the Viennese critic Sonnenfels in the famous "Briefe ueber die Wienerische Schaubuehne" ("Letters about the Viennese Stage") of December 31, 1768, — might be worth mentioning. The opening march represents Don Quixote's merry departure; pieces for dancing of a lyrical character alternating with brass march rhythms depict the gallant love adventure of our dare-devil hero and a grotesque funeral march illustrates the hero's sad exit after a lost fight. Then comes a Bourrée with its grotesque melody in B minor, supposed to refer to a certain scene in which Noverre wanted to give a blow to a rival in Vienna (probably Hilverding or Angiolini).

Don Quixote in a duel has defeated the knight who fled to a mountain. From there he was removed by a machine and thus escaped the persecution of his victor. The latter, Don Quixote, rides on his Rozinante to the summit of the mountain, does not find the defeated opponent but contentedly descends to the plains again . . . Sancho Panza, on his "Arcadian mare" is just about to reach the heights upon which he perceives his hero, but his donkey stumbles at every step and, at the end, shamefully slides down the mountain.

Whom did Noverre want to depict in his work? Himself or Angiolini?

"Don Quixote" shows markedly characteristic Viennese march rhythms which Abert in his study about Noverre considered as a sort of "rhythmical Leitmotif". But only in the ballets "Roger and Bradamante" and "Rasender Roland" ("Roland running wild") does Starzer accept Noverre's requirements to their full extent. The framework of the dance forms is enlarged and large space is given to illustrating music. In his "Roger", however, Starzer proceeds one step further. Just as Beethoven in his Ninth Symphony trespasses the framework of the Symphony by using the articulate word, "the Hymn to Joy", Starzer on a smaller scale does the same in this ballet. In the closing scene of the second act Bradamante is given the magic ring with the words: "Bradamante, prends cet anneau et tu detruiras tous les charmes!" ("Bradamante, take this ring and you will destroy all witchcraft!") In this adagio phrase in c minor, following the pattern of Neapolitan ghost scenes, horns are heard, but then those words are recited to a melody full of pathos played by a unisono of strings calling oracle scenes from contemporary operas. The result is the inevitable strong effect of a transition from one form of art to another — provided that it is done in the right way and in the right place. The loosening up of rigid forms of dance into more freely treated structure for the benefit of dramatic expressiveness is indeed an early parallel to Wagner's artistic set-up. This put the ever-flowing "endless melody" in the place of the old principle of making an opera consisting of a number of separate pieces, each of them rounded off and complete in itself.

It is a significant fact that of all those "tragic" ballets of Noverre's school, only one work has reached world-wide fame, namely Gluck's "Don Juan".

In 1758 the choreographer Hilverding, whom we mentioned before, was appointed to the Russian Court at St. Petersburg. He left Vienna, and Gasparo Angiolini became his successor at the Burgtheatre. The latter's wife was the famous dancer Maria Theresia Fogliazzi, mentioned also in the memoirs of Casanova, who was so madly in love with the beautiful dancer that in 1754 he stole her picture and eloped with it from Vienna to Venice. At that time Gluck was supposed to deliver his ballet-music to the Burgtheatre. Much information may be gathered from the diary written by Count Khevenhueller who was well informed about all that was going on at Maria Theresia's Court with regard to society and art. Ballets of the period were "La Promenade", "La Foire de Lyon" ("The Lyon Fair") and a "Chinois poli" ("The Polite Chinaman"). In the beginning Angiolini kept his ballets within the customary framework of simple entertainment. But soon Gluck's influence became noticeable, and Angiolini planned to amplify Hilverding's ideas — a phenomenon obviously parallel to Noverre and his ballet. He conceived the ballet "Le Festin de Pierre" after Molière's "Don Juan", a drama, which at that time had greatly impressed the theatre-goers of Vienna. This was also a subject to suit Gluck's taste, and on October 17th, 1761, the performance at the Burgtheatre took place. The audience was puzzled. What? Those terrifying and tragic happenings which made blood freeze in your veins, were to be the subject for a ballet? But soon the audience ceased to be baffled, the ballet was a big box-office success, and the scene in which the statue preaches conversion to Don Juan was soon considered very impressive. On November 3rd the rush of the public was overwhelming and it was on this day that the Burgtheatre was completely destroyed by fire. About a century later, when the fire which consumed the Kaerntnerthortheater broke out on occasion of the performance of Offenbach's opera "The Tales of Hoffmann", the superstition arose among theatrical people that sinister and overromantic subjects bring bad luck.

Angiolini wrote a foreword to his scenario discussing his ideas about the tragic ballet pantomime. He considered this ballet as a work of art in the style of the old Greeks: "Whoever has read Greek and Latin authors knows the famous names Pylades and Bathyllos from the times of Emperor Augustus — those representatives of the pantomimic dances . . . As a sample I have chosen a Spanish tragic-comedy approved and applauded by all nations. The plot is splendid, the catastrophe terrific and, in our opinion, all happenings have a great resemblance to reality.

"The decorations of this ballet were made by Mr. Quaglio with great understanding. Mr. Gluck has set the music. He has fully grasped the terrific elements of the plot and has tried to express the passion as well as the horror which dominates the catastrophe. *In a pantomime the music is the main thing.* It is the music which speaks, we dancers make only the movements in the style of the actors of the old tragedies and comedies (who had the stanzas of the play recited by others) and only make the gestures. It would be almost impossible for us to make ourselves understood without the music, and the better the music fits that we wish to express, the better we are understood. About this phenomenon I want to speak in greater detail on another occasion.

Gaspar Angiolini."

Now about music: A brief "symphony" in the form of a simple sonata introduces the ballet; it is similar to the ballet symphonies by Rudolph and Deller, (the latter being somewhat shorter). Later on this music was included within the ballet-music to "Iphigenie in Aulis", on which occasion some changes towards a more regular four-bar periodicity were made. It is a very characteristic piece in which threatening trumpets prepare the dramatic action. Whereas we saw that Starzer in his "Don Quixote" used some sort of Leitmotif, we see here that Gluck in his "Don Juan" carries, so to speak, a "red thread of melodies" right through the whole ballet. The main motif appearing in Nr. 1

appears again in the Gavotte (Nr. 7) at the opening of the second act, in Nrs. 13, 18, 23, 24, and in some other places. Thus we find here another reminiscence of the old variation-suite. It seems that a more "streamlined" dramatic conception tends also towards a greater unity of motifs. This has been made clear by Monteverdi's "Orfeo" and later on by the romantic operas and Wagner's musical dramas. When the musicians play in front of Donna Elvira's windows we hear a serenade in the rhythm of a Siciliana. Its pizzicati indicate the playing of Spanish guitars and alluring Neapolitan sixth-chords are supposed to infatuate the Commendatore's daughter. The Commendatore appears and challenges Don Juan. A duel results. The Commendatore is hit. Breathless pauses! But quickly he pulls himself together and makes a new assault. In vain. He sinks to the ground . . . and while the motifs of assault are heard in quickly rising hemidemiquavers, the motif of the dying man sobs in diminished seventh-chords and finally in descending unison passages. The second act opens with dinner-and dance-music: A gavotte, a contradance, and a minuet-laendler, followed by three pieces of dinner-music. This last piece is interrupted as the marble guest knocks at Don Juan's door (six-eighths in top-speed). Don Juan himself opens (graceful music which later changes into an expression of excitement) and the Commendatore appears. Don Juan, his drinking-cup in hand, welcomes him, and the leading motif of the presto-movement — copiously taken over by Starzer in his "Adelaide von Ponthieu" — might perhaps be considered as a musical forerunner of Mozart's "Champagne-Aria".

As the ghostly visitor approaches, rolling and dismal demi-quaver-triplets sound in unisono. Again in a dismal unisono he turns to the somewhat amazed host who hesitates at first, but then in a triumphant movement in A major — later on used in Paris for the ballet music of "Cythère assiégée" (Besieged Cythère) — invites the statue to stay with him for dinner. It is interesting that the Commendatore responds to the invitation by a noble minuet, whereupon, escorted by Don Juan, he leaves to the strains of another minuet. No doubt this piece served as a pattern to Mozart's famous minuet in "Don Giovanni".

In the last act, the short scene at the graveyard (scene 23), the horrible location, is introduced by fanfare-like phrases played by the strings. Don Juan enters at top-speed, very energetically, but shivers obviously (a unisono passage in diminished sevenths). In the next scene (24) the Commendatore, to the strains of a solemn minuet, descends from his platform, and (25) scolds Don Juan in quick semidequaver-passages on account of his evil way of life (to the strains of the same theme which was played when the seducer invited the Commendatore to dinner). The following scenes (26-29) depict Don Juan's determination, his pride, frivolity, and courage — symbolized by the repetition of No. 62. This musical characterization of what is happening in Don Juan's mind is one of the climaxes of the entire ballet. Then a solemn introduction indicates the tragic turn, the judgment over the malefactor. After the last admonition and the threefold rigid "No" from Don Juan's lips the earth opens and devours him. Threatening sounds of the trombones are heard as well as the motif of the slaying of the Commendatore. These terrifying strains then change into Gluck's "Feuerzauber", the famous dance of the furies, which Gluck included into his "Orfeo". The old passacaglias by Lully form the pattern for this grand orchestra piece, built up in stanzas. Again and again the horrors of hell resound in dismal unisono-tremoli. In sharp diminished sevenths, sulphur-foam splashes from hell to heaven, accompanied by stirring violin-passages and threatening horns. A breathless general pause—and again the masters of the inferno begin their terrible game, the hellish spectacle starts anew— but the strains weaken . . they fade away . . and Don Juan has breathed his last.

Just as Starzer often uses Austrian folk-music in his ballets, Gluck, in the interest of local color, occasionally borrows from the motifs of the Spanish folk-dances. No. 22, for example, is an only slight variation of the "Matachin"-dance, well-known in 18th century Spain. (We wish to indicate in passing that already Arbeau mentions this dance identifying it with the Buffo-dance). "Il matacino" was a comical and awkward character of Italian comedy and the Matachins appear often in the French operas as well as in the ballets of Schmelzer. When mentioned by Arbeau, this dance was still a sword-dance like the Moresca which — with accessories such as jingle-bells, swords, helmets and a funny little skirt — was danced to the strains of the following melody:

a melody which was known in France as late as the 18th century, where it appears among the airs of the "Parodies du nouveau theatre" (1731, vol. I., p. 48). In Spain however the "Matachin" — according to Pedrell's "Cancionero Musical Popular Espagnol" — was played in the following way,

and Gluck's dance goes as follows (almost identical with the "Matachin") etc.

More famous became the Fandango (No. 19) of the dinner music which was used by Mozart as a ballet in "Figaro", when the peasants appear before the Count to pay homage to him. This Fandango was a genuine Andalusian melody, which had however been known in Vienna for a long time, in fact so long that contradances were danced to its strains and that the German expert of gymnastics, Gerhard Ulrich Vieth, quoted it in his "Versuch einer Enzyklopaedie der Leibesuebungen" ("Encyclopedia of Gymnastic Exercises") (1794-1818).

In a later chapter we shall return to the Fandango which brings our discussion to that period of History of dance music when new and forceful dances, rooting in the rhythms and melodies of the people, were about to develop. It was the time when strong national feelings and class consciousness arose and mirrored themselves in both the way of living and in the literature, the music and art of the people, — and naturally also in their dances and in their dance music.

Among all the contributions offered by Europe's manifold nations, among all those characteristic dances and colorful dance tunes, it is the Waltz — a contribution of the German people — which deserves no doubt the prize.

CHAPTER XI.

THE AGE OF THE WALTZ.

THE waltz is not a product of the 19th century, arising spontaneously at this time, nor is it true that for the first time a
waltz was heard in Vincente Martin's opera "Una cosa rara",
which appeared in 1786. One needs only to compare this "first"
waltz of the Spaniard Martin with one of the many airs

written by Schmelzer to see what nonsense such an assertion
is. The fact is that the waltz was born in the suburbs of
Vienna and in the Alpine lands of Austria, and that the first
waltzes, having a definite artistic musical form, were played
for the ballrooms of the Austrian Court around 1660. Even
before that time the "Weller" had been danced by peasants
both in Austria and in South Germany. When the connection
between Schmelzer and Johann Strauss, — between the musical periods of the Baroque age and the so-called Biedermeier
(we might call it "early Victorian") — has been uncovered, I
trust that this question concerning the origin of the waltz will
be settled once and for all.

In spite of early roots of the waltz, the true "waltz-period"
did not begin until the cultural background was ready for it.

The plea for "a return to nature" found, as far as the dance was concerned, its most radical expression in the adoption of the waltz. The "Contre" was only a transitory phase preparing for a new democratic period and stood for it. Yet it fell into disuse. A dance calendar of the year 1801 states that "the English dances have no character. All they consist of is kicking and leaping to the measure, and this is falsely called dancing". The transformation of society — so bloody in France, so apparent in the rest of Europe — had to bring along a revolution of the dance. New spirit, new movements were necessary. No longer could the formal artificial minuets and gavottes, the dances of a now rejected, courtly and aristocratic civilization prevail. This trend to a freer, less hampered emotional expression of bodily movements, such as we found it in the Baroque "Wirtschaften" (hoteleries) and peasant weddings, had shown itself only in the intimate closed entertainments of aristocratic society. But now with the rise of the "third class" it became more universal. Natural and spontaneous dancing became "the fashion"; and the German, — that is to say — the South-German, - Austrian form of the peasant dance, was taken over. What this revolution meant for the life of society is seen in the wild discussion pro and contra. At the head of the party against the Waltz stood the dancing-masters who for the first time saw themselves ignored. Chavanne, writing in 1767 in his "Principes du Menuet" says that the waltz has no relation whatsoever to "la bonne danse", and the author Vigée exclaims: "I can imagine that the mothers are fond of the waltz, but not that they permit their daughters to dance it."

But what was the good of all this antagonism? "Une valse, oh, encore une valse", was the cry of the young people of Paris, according to a report of the German writer and traveller, E. M. Arndt, in 1804. "This love for the waltz and this adoption of the German dance is quite new, it has become one of the vulgar fashions since the war, like smoking". Surely, this is a recognition of the psychological background for the vogue of the waltz, and it is not surprising that the court circles obstinately held out against the waltz even down to our own time. The Princess Radziwill in her "memoirs" tells us that the two Princesses of Mecklenburg, (one of whom the famous Queen Louise), were the first who dared to dance a waltz in 1794 at a court ball in Berlin. Though the old King was charmed, the Queen turned away her eyes in disgust, and forbid her daughters to imitate the princesses. This ban of the waltz prevailed at the Berlin Court down to the time of William II. At the Russian Court waltzes were not introduced until after the death of Catherine I., not until 1798, when the mistress of Paul I., Princess Lapuchin, danced the condemned steps for the first time. In England, the land of strict morale adhering to its "contre", it took even longer. Boehn tells in his book "The Dance" how the young Count of Devonshire returning to London from Paris, long after Napoleon had been sent to St. Helena, expressed his surprise that the young English ladies did not dance the waltz. But when he found at his next ball that his admonition had been followed and all the young women were swaying languidly to the strains of the new dance, he turned away shocked, and vowed never to espouse one of these "shameless creatures". When the first official sanction was given to the waltz by its inclusion at a ball given by the Prince Regent on July 13th, 1816, the London "Times" published a violent outcry against such immorality, and even Lord Byron, elsewhere not afraid to offend English sensibility, was not slow to condemn the waltz in strong words.

But in spite of all this the waltz ran its triumphant course. At the congress of Vienna 1814-1815, it was danced again and again. It was native there, and had been danced for a long time as "Laendler", "German", and "Langaus". (The "Langaus" was a distortion of an old folk dance in which the couples danced to a two-beat measure through a large space, but with the smallest possible number of turns.) The old dance forms had been danced on unpolished floor with hob-nailed shoes beating the ground: here, in society, the dance took up the gliding, sliding step. Thus the "high" (hopping) dance became a "low" (sliding) dance. The wide paces became small ones. But in its essential character the waltz remained what the laendler had already been: a ternary dance with a strongly accented first beat, to which the couples, in close embrace, turn on their own axis, at the same time circling around the room. Sachs has pointed to the fact that this movement resembles that of the course of the stars, and one might at this point remember the old astral dances, imitating the movements of the heavenly bodies.

Has not the impulse of the waltz perchance in its primitive origin some mysterious connection with that great cosmical law?

The shaping of the waltz, as we know it today, took some time. In the beginning the old fashioned form of leading the lady to the dance was customary and Vieth says in his "Enzyklopaedie der Leibesuebungen" (physical training): "Many different couples can waltz around one behind the other, if all of them follow one couple and keep well on the circumference of the circle". This is a sort of "Dictated" transition period of the waltz in which one couple is chosen to take the lead. During this phase the circling of the couples may still lead to confusion. But soon balance and harmony are introduced especially in those countries where the dancing masters give their attention to the waltz. The new and characteristic feature is that the couples dance in close embrace, no longer using the arm and hand interlocking gestures of the Laendler. Yet there are many transitional forms. Thomas Wilson in 1816 distinguished two kinds of waltzes, the French and the German: the French has four paces forward at the beginning, the German skips these. It is impossible, however, to give in detail all the variations through which the waltz passed in the course of the nineteenth century. Let us rather dwell on the music.

In the previous chapters we have pointed to the extrovert and wide paced character of the minuet of the eighteenth century. We have, however, seen that already in the seventeenth century Schmelzer's dances, influenced by the instrumental music of the Alpine regions and by the "yodler" showed wide spaced forms of dance-music. Let me point here to a "Braderdantz zu Wienn" of the year 1681, which I published in the

"Denkmaeler der Tonkunst in Oesterreich". This is already an example of melodic line with wide intervals

In this respect it resembles the greater part of the Viennese dances of the seventeenth and eighteenth centuries.

In the countless musical comedies appearing around 1750 which are our sources for the folk art of that time, written by the famous Viennese clown Felix von Kurz, called "Bernardon", we find numerous waltzes even designated by name as such "Walzer". To this example

the clown sang the words:

"Bald walzen umadum
Mit heirassa drum"

("Turn about waltzing and
Cheer as you turn")

It may be assumed that the composer of this music was Joseph Haydn who occasionally wrote the music for contemporary comedies. This surely dismisses the legend of Martin's "Cosa rara", not to speak of the fact that not only on Kurz's stage but at the court-performances of Leopold I. waltzes were played and danced. Indeed, all these waltzes are wide-spaced dances and resemble each other, from Weber's "Invitation to the Dance" and the waltzes in his "Freischuetz", on to Strauss' "Blue Danube". The folklore and musical research of the Austrian musicologists Pommer, Zoder and Kronfuss have shown that many waltz airs can be traced back to simple yodeling melodies. This is surely the case in that "waltz of all waltzes" "The Blue Danube". Conversely many waltzes written by Austrians have in their turn shaped the character of Austrian folksongs. This intimate connection of the Alpine Yodler with the Viennese Waltz shows us clearly how the virile, peasant cultural character shapes musical history, and how the primitive erotic strength so clearly seen in the Alpine melodies influences the new forms of dance music. Even Bach did not disdain peasant dance music. In the overture to his "Bauernkantate" (Peasant Cantata) he has a true rustic waltz, such as was danced customarily in the Province of Lausitz, where there was a strong Slavic peasant element.

Permit me to interpolate a few remarks on the word "waltz". The derivation from "volta" which we found in some dictionaries has been recognized as an error. In old German "walzen" means to "wander", to stroll. Another meaning of the word is to turn, to roll, to glide (schleifen). In 1760 the word occurs in a "Verbot gegen walzende Taenze" (prohibition of waltzing dances). Goethe in his poem "Hochzeitslied" uses the word "walzen". But it seems to me that the Kurz-Bernardon quotation given above, is the earliest instance. The name spread over Europe as quickly as the dance. Gretry in 1784 entitled a piece in 3/4 time "air pour valser".

At the beginning of the 19th century the designations "Deutscher Laendler" and "Walzer" were used indiscriminately, but the "Laendler" was played more slowly than the waltz, and the Czech composer Vincenz Maschek, (famous for having made the first piano score of Mozart's "Figaro",) published a collection of these dances in 1803. The critic of one of the music journals of the time thought it was a good thing that Maschek had added to his "Laendler": to be played more slowly than the "German dances".

In his treatise "Zur Entwicklung des Walzers", Ignaz Mendelssohn has pointed out the importance of the composer F. H. Himmel (1765-1814). This musician, known as the composer of songs and operas and of the operetta "Franchon" was one of Goethe's friends, who met him frequently in Karlsbad. Himmel, a most exuberant and lively personality, a man of great girth and, as Goethe says, "improving the tone of the poorest instruments when he played on them", followed the slogan "carpe diem". Goethe wrote about him in 1811 to Zelter: "I haven't had much opportunity to see or hear him because he leads such a gay life." In 1810 Himmel wrote as op. 30, "Sechs grosse Walzer fuer Liebhaber des Pianoforte". Twenty years before Strauss and Lanner made the waltz with six divisions to be the general type, Himmel wrote a sequence of 6 waltzes, joined to each other by the interrelation of their respective keys: C major - G major - C major - F major - C major. Besides, the "da capo-form" of the Viennese waltz which we meet in later compositions is already indicated here. Himmel, who stayed in Vienna in 1802, surely must have heard the musicians of the suburbs of Vienna: Grinzing and Moedling; and bits of his waltzes give us a premonition of Johann Strauss. It must be said, however, that dances with 6 divisions are found already in Mozart's German Dances, together with coda-and da capo-forms. It was not at all unusual to join six dances. F. H. Himmel should not be confused with Johann Nepomuk Hummel, the renowned pianist, who also had his share in the development of the Viennese waltz, writing a series of such dances in 1808 for the Viennese "Apollo Hall". He wrote gracefully constructed "Germans" with delicate trios and brilliant, independent codas with flourishes of trumpets and rolls of drums. As pianist of great virtuosity Hummel knew how to write dazzling bravoura passages, but lacked all the convincing melodic charm of the Viennese "Walzerer" (waltz composers). One cannot dance to the coda, nor are the dances organically joined one to the other.

All during this time before and during the Viennese Congress, dancing was the most popular form of amusement, and a large quantity of dance music was published: Emanuel Aloys Foerster (1747-1823), published simple, tuneful dance music in his "Tedeschi per il clavicembalo": Anton Eberl, adhering to his idol Mozart, wrote many minuets: the Prague composers Vinzenz and Paul Maschek, Franz Duschek, Beethoven's famous copyist Volanek, and J. J. Ryba also imitated Mozart. Nikolaus von Krufft (1779-1818), wrote dances, paying great attention to the elaboration of the middle parts, while Joseph Woelfl (1772-1812), contemporary of Beethoven, and his rival as a piano virtuoso distinguished himself by tunefulness. Anton Diabelli (1781-1858) made immortal by Beethoven's variations on his waltz theme, should be mentioned here. Among the composers let me enumerate a few more: Hofkapellmeister Joseph Eybler (1764-1846), a friend of Mozart's, the guitarist and composer J. Amon (1763-1825); J. J. F. Dotzauer, and C. H. Rink. Far above the crowd of musicians tower the figures of the two great Romantic composers Karl Maria von Weber and Franz Schubert. Weber in his "Freischuetz" (1819) gave us a waltz of such compelling natural charm that it may be ranked together with his "Invitation to the Dance" among other classic waltzes as we find them in the compositions of Schubert, Lanner and Strauss. Their common characteristic is an introduction of 3 bars with the typical apoggiatura on the dominant, the fourth bar having the typical waltz upbeat, followed by three periods of eight bars each. The accompaniment is the characteristic bass of the guitar accompaniment (popularly depicted as an "m-ta-ta, m-ta-ta") which originated in the instrumentation of laendlers and waltzes in Upper Austria, with 2 violins, guitar and bass—an ensemble still used in the taverns selling new wine (Heurigenschaenke). This kind of accompaniment was used as early as in the 17th century, as shown in the musical example of the Viennese "Braderdantz". There is also a connection with the yodler. But we should not forget that it originates in the triademelodics.

The melody of the "Freischuetz-Waltz" had been known in Bohemia for a long time, and it was not surprising that Weber, who drew upon Bohemian folk-lore sources, should have received his inspiration from there.

But the "Invitation to the Dance" was even more influential in shaping the form of waltz composition. The slow introduction led directly to the development of Strauss' waltz introductions. Here in Weber's work the masses definitely accentuate the first quavers, and the "guitar bass" is perceptible everywhere. In spite of its rondo form, the waltz was admitted for use in ballrooms and we have here an example of highly cultivated dance form used for practical purposes. Also here, the idea of the suite is retained. Just like the dances in Beethoven's Seventh Symphony, Weber's masterpiece is a poetic treatment of dance forms. Weber himself later gave the piece the well-known programmatic notes in which he described it as an idealized form of a courting dance. What force, grace and tenderness is expressed in its rhythms and melodies! Indeed, Weber, one of the great talents in the history of dance music, expressed in it all his exuberant joy of living and the dynamic force of his emotions.

Let me interpolate at this point a little-known episode dating from Weber's stay at Prague. I have already drawn attention in the "Zeitschrift fuer Musik" to an unknown Ecossaise by Weber which was probably composed in Prague and published in the "Almanach" of 1830 for the Prague Carnival (at S. W. Enders, Prague).

A Prague source reports that Weber was, like Mozart, passionately fond of dancing and occasionally improvised ballets himself. For the eve of Lent in 1814, he arranged a procession of masks; musicians carried instruments covered with black crepe with the device on their caps: "No more fiddling". Harlequins carried a charming Columbine on a litter, weeping women followed in the costume of Pierrot. Behind the mask of "Carnival", impersonated by a fat and sallow innkeeper, came Death himself in the person of Karl Maria von Weber, munching a cruller and carrying a sign with the words: "No more dining, no more wining, no more dancing"! Three masked characters followed representing bankruptcy, a "hangover" and the pawn shop. In this fantastic representation we see the converse of the sensitive and emotional poet-musician. It represents in crude and coarse form that state of mind of the Romantic writers and poets: Death lurks behind the sweet pulse of life. This is no longer the optimistically triumphant strength of the classical masters, challenging Fate, — but a philosophy conscious of enforced resignation that follows joy and gaiety. Weber typifies that longing for a world beyond reality, a world of fairy creatures, far removed from the pains of actual existence.

The second of the great Romanticists was Franz Schubert. It was he who actually presented the Viennese waltz as a gift to the world. However, there was no innovation in form, because in the introduction and the coda Schubert kept close to the tradition. His dances consist of 8 - 18 bars; for, not adhering to the number 6, he wrote as many as he pleased. But when he combined them they formed an organic whole. His "Germans" and "Laendlers", his "Waltzes" (which he once calls "Originaltaenze op. 9") are in truth nothing but suites conceived in the modern spirit. The mood of any one dance passes over smoothly and naturally into that of the next, and this transition always obeys psychological laws. It has been noticed repeatedly that Schubert's instrumental works express much more clearly the joys and pains of his own life than his songs in which the limits set by vocal expression constrained him. In his piano works he unfolds harmonies which, by the vigor and tempestuousness of his figurations, give us insight to the dreadful battle within his mind. This mighty struggle with its overwhelming massing of sound is followed by melodies expressing sweet and deep melancholy.

The same quality shows itself in Schubert's waltzes and laendlers. As no other composer he encloses all the sweetness and all the bitterness of life, in his rhythms and melodies. The series of waltzes, op. 18 (waltzes, laendler, ecossaises) begins with those triumphant "Atzenbruck dances", whose vigor recalls the glamorous parties of the Vienna Congress: Full and rich chords in bright E major, ominously shifting over to a minor key, — a beautiful trio follows and listening to it, we all of a sudden find ourselves out in the country, in Poetzleinsdorf, the lovely and picturesque village near Vienna . . . languidly we give in to its charms, but surprisingly, with triumphant double octaves, appears a solemn A minor part, just as if the composer did not want to be too sentimental and too sweet. But soon again the energetic sound of the A minor octaves plays into a friendly and mild A major, leading our feelings back to nature and peasant life . . . a delightful C sharp minor part follows.

"Pull yourself together with all your might" is the call of these giant chords. A transitory G major episode surprises here, followed by the miracle of a waltz in b minor, telling about all the sorrows and blissful memories granted to a humble human being.

Out there in Grinzing, situated on the outskirts of Vienna and overlooking the city as well as the lovely mountains and woods and the silvery shining ribbon of the Danube river, — Schubert listens to the awkward fiddling of the "Heurigen"-musicians, and, surrounded by his friends, — his glass of "Heurigen" wine before him on the table, he would see the world in rosy colors, — yet, at the same time he feels deep in his heart the futility and the quick fading of all the beauty around him. . . .

Technically, and in the terms of our theory of the suite, we have to stress again the old principle of contrast. Let us, for example, take the "Valses nobles" op. 77, the brilliant flowering of the waltzes in C major, A major, and A minor, immediately followed by a languidly swaying waltz in F major! Theme and mood of one waltz organically blend with that of the next one, just as it is the case in No. 9 of the "Valses nobles" in A minor — which most distinctly harks back to waltz No. 5 also in A minor (Liszt has used it in his "Soirées de Vienne"). How often the moods shift over from major to minor, how harassing are the modulations into and from distant keys! These different moods are like the changing moods in Schubert's heart. He loves life, — it seems to him ever so new, ever more beautiful, ever more sweet, — all the more that he knows how soon all will be over, how soon after the blooming and gay Spring and Summer, Winter and death will come . . . Schubert's famous song "Der Wanderer" and his wonderful "Wanderer Fantasy" are the true pictures of the master's life with their words and motto: "Where you are not, there dwells the happiness of life". . . .

When we turn the pages in the manifold volumes of dance music in the Austrian libraries we are liable to find numerous dances whose composers are forgotten today. There is, for instance, a certain Martin Schuller, who in 1818 wrote "Graetzer Redoute — Deutsche" (German for the balls of the town of Graz), of Karl Eduard Hartknoch (the name means "hardbone", but had obviously no effect upon the composer's character, who dedicated his "Six Waltzes" to Mme Fanny Mendelssohn). André Spaeth, Albrecht Gottlieb Methfessel, and the Czech composers Jan Horzalka and Anton Krch should, at least be mentioned. About the latter, the famous music historian of Prague, Ambros, asserts ironically that only the impossibility to pronounce his name has barred him from becoming famous. Altogether, the Czech composers ·have an important part in this early era of the waltz. We find such Czech names as Wrba, Pichl, Cibulka, Neruda, etc. It is strange how little German musicians — with the exception of Weber — contributed to the development of the waltz, compared with Austria. However, the names C. Goerner and Otto Karl Claudius should be mentioned. Their dances are written in primitive periods of eight bars, and sound somehow stiff.

More important are the immediate predecessors of Lanner and Strauss, — Ferdinand Gruber and Michael Pamer. The former wrote waltzes whose introduction comprise 10-14 bars, and often uses themes of laendlers with those typical Lombardic rhythms, which later became popular through Lanner and Strauss, for example in Lanner's "Schoenbrunn Waltz",

As Lanner's immediate predecessor, however, we may consider Michael Pamer. He wrote "Dances of the Town of Linz", (Linzer Taenze), Upper Austrian laendler, series of waltzes with introductions called "Entry" or "Tusch" (flourish). "Tusch" is the German form of the French word "toucher" (English : touch) which, here, means "to blow", ("toccare" in Italian). (Compare Monteverdi's "Toccata", an introduction to his "Orfeo", written for wind-instruments). But the single waltzes are still in one and the same key. The most interesting piece of work is Pamer's collection "Verschiedene Taenze, Ekkossaisen, Monimasques, Madratura, Mazurka, Milaneise, Altvater, Kallopade, boehmischer Konfusionstanz, Calamaika, komponiert fuer die grossen Gesellschaftsbaelle fuer den Karneval 1818". (Different dances . . . written for the great balls for the Carnival of 1818"). I could not determine what "Monimasques" means. It might be a special kind of masquerade. Madratura seems to be a Slavic dance, no longer existing, and therefore hard to define. Calamaika is a Bohemian folk dance in 2/4 time, originating in Kolomea in Carpatho-Russia, where it is danced with a heavy "Dumka" as introduction. The Bohemian Confusiondantz (confused dance) might be the "Beseda", the Czech form of the contradance, whereas the Kalopade is, of course, nothing else but a Galop, — that fast round dance in 2/4 rhythm, obviously no North German invention of around 1825, as Junk's "Lexicon of the Dance" asserts. It is the simplest round dance and consists of alternating sideward-steps and waltz-like circles. It is always danced at the end of the ball, and therefore recalls the fast hopping-dance of the old suite confirming our theory that the fast hopping dance is a consequence of the rising excitement of dancing. Finally the "Altvater" ("Old father") should be mentioned, most probably the old "Grossvatertanz" (Grandfather's dance), which has been mentioned repeatedly.

But let us come back to the waltz. Every visitor of Vienna will recall the monument erected in honor of the two kings of the waltz, Lanner and Strauss. Franz Lanner's life was very simple. He was born in 1801 and died in 1843 in Vienna, which he never left, except for Milan, where a festival of the Vienna Court took place. He was never a man-about-town and was better at playing dance tunes for the ladies than at courting them. Once, at a court ball after a long and strenuous performance of a minuet he tried to show an archduchess how wilted his shirt was from perspiration. The noble lady was shocked

—can you imagine—and his career came to an end. He began as a violinist of a quartet, just like all the tavern fiddlers of Doebling, Grinzing and Poetzleinsdorf; later on he played with great success at the "Waellisches Bierhaus" on the "Praterstrasse", and still later at the "Rebhuhn" ("Partridge Inn"), where Franz Schubert and his friend, the famous painter Moritz von Schwind, liked to listen to him. Soon his quartet was enlarged into an orchestra, which quickly became very popular. His colleague was Johann Strauss — not yet the waltz king, but his father. Strauss was only three years younger than Lanner, and was the son of an innkeeper in the Viennese suburb, "Leopoldstadt". When a little boy, he often heard the "Linz Fiddlers" who accompanied the boats coming down the Danube from Linz, playing their old Laendlers. Those musicians and later the old Pamer — who by the way was famed for his insatiable thirst — were his teachers. Johann Strauss joined the Lanner orchestra as violist and soon a most harmonious friendship and collaboration developed. Why both parted at last is convincingly told by Johann Strauss, the "Waltz King" in the complete edition of his father's works. There we obtain some interesting insight into the method of work of those Viennese dance composers: "To write music seems to have been an easier art in former days than nowadays. You had to have an idea, and — strange as it seems — you always got one. Self-confidence in this respect was so great that we often announced a waltz-party for a certain evening, though in the morning of this very day not a single note of the evening's music was written. In such a case the orchestra members usually appeared at the composer's apartment. As soon as he had completed part of the new score, the musicians prepared it for the orchestra, copied the parts, etc. Meanwhile the miracle of inspiration repeated itself upon command within the composer's mind, he wrote the remaining pieces and a few hours later the whole music was finished. Then it was re-hearsed, and its performance on the same evening met with an enthusiastic response. Lanner, light as he was at heart and in mind, never had trouble in inventing his charming melodies. But one morning it happened that he felt very ill and incapable of work, although a new waltz party had been announced for the same evening. Not a single bar of it had been written! So he sent a message to my father: "Strauss, see that you get some inspiration, will you?" The same evening the waltzes — featured, of course as written by Lanner — were performed and enthusiastically applauded. This fact, together with his getting married in the same year, caused my father to be on his own from now on."

However, there are rumors saying that this separation had not taken place in such a peaceful way. Strauss was very ambitious, and Lanner was a pocket-size autocrat. At the "Bock" ("Ram's Inn") on the "Wieden" (a suburb of Vienna), their last joint appearance took place. And right on the platform the breach in their friendship occurred, caused by a fiery argument — and, as on the occasion of the "box on the ear"-scene between the singers La Cuzzoni and Faustina Hasse in London — the guests looked on as though they were witnessing a coup d'état. Bows of violins soared through the air, flutes and clarinets served to keep the enemy off, and a row of the first "musical" order developed, acclaimed by some ladies in the background of the hall.

Just as Heine made his "little songs out of his great pains", —Lanner wrote his "parting waltz" out of his grief about the separation, and from this evening on, Vienna had two leading orchestras,—the new one of course the "Strauss Orchestra". When Lanner died, twenty thousand Viennese people followed his coffin, and the slogan sprang up: "Lanner oder Kaner!" ("Lanner or none!"). There are many who rate his work above that of the waltz king "Johann II".

Johann Strauss tried to conquer Vienna first from the suburbs. His "Taeuberln Walzer" ("Waltz of the Little Doves") op. 1, was, — together with some other works of his — considered worthy of being included in the "Denkmaeler der Tonkunst in Oesterreich" ("Monuments of Music in Austria"), edited by Hans Gal. It recalls his first triumph at the inn "Zu den zwei Tauben" (Inn of the Two Doves). From then on, his fame rose rapidly. Everybody talked only of Strauss, everywhere his waltzes were played, — the street urchins whistled the new melodies.

In the fall of 1830, Chopin came to Vienna, He noted regretfully, "you can't find much seriousness in Vienna. The music of Lanner and Strauss drew out everything else."

Two years later the nineteen year old Richard Wagner was a guest of the Austrian capital. His instinct made him prize the genuineness and originality of Lanner's and Strauss' strictly Viennese melodies. His most important experience was "that strange man, Strauss, whose violin casts spells on the people is the incarnation of Vienna's popular spirit".

While Lanner hardly ever left the limits of Vienna, Father Strauss tended more towards other lands. He visited the court of the King of Prussia, and when—33 years old—he went to France, defeated the national idol of Paris, Musard, (though supported by an orchestra considered inferior to that of Musard), and charmed such musical heroes as Cherubini, Halevy, Meyerbeer and Berlioz. Auber threw flowers at him, and Paganini embraced him in front of the audience. At the head of his "victorious army" he crossed the Channel and conquered London, where the coronation of Queen Victoria took place to the strains of Strauss' music. It was then that he considered a trip to America, but his musicians, succumbing to home-sickness forced him to return to Vienna. Here he had in the meantime become an authority. Everybody knew him, — the lank and elegant musician with the distinctive head, the coquettish little moustache and the tuft of bushy hair.

This was "Johann I.", the father of Johann II., who was called the uncrowned "King of Austria". Father Strauss was only 21 when his son was born. The gifted youngster, at the age of six, wrote a real waltz, with a somewhat limping rhythm (as he put the upbeat on the first of the three quarters), but still showing obvious originality. When Johann — called "Jean" in the French way (modulated into the Viennese form "Schani"), was grown up, he published it under the title "First Inspiration".

Father Strauss did not want his three sons: Johann II., Eduard, and Joseph, to become musicians. In vain! "Schani" learned secretly to play the violin — and finally his father could not object any more. It even happened at times that the son helped him in writing music, and this with full success.

The life of Father Strauss was indeed not easy. He was more than tied up with work. He was the leader of three orchestras, and as most of the time all of them played at the *same* time, he had to hurry from one place to the other. When appearing, he was frantically applauded, played one or two waltzes himself, then left his orchestra under the guidance of his first violinist and hurried to his second orchestra. And thus it went on and on. There was little spare time left for his private life. His wife Anna Maria, incidentally, had some Spanish blood in her veins, and was born in Madrid. We know very well that the influx of foreign blood often helps to bring out the best and strongest national elements. Thus specifically· Viennese quality of the Strausses is most probably enhanced by their Spanish ancestry, just as Schubert's Viennese mode of music is enhanced by the few drops of Czech blood in the veins of his parents.

The Father was so preoccupied by the excessive amount of his work, that he lived more without than within his family; moreover, the Viennese musician's blood stormed through his veins in a somewhat frightening manner. He was immensely spoiled by the ladies, who saw in this elegant musician the incarnation of the gods of love and pleasure.

In the meantime Johann, the son, had yielded to the urge of his creative musical genius. He established an orchestra for himself and became ever more famous. The father was partly proud, partly felt himself threatened. His last success was the "Radetzky March" which raised his popularity beyond all measures. Then, on the 23rd of September, 1849, he died, a year after the "bourgeois revolution".

While Father Strauss had adhered to conservative ideas, being "Imperial Court-Ball-Music-Director", the son was a revolutionary, and orchestra leader of the National Guard. It took a long time until the Court had forgotten and forgiven the sins of his youth, and appointed him Court Ball-Music-Director (1864).

Is it possible to draw the outlines of the most abundant and successful life of a musician, only devoted to dance music? Those twelve summers in Russia, (from 1855 on) where he aroused unequalled enthusiasm, seriously endangering the court's moral code and infatuating the hearts of the ladies with his Viennese rhythms . . . his unsurpassed triumphs at the "Paris World's Fair",˙ when Johann Strauss and "Le beau Danube d'azur" became the talk of the salons and cafés! . . .

Let me only tell briefly about Strauss' American tour. In 1872 Boston celebrated the hundredth anniversary of Massachusetts' movement for a separation from England. Monster concerts were planned, and Strauss was invited to conduct them. Free transportation for him, his wife and his servants, and a $100,000 salary, deposited with a bank in Vienna, were offered to him. In Boston he was greeted by colossal posters showing him as a King, enthroned upon the globe, waving his baton like a sceptre above the universe. These posters contained more than a grain of truth. According to his contract, Strauss had to conduct 14 concerts, which was easier to promise than to carry out. The concerts took place in a gigantic hall, built of wood, with a capacity of 100,000 people. The crowd lost all discipline. Women kissed the seams of his coat, he was besieged by autograph hunters! Young and less young women applied for a lock of his hair, until Stefan, his valet, feared "that the handsome Newfoundland dog from whom he cut away the beautiful 'original locks of Strauss' hair would return to Europe with a bald body." Twenty-thousand singers sang the Blue Danube waltz. In order to control them, Strauss had to post 100 subconductors at different places, who followed his beat and directed the multitude. "However", writes Strauss, "only those nearest to me could make out what I was doing, and all the rehearsals were useless as far as an ensemble of performance and a unified artistic whole was concerned. What a situation, facing an audience of 100,000! There I stood, not knowing what was going to happen and how it would end! A roar of cannon was the signal for us, twenty thousand, to begin, a tender reminder, indeed! I raised my baton, my sub-conductors followed me as swiftly as they could, and a mighty noise broke out. I'll never forget it as long as I live. As we had all begun to play and sing at about the same time, my only anxiety was that we should all finish at approximately the same time, and with God's help I succeeded!" ·

This is Strauss' report of the performance. On the 13th of July he landed safely again in Europe.

Strauss was married three times. His first wife, Henriette Treffz, was several years older than he and an ideal companion devoted to him. His third wife, Adele Deutsch, whom he married at the age of 58, was dearly beloved by him and served as an unending inspiration for his later work. Even in his later years, the joy of living, the spirit of making the most of the great and small delights of life, never left Strauss. He wrote to Adele with the same ardor that filled his days as a young man: "Let us be gay, man lives but once!"

These words may be taken for the watchword of this eager and ardent musician in whom primitive and unrestrained impulsiveness were combined with the highest forms of civic and courtly culture.

As Bach's ancestors had clung to the organ for decades and Mozart had, as it were found the conductor's baton in the cradle, so was Father Strauss born in the atmosphere of Viennese music. He had, as a child, still heard the Alpine airs on the barges carrying goods from the upper reaches of the Danube river — airs which had been shaped by the cries of the herdsmen in the mountains of Austria and Styria. The history of the Strauss dynasty is practically that of the waltz, from its beginnings as a mountain dance and song to its acceptance as a dance in the ballrooms of the Imperial Court.

When Strauss was buried on the 6th of June, 1899, by the side of Franz Schubert and Johannes Brahms (who by the way had called him "the most musical brain of Europe") his funeral was that of a King. His musical dictatorship of Austria was unprecedented, and his .Waltz rhythms unsurpassed.

In analysing the waltzes of Lanner and Johann Strauss senior we find these characteristics: Both of them have expanded the form of the waltz, developed its instrumentation, enlarged the introduction and the coda, and thus laid the foundation for the new melodic line of the waltz. Their first compositions still adhere to the old eight bar periods. Then these periods are expanded to include twelve and sixteen bars, until with Johann Strauss the younger, periods of thirty-two measures became prevalent. Even more remarkable is the expansion of the instrumentation. Beginning as tavern musicians, Lanner and the elder Strauss wrote their first compositions for a quartet, some of them for piano only. Gradually with the addition of ever more musicians the number of the instruments in the classic orchestra was finally reached, and in 1825 when the partnership between the two was dissolved there were two full dance orchestras left: The leading voice was taken by the first violin, the second violin gave the accompaniment or reinforced the first violin in a lower octave. The viola together with the second violin, — wherever the latter is accompaniment — provided the harmony for the weak parts of the measure and this same function was fitted by the cello. The double bass serves as an accompaniment. The woodwinds reinforce the strings, but occasionally appear independently, and the bassoon is merely an accompanying instrument. The brasses too are used for accompaniment except where the trumpet becomes the leading voice in fortissimo passages. Tympanum and small drums serve to give accent to various parts of the bar. The tympanum beats the "one" and the drum goes on with "two" and "three".

We have already noted that Pamer, the teacher of Lanner, was accustomed to introduce his Laendler with passages which he called "Tusch" (flourish). His pupils took over this habit as a matter of course. The introduction to Lanner's opus 4, "The Jovatsdorfer Laendler" with its lively marching rhythms in 4/4 cannot be mentioned in the same breath with those used by Weber in his "Invitation to the Dance". Such "Tusches" were the offspring of the old entries, (intrada), though, in fact these had never ceased to be used, as the custom had continued to sound a flourish, to call the dancers to order, before the dance itself began. As time goes on, these introductions became more and more important, until, viewed from a musical point of view, they actually constituted the nucleus of the waltz itself. Schubert, too, introduced his "Zwoelf Laendler" with an oversized laendler, the purpose of which is to call everybody to attention. Appealing to the ear, the themes of the dance which was to be played were indicated, and the mood of the dancer set for what was to follow. Pamer even went so far as to repeat the four measures of the introduction before each one of the dance parts, apparently to give the couples an opportunity to "pause and rally".

But later practices have a different purpose. Entry-like marching rhythms in vigorous 4/4 measure used in the "Introduction" alternate with bars in 3/4 time. In this way, Lanner has shaped the introduction to his "Pester Walzer" (Waltz of Budapest). After marching to eight bars, the post-man's horn plays the farewell. Then the movement grows faster, as "one approaches the Hungarian capital", which is reached after 28 bars, and now the waltz begins.

Another example is Lanner's "Hymen's Feier Klaenge", dedicated to the Archduchess Maria Theresia. The flourish of trumpets indicates the wedding procession followed by the triplets of the violins, and finally an Andante sings the melody of the German folk song: "Farewell, oh home of quiet peace" (So leb denn wohl, Du stilles Haus). But the repetition of the jubilant notes soon follows this sentimental farewell. We have here a replica of the form of the old Italian overture with its scheme of "fast — slow — fast", and we find ourselves again in the presence of the suite. Remembering the pageant type of the suites used in the Baroque period, with an intrada at the beginning and a retirada (leave-taking) at the close — we cannot overlook the close resemblance between these "Suites" of the 19th century and the old forms. For example, the

waltz called "Die Petersburger", which Lanner dedicated as
"Russian National Waltz" to Czar Nicholas I. begins with a
solemn Andante harking back to Russian folk-lore. The dances
that follow are quite neutral except for the fifth which reproduces the Russian hymn of the Czars in lively waltz time.

Speaking of Johann Strauss, the son, we find these introductions turned into veritable tone pictures. Take the "Blue
Danube", for instance, with its introduction, (slow - fast)
where the rising waves are depicted against a background of
floating string tremoli. The landscape is enlivened, water sprites
appear and finally join in a round. A similar use of the triad
is made by Wagner in his "Rheingold", apparently it is the
"Urmotiv" (Primary motif) for the portrayal of moving
water, (compare also the "Vlatava" by Smetana with its divided
triads!)

The "Blue Danube" was composed for singing voices, except
for the introduction, but there is no doubt that it was conceived
from an instrumental point of view, in spite of the silly text
used for it. It was not exactly the happiest time in the history
of Austria when the waltz resounded in Vienna for the first
time, in 1867. Austria had just suffered a severe defeat at
the hands of Prussia, and the process of disintegration of the
Austrian Empire had begun. The text of the waltz reminds
one vividly of the political and economic depression, even
though the melancholic background has been twisted voluntarily
into something comical. After the financial depression resulting
from the war everybody was on the look-out for the famous
silver lining to show itself, preferably in the stock market.
But nothing of the sort was to be seen, and so the Viennese
"Maenergesangsverein" sang the waltz to the following text:

"Wiener seid froh."	* "Viennese, be gay."
"Oho, wieso?"	* "What's that you say?"
"Ein Schimmer des Lichts. . ."*	"A shimmer of light. . ."
"Wir sehen nichts".	* "There is naught in sight."
"Der Fasching ist da. . ."	* "The Carnival is here. . ."
"Ah so, na ja. . ."	* "Well, well, hear, hear."

"Was hilft denn das Trauern * "What helps then your fretting
Und das Bedauern?"   * And all regretting?"
"Drum froh und heiter seid." * "Hence gay and merry be."

Who does not feel the eternal truth in this somewhat stupid text, now after almost 80 years have passed? But the music of Strauss stabs through all melancholy, all weakness, and all doubt, in a victorious, sunny and yet so simple major chord.

In another Waltz, "Wein, Weib und Gesang", we have the same kind of programmatic introduction. Here various moods are shown in the themes, ending with the German song, which provided this waltz's title. In the waltz "Morgenblaetter" (morning papers) we have a programmatic imitation of the drone of the printing machines. Offenbach wrote a waltz called "Abendblaetter" which obviously inspired the title of this composition.

*   *   *

The coda which was already used by Mozart customarily made use of the thematic material of the preceding dances, usually of the last one in order. It was Strauss' artistic achievement, to know how to make the coda the most brilliant part, the climax of the whole piece. In the coda, each waltz of the series, each in its own key, was passed in review, re-appearing in veiled form, like reminiscences of a dream.

It was the violin which determined the melody of the Strauss waltzes. The melodic line which he used was based directly on the thirds and sixths, the legato, the passionato sforzato, the whispering dotted notes, the sentimental and song-like tone of the violin with its energetic yet tender accentuation. It was a melodic line which could appear only on a soil inhabited by emotionally fervid and gifted peoples, by a mixture of racial stocks — all of ardent temperament.

*   *   *

In defining the Waltz, we should not neglect to emphasize the relation between it and the oldest forms of the dance. With the Austrian Waltz — rooting in the musical expression of the Austrian peasants — we are reminded of Curt Sachs' theory, namely that virile cultures preferred the pantomimic forms of the dance, while the more feminine cultures tended to the non-pictorial dance. The Waltz is — in this respect — a combination of a dramatic picturesque introduction, followed by a non-pictorial series of Waltzes, and thus a reminder of primitive times. The male partner only leads his lady to the dance; he no longer reproduces that pantomime of courtship which preceded the dance itself in ancient days but that idea of courtship still persists in the subconscious, and the substitutes for the expressive gestures of olden times are now the light tone of talk, the glances, the pressing and clasping of hands. To my mind, the lasting quality and the force of the Strauss Waltzes is based on the picturesque, pantomimic background of the music. The fire and glow of Viennese temperament could surely not be better expressed than Strauss expressed it in his "Wiener Blut Walzer" (op. 354), where the thirds are swung to an interval of a sixth, and the prolongation of the first accented note sets the pace. In the "Voices of Spring" the gliding and leaping passages evoke the elves of the spring moods.

Strauss naturally had a large number of followers and disciples. There were his own brothers, Joseph and Eduard, the composers Suppé, Milloecker, Zeller, Reinhardt, Oskar Straus, Lehar and Stoltz among many others. None of them attained the natural force and the intensity of Strauss' music.

* * *

Although the waltz was unquestionably the most important dance of the 19th century, it was not the only dance performed at balls, and definitely had a number of important though minor rivals. Usually the balls of Society were introduced by a polonaise followed by waltzes, polkas, mazurkas and quadrilles (square dances). The final number was a "galop". We see here again the old principle of the suite applied in greatly expanded form with the polonaise taking the place of the ancient intrada, and the last number, the galop standing for the retirada. When we remember that in the 17th century a succession of the branles was used in the framework of a suite,

we see now, in the 19th century, the sequence of waltzes, —
a kind of suite — between the polonaise and the galop. But
the modern order never reached a point where the succession of
dances was strictly laid down by musical laws as it was in
olden times.

*

Let us now take up these other dances used in the 19th
century. Why did the polonaise obtain the place formerly
occupied by the intrada?

Polish dance melodies were known already in the 16th
century, when we found paired dances, consisting of one dance
in binary time, with a second hopping part in three fourths
time, both of them based on the same themes. Doubtlessly
these were performed as paced and leaped dances, like the
complementary dances pavane and gagliarda, and allemande and
courante. The first Polish dance which I know of, appears in
the previously mentioned lute book of Hans Neusiedler of
1544, a very early record. The characteristic of Polish folk-
lore is the lack of an upbeat and the Polish "jambimetre" — the
syncopation. Mattheson in 1739 describes the polonaise in the
"Vollkommenen Kapellmeister", but he has the form of the
later mazurka in mind. As an example he indicates how the
melody of the song, "Ich ruf zu Dir, Herr Jesu Christ" should
be treated when played as a polonaise.

Gradually a rhythm is developed which resembles that of
the sarabande, a feature of which is the frequently recurring
syncopation. In other polonaises we have a different rhythm.

The typical closing phrases of the polonaise appear in the
earliest Polish dances, in the 16th century. The second, the
"Nachtanz" with its ternary rhythm became an independent
dance, — the mazurka, with the three quarter rhythm, all
pointing to the old sarabande. On the other hand the Polish
dances with phrases like this:

or like those of Joseph Sychra (1772):

led to the polonaise of the 19th century for which some writers claimed Spanish origin.

It is said that originally the polonaise was a triumphal procession of old warriors and that women were not allowed to dance it until a later period. At any rate it was a stately, ceremonial round dance, strictly regulated as to the order of the dancers according to age and rank. Solemnly the gentlemen, with sword at their side, and the ladies, holding their long trains, marched to the sound of the polonaise. The only interruption of the procession was made when the male partner bowed his knee to the lady, or led her across to his left side, or when the whole line formed geometrical figures, like those "inventions" described by Praetorius, such as shells, stars, fans.

In 1719, the Saxon-Polish King, August the Strong, led the polonaise with the Queen at a great ball in Dresden. "To the sound of magnificent music, the King went ahead and the ladies and gentlemen followed. Before him walked four marshalls with their wands, and when this procession had lasted for about half an hour, the royal couple and the ladies sat down again. Thereupon the prince asked his consort to dance a minuet and after this there was English and German dancing".

Boehme believes that the polonaise never was a Polish national dance, but was merely developed at the Saxon-Polish court. Sachs however does not agree with him in this matter and to prove his point, he quotes a passage from the famous novel of A. Mickiewicz, "Pan Thaddeusz", which says, "here in the court of the castle, couples were crowded, ladies and officers, nobility and peasant people, and 'On with the polonaise!' is the cry of them all". The argument is not very strong, for it might readily have been possible that, by the 18th century, the court dance had been taken over by the people. One thing is clear, that this dance was particularly popular at the Saxon court and was greatly developed in the 18th century. It is therefore not surprising that in the Saxon collection of folk music of the 18th century, called "Die Singende Muse an der Pleisse", as well as in the work of Bach and of Handel we find numerous polonaises in 3/4 time which have the rhythm of the old "Moresca"

or the rhythm of the Spanish "Bolero",

which, by syncopation, finally arrives at this rhythm:

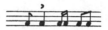

All these resemblances to Spanish dances have been noted frequently, and it may be true that similar influences, derived from the near East, swayed both the Slavic and the Spanish forms. We know that the same folk melodies not infrequently have appeared both in Spain and in the Slavic countries, as for example the Spanish folk song, "Virgen de la Cueva", the melody of which reappeared in the Jewish national song "Ha Tikva" as well as in the Polish song "Pod Krakowem". Smetana must have heard the tune sung by his countrymen before he used it in his symphonic poem "Vltava". We can still hear it in South America taken from Spain where the natives sing it to the rhythm of a habanera:

* * *

It is quite characteristic that Chopin put his hand to the composition of a bolero and that both Maurice Moszkowsky, the Russian Glinka and others, felt equally at home in the compositions of Spanish and of Slavic dances.

Be that as it may, the polonaise was one of the most popular dances of a long period, from the 16th to the 20th century. It was a favorite with the Renaissance composers, Hans Leo Hasler, Christoph Demantius, Valentin Hausmann. The German composer, Heinrich Albert, wrote polonaises. Even Johann Sebastian Bach wrote about 45 polonaises of which the most splendid is the one in the B minor suite. We have also a Polacca in one of the Brandenburg Concerti. Handel wrote a polonaise in E minor for the Third Concerto Grosso. Also Wilhelm Fr. Bach wrote twelve polonaises and so did J. Th. Goldberg (after whom J. S. Bach's famous variations were named.)

Mozart gave us a Rondo "en polonaise", in his D major Sonata. Surely he must have had Polish dance melodies in mind when he wished to write "exotic", that is, Turkish music. At any rate the second part of the Polonaise No. 85 in the "Diverse Danses pour le violon par Monsieur Nahler", Leipzig 1800, is that very famous aria of Monostatos from the Magic Flute and it is quite possible that Mozart heard the melody in Vienna or in Prague where it had already become popular by 1791. Nahler:

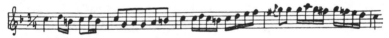

etc.

Beethoven too, wrote a polonaise, opus 89, dedicating it to the Empress of Russia in 1815, and a polacca included in his Serenade for Strings, opus 8, written in 1797. Schubert composed the magnificent polonaises, opus 61 and opus 75 for four hands. Weber's polonaises were great favorites. Ludwig Spohr incorporated a brilliant polonaise in his "Faust" (1818) which was on all the dance programs of the time, and Kreutzer's polonaise in the "Nachtlager von Granada", 1834, was equally popular. Wagner composed as his opus 2, in 1830, a polonaise for four hands.

Among the original Polish polonaises, the most renowned at the beginning of the 19th century, both in Europe and in

America, was the "Kosciusko" polonaise, so called after the
Polish hero who had fought at Washington's side during the
American Revolution. According to Boehme, this piece appeared soon after 1794, but its melodic line has little of the
folk quality of Polish music and altogether it seems somewhat
of a patchwork. After the introductory measures, we hear, in
changed form, the old "Marlborough" song, which is still sung
these days to the words, "We won't go home until morning".
There was also the "Totenpolonaise" by a well-known musician
of the time, Count Michael Oginski, (1765-1833), who is said
to have shot himself after the composition of this piece. The
Warsaw conductor, Karl Kasimir Kurpinski (1785-1857) is
also known as the composer of many polonaises.

Not unlike the suite of the Baroque Period which contained
dances of various nationalities, including German, French,
Spanish and English, — the music played at the balls of the
19th century, was made up of different national dances, including Polish, German, Czech, French, and English ones, i. e. the
polonaise, the waltz, the quadrille (contredanse), the polka and
the galop. Boehme doubts that the polka was a Czech dance
because the shift from one foot to another was customary in
the "Ecossaise". But we find this step already in the old
"Fleuret", and in the "Pas de Bourrée": it was in fact one of
the basic choreographic devices. The name of the dance is
Czech and means "a half step", (pulka), which signifies the
shift to the other foot. The Bohemian historian Alfred Waldau
tells us in his little book (published in 1859) about the Bohemian dance, that it was invented by a peasant girl who danced
it for her own amusement one Sunday afternoon. The teacher
of the village made a transcription of the melody, and in the
thirties the pulka was danced at the village festivals. In 1835,
it was first introduced in the ballrooms of Prague. A group
of musicians, going to Vienna, under the leadership of the
conductor Pergler, introduced it there, and immediately it
became a great favorite. In 1840, Raab, a dancing teacher of
Prague, danced this Bohemian polka at the Odeon Theatre in
Paris, and from there the new dance started its triumphant

career through all the elegant ball-rooms and in the high society of the French capital. The authority in the field of Bohemian dances, Zibrt, has corroborated this story. Waldau also reports that the first polka finding its way into the music shops was by Franz Hilmar, teacher in a small town near Koeniggraetz. This piece was played at the Scala in Milan and danced by the prima ballerina who won great applause "with the simple Bohemian dance".

The meter of the polka is 2/4 with the dance divided into four parts each consisting of 8 bars. There is also a trio. The "galop" is actually merely a polka in very fast time. On examining the melodic line of the polka, we find the same wide intervals used in the waltzes and the laendlers, which point to a common rustic origin. Czech dances have been recorded from the time of the Middle Ages. We also find them in the frequently mentioned Archives of Kremsier. In these "Hanakische", the polka rhythm is clearly indicated, as for example in the following:

Another instance of the early record of these rhythms is in the tablature for stringed keyboard instruments, set down by the "Jungfrau Clara Regina Im Hoff" (Ms. 18491 of the Vienna State Library). The following polka rhythm is intimately con-

nected with the shift from one foot to the other. We must also enumerate among the Czech dances a dance called "Rejdovak", which some have considered a derivation from the old "Ridevanz". It seems, however, much more likely that the name is connected with the Czech word rej, which means a round dance. It is also related to the Czech words which mean a place in which to turn about, to frolic. Like the polka this dance overran the European ball rooms, and created a furore not only in Paris, but even as distant as in New York. We find both redovas and polkas in early American publications.

There is the Redova: "A new Bohemian Waltz as danced
in the Parisian and London Saloons, and taught by Mr. Wm.
Whale. The figures by Cellarius composed by Ph. Cawlikowski,
edited by Riley & Co. 297 Broadway, New York". The
title page shows a Czech couple in native costumes. "Eight
Favorite Polkas" were published by E. Ferret & Co., Philadelphia, in 1845. Among the composers is listed also Labitzky,
the famous composer from Carlsbad with his "Russian Polka".
Waldau writes about the "Rejdovak": "Many of the well-
known dance composers apply themselves to furnish this fashionable dance with interesting music", . . . But though, now
(in 1859) it has somewhat lost in popularity, it has re-appeared
in Paris, where Musard's orchestra played the good old Bohemian "Rejdovak", alias "Redova". It is vain, however, to look
upon it as a graceful and courtly dance. The movements are
bizarre and angular, particularly those of the male partner,
and a German observer compares such a dancer to a neighing
horse or a charging bull, so violent appear his gestures. It
is danced to 3/4 waltz time, the "Rejdovačka" to 2/4, polka
time. It is clear that the relation between the here mentioned
dances is that of step-and hop-dance, with the first in slow
laendler time, the second in fast polka time, just as was done
in the case of the old "Grandfather dance" and the so-called
"Laendler-halbe" (slow 3/4 and fast 2/4).

(It is exactly the same melody which appears in the New York publication).

It is interesting to note that the name of the first of these dances (the ternary dance "Rejdovak") has the Czech male ending, the binary dance "Rejdovačka", the female ending. I suppose that the two-beat dance was originally a paced dance, and the three-beat dance a leaped one, but that later on this was reversed. As a rule the "Rejdovak" consisted of three parts with repetitions, but many of the "Redovas" played in the ball rooms have a more expanded form. Among the composers who favored the "Redova" we should mention: Friedrich Burgmueller (1806-1874): "La Sicilienne - Redova", Ferdinand Beyer (1803-1863): "Les Belles de New York", "Three Redovas", "Moonlight Redova". A "Redova Waltz" by the same composer was published by Jules Martin in Philadelphia. Furthermore H. Rosellen (1811-1876): "L'Oriental Redova"; Charles Voss: (1815-1882) "Rosalie Redova"; Anton Wallerstein: (1813-1892) "Redova célèbre", etc.

Among the Czech dances which arrived on the polished ball room floor, we ought to mention the "Strašak", called in German the "Schrecker", (Scare-head), based originally on the pantomimic theme of an interchange of female partners, in combination with the courtship motive. After dancing to a polka rhythm for 16 bars, the male partners let go their ladies, threaten them with the index finger and stamp the ground 3 times, and after that repeat the pantomime with the lady partner of the neighbor to the left, until each male partner has performed the passage with all the ladies participating.

Today the "Strašak" is danced as a children's game, with the gestures of a raised finger, and became also part of the Czech national dance "Beseda".

Every student of music knows Haydn's Symphony No. 2, in D major with the "Finale a la musette" and its first theme of a lively folk song. The Croatian student of folk-lore,

Kuhač, has maintained that this song is Croatian. But those, versed in Central European musical folk-lore, recognized im- mediately that here is a Czech dance, known as "Okročak" since the 18th century. Also in this dance the male dancer circles around his partner. The first bars of such a dance, according to the collection of Jaromir Erben go like this:

"Do not leave, stay with me! Here you find a happy resting"...

Just as numerous as the Czech folk songs and Czech dances are the Russian dances, all of which have the common charac- teristic that the male partners stamp on the ground, move back and forward with knee deeply bent, dance on their heels and then throw themselves flat on the ground (prisatky). The girls also stamp with the feet, waving brightly colored kerchiefs. The best known of these national dances are the "Kosaček" and the "Golubetz" (the dance of the doves), and here the pantomimic element is strongly apparent.

To return to the social dances of the 19th century: we have the "Ecossaise" or "Scotch", one of the favorite dances of the declining 18th, and the beginning 19th century, for which music was composed by Beethoven, Schubert, Weber and many others. This was a kind of contra dance with a number of figures: "Moulinet", "Chaine", and "Balancé" performed by the single couples and then by all of them together. The "An- glaise" was similar, except that it was danced with a double step, while the "Scotch" used the polka step. Much less brisk and lively was the "Française", performed in 6/8 time. In South Germany it became interfused with native folk dance elements and kept its place through to the 20th century. The pattern of a "Scotch" is the old dance of the "lieber Augustin", which was turned into 2/4 time, and danced this way around 1820, all over the world.

*   *   *

The list has by no means exhausted the catalogue of dances of this period. We should not forget the dance forms arising in Paris, for example the "Cancan", also called "Chahut", which was popular after the accession of Louis Philippe in 1830, and was in fact an imitation of the "Fandango".

Though first only a figure of the "Quadrille," it soon won its place at all public balls. Its invention is ascribed by some to Chicard, the "bon garçon, joyeux viveur", while others believe that it was first danced by the comedian Masarié, who executed the grotesque movements of this dance impersonating "the monkey Joko" at the Theatre St. Martin. Though at the beginning without any of its later offensive character, it was finally banished from the dance floor of good society, and left to the public balls, the vaudeville houses, the ballets and the comic operas of Offenbach. In "Orpheus in Hades", Offenbach has emphasized the contrast between two centuries and two ways of life by this juxtaposition of a minuet and a cancan and has at the same time given a musical portrait of the forces prevailing in the French Empire at that time. Following upon the tender and light minuet in the ball-room scene, he gives as the "galop infernal", a cancan, as a violent contrast. One of his contemporaries voices his impressions as follows:

"This famous dance in Orpheus has carried away our entire generation as would a tempestuous whirlwind. Already the first sounds of the furiously playing instruments seem to indicate the call to a whole world to awake and plunge into wild dancing. These rhythms appear to have the intention of shocking all the resigned, all the defeated out of their lethargy and by the physical and moral upheaval which they arouse, to throw the whole fabric of society into confusion. This seemed to be the impression upon the listening public when the gods of Olympus and those of the Hades were driven to frenetic dancing".

Offenbach's position in the era of Napoleon the Third may indeed be compared to that of Strauss in Vienna, in the era of Francis Joseph, the Austrian Emperor. He was like Strauss the interpreter of his environment, translating into musical phrase, in his cancans and galops, the overflowing joy of living of his era. Yet the musical manifestations of both countries were quite different and in every case mirrored the people for whom the dances were intended. In Vienna, the tender, sentimental flowing rhythms of the waltz, — in Paris, the dynamic stirring measures of the cancan. In Vienna, the rustic melodies of the wine-taverns, — in Paris, the intoxication and recklessness of the mood induced by bubbling champagne. In both instances, we have an immediate and realistic expression of the vigor and native strength of temperament of the people.

It was perhaps for the last time that the vigorous, erotic way of life of both Austrian and French nations became personified in dance music. This, to my mind, is the historical significance of the work of Strauss and of Offenbach.

CHAPTER XII.

THE DANCES OF THE ROMANTIC COMPOSERS

AND OF

THE NATIONAL GROUPS

A BACKWARD glance at the beginning of the 17th century brings back to our minds the fact that at this time the German composers Hausmann, Franck, Hammerschmidt and others, no longer tied their dances together, in bouquets as it were, thus making a suite of them, but offered them separately as "Intradas", "Courantes", and "Gaillards", without combining different varieties into a whole. This was, however, a transitional stage, and in the latter half of the 17th as well as in the 18th century, the principle of the suite underwent a revival.

Around 1800 we note a phase of musical development similar to that of 1600. At the time, the suite was replaced by the sonata, and dance forms descended to second rank of impòrtance in the Classic period. In the dance music played for actual dancing, single types, waltzes, contra dances were combined. On the other hand we find at this time that the "characteristic pieces", the "Intermezzi" were taken from the suite and became even independent.

I have already pointed out in a study published in "Music and Letters" in January 1942, how important was the influence of the Czech composers Johann Wenzel Tomašek (1774-1850) and Hugo Voříšek (1791-1825), who were the reformers of the lyrical pieces for piano, which later played such an important role in the hands of Schubert. The type developed by these two composers might have harked back to that of another Czech composer, Joseph Mysliveček, who composed six "Divertimenti per cembalo" in 1770. Mysliveček was a friend of

287

Mozart. Tomašek published six "Eclogues" in 1810, but the date of their composition was 1807, exactly twenty years before Schubert wrote his "Impromptus". The number "six" is retained in the "Moments Musicaux" also. Schumann adhers to it in his "Nachtstuecke", and Beethoven does likewise in opus 126, the "Six Bagatelles", written in 1825.

The most remarkable feature of these pieces is that they derived from the dance both rhythmically and melodically. Many of them contain definite dance rhythms, and some of them have trios. This is true of the "Scherzi", particularly in those of Beethoven's "Bagatellen", opus 33. But Schubert too, includes a trio in his "Impromptus", opus 90, and in the well-known "Impromptu" opus 142, which glorifies the dance with its graceful moving sarabande rhythm. We find here that exuberant imagination in the creation of dance rhythms so characteristic of Schubert, whose spirit was such a rich mixture of joy and melancholy, of conflicting emotions, that it is almost impossible to find an adequate word for it. He has the heavenly clarity of the classic composers, but also Weber's romantic longing for a distant world, his cheerfulness and lively outcries, but more than that: he is the poet of the inexpressible, pleasurably-painful, even mysterious moods.

From Schubert it is but a step to Schumann, the deeply romantic, almost pathologically sensitive artist whose conflicts of soul found expression not only in the musical characters "Eusebius" and "Florestan", but also in his tragic close, as a victim of dementia praecox. Unlike Beethoven, his fight against relentless fate was not a triumphant one. Enveloped in the pessimistic philosophy of Schopenhauer, he struggled against the "senseless unceasing will", against the treachery of the world around him and the demons of his inner life. If we may say that Schubert's world is that of the Conscious, invaded continuously by the Unconscious, — then that of Schumann is that of the Subconscious, the soul itself arising to meet the light, but disappearing into the depth of its own darkness.

Just as the rolling melody of the "Baroque" and the thorough bass express the eternal super-human powers, so the ostinato rhythms of the Romanticists symbolize the relentlessness and "senseless" will of Fate.

If we use the symbol of the ever-rolling wheel to characterize the music of Bach, we may designate that of Schumann as that of an intricate web, particularly his polyrhythmic music for the piano. This may serve to explain his ostinato dance rhythms, his polyrhythmic formations, his complementary rhythms, which hark back to the lute style of Bach. Schumann indeed derives his structural style from times that are past. His "Carneval", f. i., is a reminiscence of the old variation suite.

Taking the name of the old town of "Asch" in Bohemia, the residence of his beloved friend Ernestine von Fricken, as the subject of his dance suite, he based a composition on it. The

"Scènes mignonnes" are introduced by a magnificent and majestic Intrada, in which all the persons appearing in this idealized pantomime make their first bow, the close is a Retirada, the march of the "Davidsbuendler" against the "Philistines", depicted by the quotation of the provincial "Grandfather Dance". Between these two cornerstones all the dance forms of the time have their place. Among them are the "Waltz", the "German", (here called "Valse Allemande"), and the "Polonaise". The "Waltz" prevails, while the pantomimic element is given an outlet in the numerous "Characteristic pieces".

The Viennese waltz charmed Schumann no end. In opus 26, "Faschingsschwank aus Wien", he paid special homage to it, idealizing the life of gay Vienna in these pieces but in his own romantic way. Schubert's dances and the laendlers of Lanner and Strauss excited his admiration. His letters to Clara Schumann about the women of Vienna, the delights of the Carnival there, show his susceptibility.

The "Faschingsschwank" has the form of a suite. It begins

with a pageant of solemn and gay masked figures. The prince of the feast, Prince Carnival, is led out in solemn procession, but the thoughts and moods of the composer lose themselves in dreamlike passages, from which he is called by the behests of the prince towards the robust life of reality. Then the picture of Schubert appears, with a "Heurigen Walzer", transformed into Schumann's style, a ghostlike apparition to one familiar with Viennese dance tunes, and now the fantastic dream-images whirl around in confusion, waltzing about in a mad masquerade, to the "Marseillaise" and a (German) dance by Schubert. The second movement, a "Romanze", is more tranquil (it represents the Sarabande); the "Scherzino" stands for the Minuet; and the "Intermezzo" even for an "Intermezzo" of the classic suite, while a brisk "Finale" resembles the fast Gigue.

*   *   *

The Romantic movement in Europe brought in its wake the rise of the cultural independence and autonomy of the smaller nations. In the field of music, it was the Czechs, who first arrived at a form of national renaissance, strongly influenced by the ideas of Goethe and of Herder. They were the first to turn back to their national past, to the old songs, legends and myths, finding in them inspiration for further national music. We already find Czech melodic line and Czech rhythms in the work of the Bohemian composers of the 18th century, Johann Stamitz, Johann Dismas Zelenka, Johann Zach, and others. But these Slavic traits are more or less unconscious, and not an important factor in the appraisal of the artistic quality of the work. With Tomašek, we find a definite stressing of the national quality expressed in the development of pastoral and lyrical piano compositions depicting the Bohemian landscape. But not before Smetana did the world learn Bohemian song and Bohemian dance.

The Czechs are not the only small nation which won universal recognition on the outskirts, the periphery of the cultural world of Europe: the Spaniards, Hungarians, Poles, Russians, Roumanians, Jugoslavs, Finns and Norwegians find a place in

this development. Melody, harmony and rhythm of the inhabitants of these areas have definite characteristic national folk
qualities. This fact is evident even in the Czech music after
Smetana and in Spanish music after Albeniz. We may even
consider the popular music of Schubert and Strauss as belonging to this group of "peripheral music", because it contains
so many and such strong alpine elements.

The first great musician who wrote national music in this
sense was Frederick Chopin. His mother was Polish. His
father, a Frenchman, spent almost all his life in Poland. In
his piano compositions, Chopin favored three dance forms,
two of them Polish: the "Mazurka" and the "Polonaise", the
third, however, Viennese: the "Waltz". He did all the more
for the development of these dances as he promoted their
revival in new forms with a new content and in his own highly
personal way. His biographers declare that Chopin's "Mazurka"
is a unique synthesis composed of three Polish folk dances:
of the "Mazurek", the "Kujawak" and the "Oberek". Around
1840 all the Slavic dances, the "Polka", the "Redova" and the
Russian dances were, like the Polish dances, exceedingly fashionable in Paris. Doubtlessly Chopin drew his inspiration
from the actual Polish dances as they were danced in the ball
rooms of the Countess Czartoryska and other Polish aristocrats,
though his own national inheritance and the impressions of his
childhood may have played their part. All three dances which
he may have seen had their peculiar quality. The "Mazurek"
is war-like and courtly, the "Kujawak" melancholic and sentimental, the "Oberek" brisk and gay, and, in truth, each one of
Chopin's mazurkas has one or more of these qualities. But
like other great masters of dance music Chopin stylized the
design and the mood of the folk dance, he crystallized its
spirit, as it were. It is incorrect to assert as do some of
Chopin's biographers, that the majority of the mazurkas have
kept only the old rhythms of the national dances and that is
all that is left of the "dance quality". On the contrary, these
mazurkas more than many folk dances emphasize the plastic,
picturesque dance elements as well as the characteristic of the

primitive Slavic folk dances, constructed on a foundation of the old courting pantomime, with its gestures of meeting, pursuit, longing and ultimate reunion. Just as Weber's "Invitation to the Dance" has this picturesque quality, so Chopin's dances combine idealization and realism. As his permanent motto we find a passionate longing for the abandonment and enslaved mother country. Only an expatriate, a refugee, straining toward his homeland, now a thousandfold more precious by its very distance, could have found such glowing expression for his feeling. And to Chopin — living in the over-refined atmosphere of Western Europe — sweet childhood memories and the songs and dances of the peasant boys and girls of his Eastern home country became vivid.

Polish shepherds playing the bag-pipe supply the inspiration for opus 6 No. 3.

Opus 24 No. 2, brings memories of the village church, where the organist played his simple melodies; following upon these, the Polish flute (fujarka) starts a primitive air, leading into a Lydian phrase which depicts the incomparable melancholy of the endless Polish steppe.

Pentatonic melodic treatment — originating in Slavic folk music — is particularly apparent in the Mazurkas. Chopin's great harmonic art is based on the purely minor melodic line and the "gypsy mode" of the Eastern Slavic peoples (augmented fourth in the harmonic minor scale).

In definite contrast to the mazurkas, which are peasant dances, the polonaises — though genuine national dances — are dances of the nobility, of festivals and of war. Weber, Chopin's predecessor in the creation of polonaises, fully appreciated the courtly character of these dance forms. But only Chopin actually knew how to make them the very essence of Polish culture in the 19th century: a revolutionary and warlike spirit drawing its strength from the glories of the past. In this respect they are the true epic of a people whose soil has been the battle ground of Europe's wars for many centuries. Their creator holds the same rank as Italy's Torquato Tasso and Dante; England's Shakespeare; and Germany's unknown poet of the "Song of the Nibelungs". The most famous of all polonaises by Chopin, opus 53 in A flat major, is a great song of Freedom. It begins with an introduction holding the hearer in suspense before the start of the gigantic battle. A brilliant picture follows portraying the past of Poland, first, beating off the hordes of Tartars and Turks; then subjugated by the Moscovites, the Polish cavalry takes up the struggle and with clangor of weapons and trampling of horses (given with an unheard-of realism) the battle progresses. There are obstacles, and after a short pause (arpeggio triads in E major) the horsemen advance to another attack which ends in a tumultuous and victorious climax. The E flat minor polonaise, opus 26, No. 2, is also a war picture, sometimes called the "Revolution Polonaise". The greater part of Chopin's polonaises portray either war, victory or political upheaval. This is not the case in Chopin's waltzes. The Austrian waltz was a foreign matter, not so close to his heart, and this explains why — compared with the Polish mazurkas and polonaises, the waltzes are un-pictorial, they do not have the realistic and dramatic power of his Polish dances. The elements they contain are rather drawn from the life of the aristocratic circles in Paris and in Vienna.

* * *

Let us return to the Czechs. What Chopin was for the Poles Smetana meant to them. It was he who created a truly national music though other Czech musicians before him had already given us a hint of it. And Smetana is so to speak a more universal type of genius than Chopin who used only the piano to glorify national aspirations. It was the past of the Czech nation which Smetana incorporated in his operas and symphonic compositions. He did not dwell on national dance forms as exclusively as Chopin did. Nevertheless he stressed the national dance in his piano compositions, and in the "Bartered Bride" and his symphonic works as well. Wherever he wishes to emphasize folk-lore character, he introduces the characteristic Czech rhythm, derived directly from the Czech language which is full of consonants, in which the vowels have special rhythmic stress and at times even seem to be jerked out heavily. As there is no article in the Czech language the down beat becomes instrumental. In combination with it syncopation frequently occurs. The waltz, the German dance, has an upbeat (corresponding to the article found in the German language), Not so the polka and other Czech dances. Only a very small number of the Czech folk songs, collected by Erben, have an upbeat. (The opposite is true of the German songs collected by Boehme and other German scholars). The stirring revolutionary rhythm found in the Czech dances receives its staccato incisiveness from the language of the Czech people. Sometimes it seems as if short stops interrupted each beat of the rhythm and brought about a sharp whip-like snapping accent on every part of the measure. Take for example any one of the dance themes from a Czech composition, for instance the Scherzo from the Trio, opus 65, by Dvořak:

Many of these dance rhythms exhibit a kind of warning challenge, as if stressed by the stamping feet, and the warning gesticulations of hands. Thus the Czech rhythm contains pantomimic elements which are intimately bound up with the beginnings of the dance and of dance music.

In Smetana's dances the pantomimic element shows itself clearly and openly, for he makes it a practice to use the traditional forms, such as the "Oves" (Grain dance), one of the peasant dances of the Czechs. Indeed the names of many Czech dances are derived from the agricultural life. There is the "Obrok" (Oats dance), the Řezanka" (the Chaff), the "Kedluben", (the Turnip), and the "Cibulička" (Onion dance). The original melody of the latter dance, performed by the onion vendors, has the characteristic accent on the weak part of the measure:

Smetana took over the original melody of the folk dance "Oves" for his famous piano composition: ("Oves"). The old folk song tells the story of a peasant girl binding up the grain and thinking of her unfaithfulness to her lover. But she pledges and vows to herself that this will never, never happen again! From this simple dance of the people, Smetana has wrought an admirable plastic little dance drama as the girl singing the naive song is overpowered by the mighty force of love and deeply disturbed by her emotions until she finds peace and repose again in the resolve within her heart.

This dance together with a number of other Czech dances, as the "Hulan" (Cavalry soldier), "Slepička" (the little chicken), are contained in the collection published in 1879, called "Tschechische Taenze". In this group we also see the "Furiant" (Dance of the Furies), which was mentioned by Daniel Gottlob Tuerk in his "Klavier Schule" (1789), there called "Furie". The word "furia" is not a usual Czech expression, and I believe there may be some connection between it and Gluck's dances of the furies. Smetana has used this wild dance in his "Bartered Bride". Its characteristic feature is the alteration of the contrasting 2/4 with 3/4 rhythm (each two bars long). Its prime motif seems to be this:

for it appears also in the "Furiant" of the Czech dances for the piano. This alteration of rhythm produces a most impassioned and wild effect. Waldau gives an interesting description of the "Furiant" and considers it identical with the "Sedlak" (Peasant). It is a fact that the "Furiant" recorded by Erben is the same as that used by Smetana for his furiant in the opera "The Bartered Bride":

"Peasant, peasant, peasant,
And once again thou peasant,
Peasant, peasant, peasant,
Art a mighty lord!"

The dance itself is the pantomime of the dancer trying to act the part of a proud peasant, with arms akimbo, stamping his feet, and taking off his coat, shoving his lady partner ahead of him while she dances gracefully before him and then around him, then turns on her heels around and around at the same place, until finally the male partner clasps her and begins to dance quite slowly and solemnly the steps of a "Sousedska" (Czech laendler). The "Furiant" which Smetana incorporated in his famous opera is intended to be a genuine folk dance and the description given by Waldau might well serve as a guide for the directors of performances, so that nonsensical choreographic interpolations could be avoided.

In the "Furiant" for piano which Smetana composed, he aimed at a musical picture in reviving the pantomimic dance subject. In the introduction he gives us the above-mentioned prime motif, boys and girls take their places for the dance and then the wild whirling of the varying rhythms begins. Then the crowd calms down and the simple laendler using the furiant motif begins. But the storm arises with renewed force until the bells of the neighboring church begin to ring and the dancers bend their knees in worship. Now the furiant motif has become that of the bells. But even then passion stirs in the minds of the dancers and they return to their furious motion. The end comes with the ringing of the bells interrupted by the quotation of the furiant motif, striking like the crack of a whip. Here we have a model description of a phase of Czech rustic culture, reproduced with plastic force.

Smetana wrote a number of polkas, also a "Dupak", a dance sharing the quality of wildness of motion with the "Kalamajka", the "Klouzák" and "Vosňák". Erben records two dupaks, one of which is 2/4 time and contains a lover's funny request to his girl: "Don't marry after your hundredth birthday". It seems to be the remnant of a somewhat coarse courting dance. This is indicated by the instrumental interlude, the "Dohravka", stamped with warningly repeated eights. The second "Dupak", which is written in more measured laendler rhythm, contains in its second division the same warning gestures with which the wooer threatens his sweetheart, vowing that he will be revenged if she ill-treats him. The Czech word used in the song is "Dupy dupy dup". "Dupati" means to stamp on the ground.

Waldau gives us the following description:

"The dance floor resembles a wheel turned swiftly by the wind. Even the quiet onlooker is swept along in this dizzy whirl. Four, five, even more couples swing about, with hands intertwined, in a circle, rush on like streaks of lightning, exclaiming and uttering loud cries of merriment. There seems to be no fatigue, no stopping or pausing to rest".

Smetana's Dupak partakes of this impetuous wildness. The stirring chromatic motif sets the dancers into the right mood of bacchantic exuberance which rises to a veritable frenzy with the rushing movement of the 16th notes. A quiet "Musette" brings the necessary relief. As a close we have another brisk and excited part with large intervals which keeps the hearer in breathless suspense. This whirling motion in sixteenths appears also in the dance and performance of the comedians in the opera, "Bartered Bride", for which Smetana possibly took as his pattern the dance of Bohemian gypsies. This is indicated by the somewhat exotic minor character of the "Skočna" ("Springing dance") which follows the whirling motion of the beginning. No other dances can rival these in expressing the joy of the senses, the pleasure of sensual life. Their unrestrained, almost maddened speed of movement reminds one strongly of the orgiastic dances of primitive peoples.

Quite unlike the dances of Chopin, these dances are constructed on the principle of variation, the theme used is varied according to the mood to be expressed. In this sense, the Czechs seem to have been the exponents and followers of the Germans, in whose dances the principle of variation was so signally carried out for many centuries.

Dvořak, though he was Smetana's successor in his adherence to folk ways and interest in folk-lore, is far removed from the latter in his aesthetic point of view and his artistic expression. Smetana had followed the ideals enunciated by

Wagner and Liszt, filling his music with ideas, with images of landscapes, of dramatic scenes and mimic representations, — in one word going to the external world for his inspiration. Brahms and the critic Hanslick determined Dvořak's artistic credo and led him more to absolute music. This disparity is equally apparent in the dances of the two masters. While Smetana makes pictures resembling the forms of national life, Dvořak in his "Slavic Dances" gives us the very essence of the dances of the Slavs. He idealizes, as it were, the forms of the Czech rhythm, giving us non-pictorial dances in which rhythm and form are decisive. These "Slavic Dances", like those of Brahms, ("Hungarian Dances") are written for piano duet. There are "Furiants", "Skočnas", "Polkas", "Sousedskas", and a dance of the Southern Slavs. By including the latter, Dvořak moved in the direction of the Pan-Slavic trends of his time and at the same time he established the unity of these various forms. This practice of Dvořak is even more noticeable in the second series, opus 72, where dances of various Slavic peoples succeed each other, and differ definitely from the Czech realism and picturesqueness of the Smetana dances. Šourek, the well-versed biographer of Dvořak, designates the second dance of opus 72 as a Polish mazurka "with all the elegance, grace and melancholy of the Polish dance". Ottokar Šourek and Paul Stefan (in their Dvořak biography) call the sixth "an idealized Polonaise", the fourth has a trace of the Ukraine, and the seventh is the impetuous Jugoslavian "Kolo". The second one, an "Odzemek", including a wild figure in which the female partner is thrown down and then lifted up again, may have come from Slovakia. According to Šourek the dance is a Czech "Springtime dance". It is in fact a "Galop", called "Skočna", accompanied by somewhat grotesque "lovesongs" such as

> "Dance with me, you'll get a cruller,
> Dance with, and you'll get two.
> Our mother baked them Sunday,
> And I stole them both for you".

Such a "Skočna" was a wild dance, often ending in a breathless whirling figure of the couples. This fifth one, a "Špacirka", is said by Waldau to resemble closely the modern parlor dance "l'imperial". ʹThe original folk dance consisted of two repetitions of eight bars each. The dancers hopped about to the first part, in the second which was played much faster they held each other by both hands and turned in a fast waltz. Dvořak, however, uses no proper waltz time in his form, — another indication how loosely he followed the traditional folk forms.

In later Czech music too the dance was a favorite of the composers. Let me mention here Jaromir Weinberger. He gave us numerous dances in his "Švanda, the Bag-piper" and has recently published polkas for the piano. Martinu, Jirák, Křička and Janaček, (the last strongly influenced by Moravian folk-lore) have all published Czech dances.

* * *

The Hungarians have their "Csalogatos" (teasing dance) and the "Magyar Kör", the Hungarian square dance. The "Csardas" (the word means innkeeper) was derived from an old dance of the Royal Life Guards, and like the Polish polonaise harks back to the heroic age of the Magyar world. Its elements are passionate pride and war-like bearing joined to the love motive, and its incisive rhythms are derived from the clinking together of the rider's spurs as he stands at attention.

The first part, called "Lassu" is a slow dance of the men circling around, followed by the brisk "Friss", a couple dance. The "Csardas" has other predecessors, the "Hallgato nota", consisting of a slow introduction to which there was no dancing, and the "Kalakas" during which the dancers brought their spurs together with a sharp click. Then there was the "Hajdutanc", the dance of the medieval mercenaries, danced with clapping of hands and shouting while the dancers squatted low on the ground.

The "Palotas" was a fairly fast dance, allegedly dating from the Middle Ages, with several movements, in 2/4 or 4/4 time and like most of these dances, a pantomimic dance. The

"Paptanc", a marriage dance, was performed as such in the church or in the courtyard of the priest's house in the province Heves. The "Puenkoesdi", like the "Whitsuntide dances" of the Germans, is a pantomimic dance connected with the choice of a Whitsun—King for the Spring festival. There are dances imitating animals, the "Rokatanc" (dance of the Fox) and "Szarkatanc" (dance of the Magpie), and courting dances using the familiar figure of the dancer kneeling on a cushion in front of his partner.

The Hungarians are surely as gifted musicians as the Poles or the Czechs are. We find Hungarian dances in the old organ and lute books of the 16th century which have been analyzed by Szabolcsi in the "Zeitschrift fuer Musikwissenschaft", volume 8, as "Choreae Hungaricae". A harpsichord manuscript of the second half of the 17th century (Leutschau Man.), shows such a Hungarian dance with the typical Hungarian accent on the weak part of the bar (in the second bar), and the repeated final notes. But in Eastern Europe dance airs float about without keeping within national boundaries. We often find the same melodies used by the Slovaks, ethnically so different from the Hungarians. Béla Bartók has noted this in his work on the "Hungarian Folksong", and we see that many Czech folk dances were and are danced and played in Hungary, sometimes even taking over the title, as when the "Kalamaika" became the "Kalamajko" in Hungary. In the Leutschau manuscript we also find a Slovakian "Klobucky Tanecz" (Hat dance), and we have a Czech "Cap dance" too, which has the following melody:

These Hungarian folk dances persisted and were practised among the people for centuries, and Bartók has pointed out how their structure and form changed in the course of time. But the art forms of the Hungarian dance did not appear until about 1790, though in 1759 we find a piano "partita" composed by a certain J. Czermak, included in a Hungarian collection. Z. Kodály speaking about old Hungarian dances said in one of his lectures that there are German, Italian and Slavic elements in this Music.

In a Viennese periodical published about 1791, in Hungarian, we find the first art-forms of their national dances. One of them has the following melody:

At that time it became fashionable to cultivate the Hungarian style. Haydn and Schubert wrote pieces "Alla Ongarese", Artaria in Vienna published "12 Ungarische Taenze" by Josef Bengraf (d. 1790) and, strange to relate, the Czech Tomašek entitled his first opus "Ungarische Taenze".

The Hungarian musicologists designated the style of Hungarian music around 1800, after the Hungarian recruiting dance ("Verbunkos", - Werbetanz), as recruiting style, referring to the practice used in enlisting the Hungarian peasant boys for the national militia. These forms are the basis of the Hungarian musical jargon used by Erkel, Liszt and Mosonyi, and at the same time sow the seeds for the "Hungarisms" of Haydn, Schubert and Brahms. The Slavic and German elements gradually disappear and under the guidance of the Hungarian violin virtuosi (Bihari, Lavotta, Czermak), the national folk elements became paramount. This style has spread throughout Europe by the gypsy orchestras, who stressed and over-emphasized its peculiar characteristics. Since the music of the gypsies is Oriental and monophonic per se, it retained down to our own times a distinctly soloistic and rubato character. It has primitive basses, tremolos accompanying a leading voice quite rich in melody, and is stressed dynamically. There is a great variety of rhythms. Syncopation is one of the peculiarities of Hungarian music, as well as a frequent change in time, and themes occur with the three and six, five and seven bars. The rhythm occurs very frequently with the short note in the strong part of the bar. There are also frequent pauses on the strong part of the measure and it is customary to suppress the balance in the bar. Compare for example this bar from Liszt's Twelfth Rhapsody

with its accented appogiatura notes on the interval of the prime (a special feature of the gypsy instrument), the "cimbalon", in the well-known opening measure of the same rhapsody. Another peculiarity is the embellishment of the final notes.

On these foundations rest the Hungarian Rhapsodies of Liszt as well as the Hungarian dances by Brahms which, although not actually dance music, contain strong dance elements. The original division of the folk dances into two definite parts has its influence on the structure of modern compositions. Whereas Brahms does not follow the rule that the Hungarian dance must begin with a slow sentimental love motive, Liszt, to a certain extent does. Because of his trend towards illustrative descriptive music he is far more pictorial and closer to the folk dance than the composer of "absolute" music, Brahms. Liszt attempts to give instrumental effects on the piano, he likes to imitate the Puszta melodies of the gypsy violins with their long spun-out melodic line. The cimbalon tones, which give heterophonic accompaniment to the air played on the violin, lead to the wild "Friss". There the peasant youth performs his fiery and wild dance with clanking spurs. Brahms is by far more reserved and quiet.

The more recent phase of the development of the Hungarian dance has been the abandonment of this "recruiting style" and the return to Hungarian, Roumanian and Slovak peasant music, neglected for centuries. The compositions of Bartók, Kodály and László Lajtha revived it. The chief characteristic of this indigenous musical style are ancient scales, such as the pentatonic scale: g, b♭, c d f g, or aeolian and dorian scale: and minor keys are avoided. A kind of parlando-rubato rhythm is also characteristic.

Other dance melodies created within the last nine decades use symmetrical periods, and the major, aeolian, dorian and myxolydian keys, rarely a minor key. And finally there is a third type which mingles the elements of various ethnic groups inhabiting the Hungarian plains. Bartók's suites for orchestra, of which the second, called "Tanzsuite", (performed at the International Musical Festival in Prague, 1925), laid the foundations for his great reputation, is based on this primitive folk style. The same is true of his dances for the piano and for chamber ensembles. In all of them we find expressed the almost barbaric wildness of these people of the steppes, who represent a striking mixture of primitive and instinctive impetuosity, combined with most modern forms of intellectual subtility. Besides these works of Bartók we find that he has made a splendid contribution to Hungarian music by his dance pantomimes "The Wonderful Mandarin" and "The Wooden Prince". In both these pieces we find the rhythmic forces which are deeply interwoven with the life of the Hungarian people, structurally simple, but filled with breath of life itself. H. Mersmann makes the following remark: "This is music behind which stretches the long line of nameless and unknown singers of the people, impelling the creative powers of Bartók to set the amorphous masses in motion".

*   *   *

It has been noted, and quite rightly so, that there are certain resemblances which are common property of all the nations living in the "outskirts" of Europe. Norwegian dances remind us of Czech dance music, and Spanish melodies are often identical with Polish ones. We have already mentioned the fact that the common Asiatic antecedents of Spanish and Slavic music, i.e. the predominance of Near-Eastern elements, are responsible for this resemblance. But a broader, more universal point of view must be taken into account, namely that in the musical culture of Central Europe, of Germany, France and Italy, folk music developed closely intertwined with art forms which were for the most part strongly influenced by religious vocal music. Even instrumental music among these peoples could regain its dynamic force and rhythmic variety, which it had in the Middle Ages, but only slowly and step by step (vide medieval dance forms). On the other hand, the folk music of the border countries was less subject to outside and "artistic" influence, and continued to retain its independence. Old-fashioned modes and asymmetric rhythms, formal embellishments, ancient instruments and styles of delivery, have been preserved among these peoples, giving their music an almost uniform character. For example the second of Grieg's "Norwegian Dances" has a remarkable likeness to a Czech folk song, and though one may object that this is just a matter of pure melody having nothing to do with old-fashioned and primitive rhythmics or harmonies, it must be repeated that the melodic form is definitely pre-determined by the similar, primitive musical cultural phase. Let us quote another instance, that of the migrating melody (mentioned on page 278) which appears in South America, Spain, Belgium, Bohemia and Poland as well as in Palestine. It is based on the primitive minor hexachord.

Another Czech folk song (Erben 509) begins this way:

and we find it in this form as a folk song in Sweden:

Indeed, both the structure and the style of the Scandinavian folk song and folk dance rest on the same foundations as the Slavic songs and dances. That is on the primitive scales, which favor a purely minor melodic line, pentatonic scales, the G scale with F natural (myxolydian seventh) and the A minor scale with G natural, etc. Moreover we have tetrachordal treatment with bag-pipe and ostinato basses. This primitive melodic line is also not dependent on the centre tone, the tonic or the dominant, as in the following example of a folk dance by Grieg, who used Norwegian folk music in his compositions and with the popular airs turned to the landscape like Smetana did, both of them aiming to picture the dancelike lyrical pieces of the home-countries.

Grieg's harmonic treatments derived from the Norwegian folk song and, as C. von Fischer showed in his dissertation on Grieg, the composer made ample use of a most complicated type of harmony, which he combined with primitive types, as Balakirev, the Russian did, and Bartók, the Hungarian. Moreover, — dissonances now no longer lead into consonances (as was the rule), they no longer express the romantic and harmonic tension. Instead they become more and more independent, very impressive — yet — "without the tension which dissonances had in both the classical and Romantic periods".

Grieg has modeled his dances mostly on those of the peasants of Hardanger, and we find that they are often idealized "Slaatters", Norwegian peasant dance music. Using mostly short but exceedingly plastic motives, he approaches the Oriental use of these forms. Rhythmically too he leans towards primitive forms in the Norwegian Dances, which, like those of Dvořak and of Brahms were composed for the piano for four hands. Consider the fourth of the Norwegian dances with its uneven periods and shifting of the center of gravity of the theme:

Such forms are common occurrences in the folk dances of the Czechs and Hungarians. In the same way the accentuation of the weak part of the bar (dating from pre-metrical times)

is very frequent in Norwegian folk music. Grieg writes a "Halling", a dance performed by two men and apparently a derivation from a sword dance, which goes like this:

Here the old Nordic shalm with the Lydian augmented fourth is imitated and accompanied by bag-pipe basses. The accent on the weak part indicates the stamping of the dancers, or the original ringing of bells or clashing of swords.

*   *   *

In Spain Isaac Albeniz (1860-1909) occupied the place held by Grieg in Norway, by Smetana and Dvořak in Bohemia, and by Chopin in Poland. His task, like theirs, was to idealize the folk music of his people and thus make it part of the musical literature of the world. It must not be forgotten that Spanish music had its place, and a considerable one, in the Middle Ages and in the Renaissance as well as in the 17th and 18th centuries. The Spanish lutenist Luiz Milan and many others introduced Spanish folk music into their fantasies, their "Ricercares" and their "Differencias" (variations), all of which were art forms. Many musicians, not natives of Spain have felt the lure of Spanish folk music. Among these was Bizet who developed a highly personal style of Spanish music in "Carmen" and the founder of modern Russian music, Glinka, whose "Jota Aragonese", as well as his "Seguidillas" (folk dances of the province La Mancha), tell of the deep impression Spanish folk dances made on him.

From times immemorial dancing has been one of the favorite amusements of the Spanish people and in ancient times we find their dancers celebrated by Roman writers for their beauty and the lascivious fire of their gestures. Pliny the Elder praises the art of the dancers who entertain the guests at the banquets. With the spread of Moorish culture to Europe, exotic dances became important. Later, after the discovery of America, the sarabanda, chaconna and fandango returned to Spain, re-imported from the "Indies". In the 16th

century the usual dances were the "Gibadina", the dance of
the hunchbacks, whose disappearance was deplored by Lope
de Vega; also the "Madama d'Orleans", a dance brought over
from France; the "Rey Don Alonso el Bueno", so called after
the title of an old romance, — the "Piede gibao", and the
"Pavana". In addition to these were a very lively "Escar-
raman" and the "Zapateado", where the rhythm was stamped
out with the flat of the foot, or beaten with the hand on the
sole of the shoe, a veritable Spanish "Schuhplattler". (This
dance is still danced in Peru under the name of "Tapada").
Moreover the "Zapateado" is one of those dances which have
crossed the ocean twice, first from Europe to America and then
back again to Europe, where it was danced by Fanny Elssler.
Its characteristic motions are the shaking of the legs and the
tapping on the ground with the heels, both of which had great
influence on the modern forms of "Stepping". Other dances
are the "Polvillo", the "Guieneo", "Hermano Bartolo", "Juan
Redondo", "Pipironda Sapona", and the "Zorongo" — mentioning only a few.

The Spanish dances as danced in Spain today arose at the
end of the 17th century and in the 18th. With its variations:
the "Malagueña", the "Rondeña", the "Granadina" and the
"Murciana", the "Fandango" came to Europe in the course of
the 17th century and has — according to present opinion — its
origin in South America, just as the "Sarabande" and "Chaconne". The Fandango was mentioned already on p. 251
(Gluck's "Don Juan"). It is a most sensual dance of courting
in the rhythm of 3/8, wherein each pair of two bars forms a
unit in the rhythm of the castanets

thereby forming a 6/8 bar. Guitar and castanets are compul-
sory. Danced and played couplets alternate with stanzas which
are only sung without any dancing. The "Fandango" is danced
by couples, and reflects temptingly the voluptuous courting of

the man and the bashful reluctance of the woman. Its performance frequently became so bare of decency that the clergy remonstrated against it. It was even put on trial in all earnestness, and the ballet "Le Procès du Fandango" by Saint Léon, arranged in 1858, deals with the story of this lawsuit. There is a difference between the Castilian and the Andalusian Fandango. Male and female dancers have their separate tours and do not touch each others hands. In Spain the Fandango fascinated old and young alike, and even the nobility succumbed unreservedly to its power of temptation. When Casanova in 1768 was in Madrid, he attended a masked ball where the Fandango was danced. In his memoirs he wrote: "I thought I knew the Fandango. Up to now I had seen it danced on the stages of Italy and France, but the dancers were very careful to avoid all those movements by which the Fandango becomes the most seductive and the most voluptuous dance on earth . . . Men and women make only three steps and shiver at the sound of the castanets". According to Casanova's story, the Fandango was danced best by the "Gitanas" — the gypsies.

The "Bolero" (allegedly from the Spanish word "volero": to fly), is a dance for a couple, created by the dancer Zerezo (1780). The movement is one of a moderately fast ternary dance, but there is occasional change of time to a duple meter with this characteristic rhythm:

The dancer accompanies himself with castanets. Where song and the guitar are used as accompaniment, it is called "Seguidilla Bolero". The "Bolero" is a much more reserved and quiet dance than the fandango. Though it is a courting dance, with the escape, pursuit and renewed flight of the female partner, it no longer has the impetuous passion of the fandango, but is rather persuasive and tender. It consists of five divisions: first: "Paseo" (promenade) as an introduction, second: "Traversias" (change of place), third: "Differencias" (change of steps), fourth: "Traversias", fifth: "Finale".

Another dance is the "Cachucha". The word is a diminutive, which may be used to name a little bird, a little piece, a little cap. This dance is related to the bolero, in 3/8 time and is to be performed by a solo female dancer. Fanny Elssler introduced it on the stage, dancing to a melody which became so popular that the German students sang a drinking song to it.

The "Guarracha", also in 3/8 time is an African dance, performed by a single person playing the accompaniment himself on a guitar, as the tempo grows faster. Guarracha means liveliness in the language of the Negroes. Auber has given us a stylized Guarracha in his opera "The Mute of Portici". In Cuba the "Habanera" is known as "Danza". It has duple meter with slow movements. The Habanera has Spanish background and was re-imported to Spain. It is little known that the famous Habanera from "Carmen" was not written by Bizet but borrowed from a song by the Spanish composer Sebastian Yradier, published about 1840 in Madrid under the title "Chanson Havanaise". In Andalusia "Jaleo de Xeres" in 3 beat measure has alternating wild and quiet gestures. The "Jota" danced in Aragon, New Castilia and Andalusia is a waltz-like dance. The couples dance opposite each other but do not circle around the room though they change place with each other.

When the "Tango" was brought to the United States and to Europe from South America in 1900, with slow crossed steps and knee bending and pauses, it turned the heads of society with its exotic rhythms.

Finally we must mention the "Sardana", a Catalonian dance which may be performed by an unlimited number of participants.

In discussing Nordic folk music we emphasized the fact of the independence of its development in the outskirts of European music, and thereby explained its archaistic and exotic impression. In considering Spanish folk music, we must not ignore the historic factor of the cultural and musical progress of the Iberian peninsula being subject to Arabian currents and influences for many centuries. We have a famous collection of Spanish folk music in the "Cancionero Musical popular Espagnol" by Felipe Pedrell, who took a part of his melodies (dating from the 13th and 14th centuries), from the musical works of Francisco de Salinas (1514-1590). The Jewish musicologist Idelsohn writing in his book "Songs of the Oriental Sephardim", has proved that countless Spanish melodies, dating from the 14th and 15th centuries have Arabic character. On the other hand, in a later period, a new type appeared which exhibited a blending of Arabic and Roman elements. Idelsohn also found that there was a strong resemblance between the Spanish folk songs of a later date and the songs of the Jews who emigrated from Spain to the Orient and to Europe and he showed similarities between the Jewish, the Polish and the Czech folk songs.

Be that as it may, the folk music of Spain has retained from these Arabic periods the predominant minor character, the sentimental-melancholic mood which it has in common with Slavic music. We find short motives which are repeated over and over again, frequently having tetrachordal character, also pentatonic and ancient scales. But the most remarkable quality is the use of the "gypsy mode" which we find in the music of the Hungarians. Most characteristic of this music is the rhythm of the guitar and castanet accompaniment, as well as the fixed and rigid forms of embellishment, as for example here:

This type is very frequently used by the Hungarians.

It would lead us too far afield to enter into a detailed discussion on the peculiarities of Spanish folk music. Albeniz introduced these forms and the Spanish folk dance in his piano suites. The principle of the suite receives new impetus from these works, in which the succession of dances represent characteristic dance forms from the various provinces of Spain. Granada contributes a "Serenata", Barcelona a "Curranda"; there are "Sevillanas" and the "Saeta" of the Easter pageant

from Cadiz, a "Legend" from Asturia, "Seguidillas" from
Castile, while Cuba furnishes a "Nocturno". These are the
parts of the "Suite Espagnole". The dances of Albeniz are
exceedingly pictorial. His "Seguidillas" are realistic representations of Spanish folk life: Guitar sounds call the singers
into the old Moorish garden of Madrid. They range themselves
in two long lines opposite each other. The female singer intunes
the first short verse, then the guitar sets in with the continuation ("seguidilla") as the dancers begin their dance, continuing it until the singer chimes in again. The dance, quiet at
first, becomes more and more fiery. (Wholetone scales). All
kinds of steps are introduced, Bolero, Fandango and Jota. In
the second part, places are changed, then the first part is repeated with slight variations, and then, when the music ceases,
suddenly the dancers remain rigid as statues.

Besides the Spanish composers Albeniz, Granados, de Falla
and Turina, also French composers, among them Ravel, Cha-
brier and others, wrote Spanish dances.

If Albeniz has been called the Spanish Liszt, Manuel de
Falla may well be designated as the Spanish Bartók. Falla as
well as Turina derive their melodies from Andalusian folk
music, but all the modern composers of Spain, of course, have
been greatly influenced by the French impressionists.

* * *

It would take us far beyond the limits set for our task in
this book to try to describe the music of all the other border
countries. We should find ourselves compelled to widen the
scope infinitely, all the more since the entire musical develop-
tók, Moussorgsky and Stravinsky uninhibited folk influences
of the folk song and the folk dance, almost as much as in the
days before the classicists and the Mannheim School. For this
new music is not only the consequence of national music styles,
but it was constantly influenced by them. All of the characteristics of old popular music: rhythmical irrationalism and
anti-harmonic melody line, as they have been preserved in
ancient and primitive scales and primitive polyphony — all
these mark, too, the new musical style. There is a deep signi-

ficance in the fact that at the end of a long development of music, an ancient folk lore should be rediscovered. With Bartók, Moussorgsky and Stravinsky uninhibited folk influences penetrate music. But it is not the melody or even the rhythm as such that are the criteria of the new music, but the unconscious unity of the composer with his ethnic group.

Behind Bartók's rhythmic system stands his race. But this dependence on his people has at the same time something international and universal. Primitiveness, a regression to primeval musical values, gives to the music something which transcends pure ethnology. The older Russian composers, Glinka, Tchaikovsky, Balakirev and Borodin, still forced their genius into a rhythmic and melodic-harmonic set of rules brought from outside. Stravinsky and Bartók created new rhythms which in their complication reach back to primeval forms. Just examine Stravinsky's "Rondes Printanières" from the "Sacre du Printemps". "In these cultic dances the tortured ear of modern man feels an audacious primitiveness and a new barbaric religiosity": (Mersmann). Let us listen to the "Russian Dance" from Stravinsky's ballet music for "Petruschka." There one finds genuine heterophony resembling the old "Faux Bourdons" of the Middle Ages or the Javanese Gamelan orchestra. Here a complete circuit is made by a train of thought which led us from the dance music of the primitives to that of modern man.

CHAPTER XIII

BALLET AND MODERN DANCE.

IT IS WITH Stravinsky that we have reached our last chapter dealing in a short outline with the history of the ballet and the dance music of recent times.

The classical ballet of the 17th and 18th centuries in France received its greatest stimulant from the two great personalities — Lully and Rameau. Never before, nor ever since, have there been two artists equally gifted as composers of ballet music.

It is strange that French predominance in the field of ballet was wrested from France about 1800 by an Italy that would boast of an ancient ballet tradition that was dominant since the days of the Renaissance but lost to France in 1660. The "La Scala" in Milan became the center of ballet development. The great dancer and choreographer Salvatore Vigano (1769-1821), already mentioned when we discussed the "Prometheus" music of Beethoven, became the leader of the Italian School. He created the mass-pantomime of "La Scala" which held sway over European theatres until the era of Luigi Manzetti at the end of the 19th century. Like Noverre, he emphasized action and psychology in dance and liked to stress the element of folklore. The only familiar score of his long career is Beethoven's "Prometheus".

Nor had the great classical period of Vienna a significant influence on the development of ballet music.

Franz Schubert who wrote the charming music to "Rosamunde", in the field of ballet was unfortunately likewise denied any influence. Of course two of the greatest German romanticists: Mendelssohn and Schumann, had very little relation to the theatre and still less to the ballet. In the Germany of that time the Romantic Period coincided with a strong nationalist movement, and the ballet was deemed something un-German and hence inferior, — a regrettable fact in view of the fine plasticity and the rhythmic force of Schumann's music. Its impressiveness was acknowledged later by Fokine when he wrote (in 1912) his ballet "Carnival" for Schumann's music. Mendelssohn's music was also adapted for the ballet-divertisse-ment "Snow Episode in the Primeval Forest" (Schnee-Episode im Urwald), — Vienna 1921 — and so was Brahms for several ballets. We witness in the 19th century in the field of ballet a phenomenon reminiscent of the star- and prima-donna system of the opera in the 18th century. As the "star system" for ballerinas became the vogue and the productions were designed to enhance individual personalities and virtuosity, music was obviously on the decline. Let us also remember that in the 17th century ballet music was composed in Vienna and at German courts (and even occasionally in Italy) by second-rank composers. Germany was never really a ballet country, and in the 18th century ballet was — in Vienna as well as in Stuttgart — merely imported French stuff. We need not be surprised therefore at the fact that at a time of resurgent national self-consciousness ballet had to become the step-child of German art.

With German romanticism at its prime, it had to enter the world of ballet in another land and through the medium of a French composer. Heine's poetry was the inspiration for Coralli's ballet "Giselle ou les Willis" (1841) — with St. Georges and Gautier as collaborators — with a score by Adolphe Adam, the one and only ballet of the period that has lasted. Compared to the music which was written during the time by Marschner, Weber, Mendelssohn, Schumann, the musi-cal value of the ballet is insignificant although the rhythmical charm and the melodic beauty of the score must not be under-estimated. Other ballets by Adam were "Faust" (1832), "La Fille du Danube" (1836) — by Filippe Taglioni for Maria Taglioni —, "La Corsaire" and "Isaura". "Giselle" held the stages of the world not for its certain degree of musical conti-nuity, but mainly for the opportunity which it offered to the ballerina. It has remained a popular ballet subject.

As far as ballet in opera is concerned, it was Paris that traditionally dominated the scene. Marschner and Weber who paved the way for the genius of Richard Wagner, did not contribute to ballet in opera. It is well known that for the Paris performance of "Freischuetz", Weber's "Invitation to the Dance" was interpolated as a ballet number, and Berlioz scored the original piano composition. Dietsch also composed a ballet music for "Freischuetz" in Paris, 1846. Later on, in 1927, Fokine choreographed the ballet "Le Spectre de la Rose" with Weber's "Invitation to the Dance" again used; Lehnert (1927) arranged "The Water-Nymph of Schoenbrunn", and Taglioni and Telle in 1876 transformed the "Invitation to the Dance" into the ballet "Rococo". Wagner's only contribution to ballet, the "Bacchanale" of "Tannhauser", was written especially for the Paris performance, and then the work failed because the ballet was in the first act, — much too early to be seen by the influential members of the "Jockey Club", which at that time was considered to be the most important group in Paris social life.

Composers for the romantic ballet were Schneitzhoffer, Gyrowetz (40 ballets), Carafa, Labarre, Talbecque, Gide and Conte Gabrielli who wrote 60 ballets not one of which is known today. Today these names are alive only in the encyclopedias. However, Ambroise Thomas, the composer of "Mignon" collaborated with two other unknowns: Benoist and Marliani, in the ballet "The Gipsy", created especially for Fanny Elssler. His other ballets were "Betty" and "La Tempête".

Even Offenbach, who was a prolific composer for the theatre, composed only one original ballet "Les Papillons" which, incidentally, was the only ballet choreographed by the great dancer Maria Taglioni. The many successful ballets which are credited to Offenbach today, are actually adaptations, designed to fit the needs of the choreographers and respective stories.

Auber adapted music from his best liked operas for the

ballet "Marco Spada" and wrote "Le Dieu et la Bayadère" for Fillipe Taglioni (1830), who staged it for his daughter, Maria. Auber's most important contribution to ballet is the opera "The Mute of Portici" in which the female lead is not a soprano but a ballerina. A rare example of a pantomimic figure providing the dramatic impetus of the entire opera. In contrast to this unique experiment, the dances in opera were mostly incidental and scarcely ever a part of the dramatic continuity, yet ballet flourished in the French and Italian opera houses.

One of the few composers who wrote equally important music for opera and ballet was Leo Delibes. Of his creations, particularly "Coppélia", one of the many "doll comes to life" stories of its time, has, like "Giselle", remained in the standard repertoire. But unlike "Giselle", its musical quality has been proven superior by the fact that excerpts are still part of the popular concert repertoires. It is the first of all the ballets of the romantic period whose music has found a place in concert programs, independent of the dance. Of almost equal popularity musically, although long dropped from the ballet repertoire, are "Sylvia" (1876) and "Naila" (1878).

The last important composer of this period, Camille Saint-Saëns, managed to create a magnificent uniformity of ballet and dramatic action in the "Bacchanale" of the opera "Samson and Delila": Another isolated case in which ballet is not only a part of, but points up the dramatic action. "Javotte" was his only contribution to ballet and this was written for Mariquita. Damiani was the principal dancer.

It may be said that — as distinct from social and folk dances which had the greatest influence on the development of national music schools — the influence of ballet on development of music in the 19th century was on the whole slight. In spite of the immense popularity of the ballet which almost overshadowed the opera, it held little attraction for the prominent composers of the day. The majority of the hundred of ballets of the period were composed by musically inferior routine composers. The ballet was a shallow form of entertainment for a class saturated with money and pleasure, and hence unable to strike "the spark of genius" . . . People adored the stars and raved about the sex appeal of the movements of their limbs, they wrote verses in anacreontic fashion about the "pas de deux", danced by Blasis and Virginia Leon and composed by Paganini. But who cared about the music when the eyes were offered such delights by the Bocci, or the Maderna, and all the others. Their names were on everybody's lips, they were then not less famous than is today Ingrid Bergman . . . Only a few names of the numerous dancers and danseuses survived. The musicians who composed for them the waltz- and polka rhythms, the "Ballabiles" and the instrumental solos, are also forgotten. A few anecdotes about the great ballerinas are, however, still current in our time, for instance the story of Taglioni's marriage. She married the Count Gilbert des Voisins who, however, "lost sight completely of this fact". When Mme. Taglioni was introduced to him casually one day as his wife, he is supposed to have said: "Après tout, c'est possible".

In Central Europe, the Vienna Court Opera was most representative in its contribution to ballet. But "Court Opera" it was from the beginning and, in spite of political changes after the First World War, its style remained that of the second half on the 19th century. Vienna was in the field of music either reactionary or extremely revolutionary. This was always so. But not even the slightest innovation was tolerated in the field of ballet. The composer who did most of the writing was Joseph Bayer (1852-1913), conductor of all the ballets at the Vienna Opera. The style of ballet in Vienna differed from the classic style of Paris by making the Viennese Waltz an integrated part of the dance. Bayer's best known ballet "The Doll's House" ("Die Puppenfee") was later used by Diaghileff in "La Boutique Fantastique", but the music was exchanged for unknown piano pieces by Rossini, and orchestrated by Respighi. Bayer did not only compose, he also made many adaptations, especially of the music of Johann Strauss, in his ballet "Around Vienna" ("Rund um Wien") — 1894 —, and "Cinderella" ("Aschenbroedel") — 1908. Sometimes he ventured even on Oriental motives, as for instance in his "Persian Divertissement", performed 1899 in Vienna in honor of the Shah of Persia.

The Czech managed to make a greater contribution to ballet than the Austrians, and it is characteristic that a whole galaxy of Czech names can be found among the Viennese ballet composers of the period around 1800. I could also point, in addition, to the already mentioned Gyrowetz and to Paul Vranitzky also — who wrote (1798) the music for Traffieri's ballet "The Girl of the Woods" ("Das Waldmaedchen"). He introduced there various national dances. One of them, the "Russian dance" served Beethoven as a theme for a piano composition. Other Czech composers too, were not unknown as ballet composers. For instance František Škroup (1801-1862), the creator of the Czech musical comedy and composer of the Czech National Anthem, but it was really Smetana who put in his "Bartered Bride" the fiery, quick Czech dances on the stage. He had a whole array of successors in the ballet of the Czech National Theatre, i. e. Oscar Nedbal (1874-1930) whose ballet "Lazy Johnny" was produced in many theatres. He won particular success with his ballets "From Fairy-Tale to Fairy-Tale" 1908, "Princess Hyacinth" (1911), "The Devil's Grandmother", and so forth. Nedbal's ballet music exhibits Czech rhythms with a Viennese touch. Karl Bendl (1838-1897) was another Czech ballet composer. He oscillates between Smetana's raciness and Mendelssohn's romantic lyricism, and wrote the ballet "Czech Wedding". Karl Kovařovic (1862-1920) came out with the ballets "Hasheesh" (1884) and "Tale of the Good Luck Found". Leoš Janaček (1854-1928) is, however, more important. The rhythms of his ballet "Racocz Rakoczy" are nurtured on Moravian and Slovakian folklore but some traces of Borodin and Moussorgsky influence are also discernible. Viteslav Novák who leans heavily on Slovakian folklore should also be mentioned because of his ballet-pantomime "Signorina Gioventù" (after a story of Svatopluk Čech who supplied also the subject to Novák's ballet "Nicotina"). We should mention finally also Bohuslav Martinu who lived for a long time in France and now is a resident of the United States. He is rooted in Czech folklore but strongly influenced by French impressionism as may be seen in his ballet "Istar", with its orchestration tending to exotic colors and the preference for oriental themes and tunes. His ballet "Spaliček" (1931) is written in the style of a variety show with rapid change of scenes and many colorful portrayals of Czech life with the text drawn from Czech folk tales.

Ballet in Russia developed fairly much along the lines of the desires of the Reigning House and was greatly influenced by the members of the court. The Neapolitan Opera and, in connection with it, the Italian ballet as well were "en vogue" until the middle of the 19th century. From that time on, Paris virtually set the style for St. Petersburg. Music and theatrical dance were on the same line of mediocrity. With Mme. Taglioni, Fanny Elssler and Cerito, came the music of Cesare Pugni (1805-1870), who settled in St. Petersburg as "Court-Composer", and worked there for 30 years. He wrote music for about 300 ballets, complying with the needs of the choreographer, without attempting creative individuality. Ludwig Minkus, Paul Hertel and A. Drigo were the other composers of the period.

Marius Petipa who came to St. Petersburg as a dancer, became the leading choreographer preceding the Diaghileff period. He was a perfectionist in execution, and thus set the stage for the immense development of Russian ballet. This development was an evolution covering many years and gradually paved the way for the creative genius of Michael Fokine. With Russian intensity, perfection of ensemble and virtuosity, Russian Imperial Ballet prepared to serve as the most influential force for the dance in the world.

Tchaikovsky and Glazounoff were the first composers of major importance to write for ballet in Russia. And it is no coincidence that Tchaikovsky's 3 ballet scores: "Swan Lake", "Sleeping Beauty" and "Nutcracker" are used by ballet companies the world over, although these are not among his best works measured in terms of absolute musical values.

In tracing the development of music in ballet it becomes apparent that the art was in need of a coordinating genius like Diaghileff in order to attain the high level which its sister-art, the opera, had established for itself. Originally planned as a kind of theatrical exposition of all branches of Russian music, opera, ballet and symphonic music, the Diaghileff plan outgrew its original intention after its great initial success.

It is an established fact that Diaghileff is responsible for three of the most important works of the first two decades in this century: "Firebird", "Petrushka" and "Rites of Spring". In spite of the fact that the latter never became at home in the theatre, its music, even today, is still considered a radical departure from rhythmic and tonal conventions; it is this very piece that has influenced the creation of music in all countries, perhaps more than any other work written in this century. Aside from playing a most important role in the development of Stravinsky, Diaghileff can also be credited with giving the world a great theatrical score by Ravel. Though not as daring a work in its general conception, "Daphnis and Chloe" is one of the milestones of French contemporary music, and can be considered Ravel's most successful work for the stage.

Russia and France contributed jointly to the creation of modern ballet: Russia through the creative power of her choreographers and the dynamism of her composers, and France through her ballet tradition and her particular musical development which in its last phase, the impressionism of Debussy, had become the most fertile soil for the ballet. It was in France that the stage was inseparably linked with dance from the beginning. But it was only owing to musical impressionism that ballet achieved its full stature as a work of art per se. It is with Debussy that verbal language became more and more indifferent. Of course from the point of view of his musical philosophy it was quite natural that the word faded away while gesture and movement assumed prominence. This is one of the most essential roots of the new ballet-pantomime.

Ravel wrote in addition to "Daphnis and Chloe" (1912) several other ballets: "L'enfant et les Sortilèges" ("Child and

Spell"), with a libretto by Colette (1912), which was also performed in Vienna in 1932, under the heading "Das Zauberwort ("The Spell"). Other ballets of his are: "Ma Mère, L'Oye" ("Mother Goose")—1912—, "Adelaide or The Language of Flowers" (after the "Valses Nobles and Sentimentales"), "Couperin's Tomb" (from the orchestra suite), and "Bolero"—1928. Ravel's works show clearly that their starting-point was Debussy. There is, first of all, the short-limbed "pointillistic" principle of form which suits the ballet to a high degree because pantomimic action is dissolved into a great number of single tiny elements of movements. Each choreographic unit gets also its uniform musical expression.

It is characteristic that Germany again did not take part in the evolution of music in the dance revolving around the guiding spirit of Diaghileff. Except for the "Joseflegende" by Richard Strauss, which never became a real success, its choreography having gone through numerous changes, music for Diaghileff's company was created exclusively by Russians and composers of the Western hemisphere. Up to this day, Germany has stayed away from ballet almost entirely; it is therefore not surprising that there are no German composers of the first rank represented in ballet. There is one exception: Hindemith's "Nobilissima Visione", created with Massine for the Ballet Russe de Monte Carlo in 1938. It cannot honestly be said that it was the world of ballet that attracted Hindemith, but rather the medieval mysticism of the subject. The work was written immediately after he had finished "Mathis the Painter", the opera which deals with a dissimilar theme, yet related through channels of religious thought. As in "Mathis the Painter", and earlier in the viola concerto, "Der Schwanendreher", Hindemith uses medieval tunes. The leading motive of the ballet is a Troubadour melody: "Ce fut en Mai".

Returning to the Diaghileff era, Michael Fokine was the first Russian choreographer destined for fame in Europe and America. Being a sensitive musician himself, he, like his forrunner Noverre, felt the need of complete fusion of dance and music. He also sensed the lack of dramatic force and continuity in the ballet scenarii. The first ballet he created for the Imperial Russian Theatre was "Le Pavillon d'Armide", produced in St. Petersburg in 1907. Its score is an original work by Nikolai Nikolajewitch Tcherepnin (the older), and is said to have a seductive quality with a hint of mysticism. With Diaghileff, Fokine's first works were based on existing music which limits discussion from a purely musical point of view. It cannot be denied though, that the popularity of the dances from "Prince Igor" is a direct result of the popularity of the ballet — a production conceived independently of Borodin's opera — which is prominent in the standard ballet repertoire of today. Another early production of the Diaghileff period is "Cleopatra", which boasts of an unusual musical history. The ballet was based on an earlier work by Fokine: "Une Nuit d'Egypt", the music of which was an original score by Arensky. In the new version, music by other composers was substituted for Arensky's in many spots. Although the dramatic needs were thus well filled, the musical unity was greatly disturbed. At the Paris première in 1909, the ballet had music by Arensky, plus excerpts from Rimsky-Korsakoff's "Mlada", Glinka's "Russlan and Ludmilla", as well as Moussorgsky's "Khovanchina" topped with a bit of the "Bacchanale" from Glazounoff's "Seasons". Fokine's creative powers reached their height, when an original score of dramatic force inspired him. "Firebird" and "Petroushka" are undoubtedly historical achievements of this period of the dance. Of equally great musical importance is Ravel's score for "Daphnis and Chloe", though it seems that the ballet itself has lost its place for present-day audiences, both the suites, especially the second, having become "best sellers" in the concert halls. One reason for lack of its continuous success as a stage work, is that the book, based on shepherd's stories popular in the days of Noverre, holds little interest for the public of today.

"Petroushka" is not only the most representative score of the era, but also an immense step forward after "Firebird". While "Firebird" is still a romantic ballet, in regard to stage work and score, the natural quality of the score and stage action of "Petroushka" is decidedly Twentieth Century. The score for "Firebird" stands in the development of Stravinsky about where "Rienzi" stands with Wagner, or "Transfigured Night", with Schoenberg. With all its dazzling sound, its dissonances in the scenes of the sorcerer, Kastshei, this score is full of the heritage of Rimsky-Korsakoff and even of Glazounoff.

This romantic heritage can also be traced in "Petroushka", especially in the final scene of the dancing crowds where Russian folk melodies are introduced. "Petroushka" is basically modern in its rhythms, its musical naturalism, and the bite of characterization in the two middle scenes. The naturalism of the milling crowds of the opening scene are musically striking. Projected with the revolutionary new rhythm of 3/8, 4/8, 2/8, and 5/8 bars in rapid succession, immediately following this new design in musical characterization, the sound of a broken hand organ is reproduced quite realistically with woodwinds, bells, celesta and piano, and an off-balance rhythm which is achieved by writing a 4/4 theme in 3/4 rhythm, thus shifting the natural downbeat once in every bar. Another rhythmical device is the piling of 2/4 on top of 3/4, the orchestra playing two rhythms simultaneously.

As is frequent with provocative new works, the excerpt which has become best known, is the least original; just as "The Ride of the Valkyries" became most popular as a closed form while Wagner was fighting to get his idea of endless melody recognized. This reference is to the Russian Dance of the three puppets; although it fits the action to perfection, it is less developed than the other sections of the score. Its simplicity makes it easy to keep in mind. In fact, its thematic material was originally intended for another piece, a piano concerto, which was never completed. Sketches for this same piano concerto also appear in the following scene, when Petroushka is locked in his cell. But here is more than mere adaptation; the racing piano passages, combined with weird combinations of muted brass instruments, give a moving picture of Petroushka's desperation, and the following little

"Adagietto" with its whimpering mood is a unique piece of characterization. The following scene "Chez le Maure", contains both natural and expressive elements. It starts with an oriental mood followed by the childish tune the ballerina plays on her toy trumpet. The mood retains this satyrical quality with the quotation of an old Viennese Waltz by Lanner (the same which is also quoted to create atmosphere in an Austrian opera by Kienzl: "The Evangelist". Students will note the opposite results of the quotations; one is satyric while the other is sentimental. Out of the Waltz develops a semi-dramatic chase, culminating in the most complex rhythmical pattern Stravinsky had conceived up to that time. In the last scene appear the already mentioned Russian themes, brilliantly woven into a fluid rhythmic form. The end, depicting the appearance of the dead puppet's spectre, using only two trumpets, two oboes and four horns, has an unreal quality which scarcely ever had been reached by a composer.

The last work of musical historic importance to be created under the leadership of Diaghileff was De Falla's "Three Cornered Hat", — a perfect blend of the Spanish and Russian spirit. By the time of its creation, Russian ballet had been in Western Europe for almost a decade and the unity of thought which Diaghileff managed to create between De Falla and Massine, was complete.

These were the great contributions made to music by the Russian ballet. The less fortunate creations (musically) were those which used music created earlier for another purpose, without too much discrimination.

There can be little objection in the use of Chopin's piano music by Fokine for "Les Sylphides"; with the score partly orchestrated by Stravinsky. But with the pantomimic recreation of "Scheherazade", a sequence of developments occurred which not only hindered the creation of new scores, but returned to the old custom of adaptations that were so prevalent in the days of Vigano and Filippe Taglioni. For Fokine's "Scheherazade", the original score by Rimsky-Korsakoff was used, but the program which the composer had given his symphonic suite, was completely ignored, and another Arabian tale, with no connection whatsoever to the original story of "Sindbad the Sailor" was superimposed.

Even worse was "Cleopatra", when Diaghileff used music of no less than three composers, resulting in an artistic unbalance which led to utter and complete failure.

The two ballets which might be held against Fokine's musical integrity are the above mentioned "Scheherazade" (1910), in the days of Diaghileff's uncontested triumphs, and his last creation: "Russian Soldier", produced for ballet theatre in 1942. Here a satyrical humorous score by Prokofieff is used for a thoroughly sentimental story. This complete lack of fusion between action and music, had made the last production of a great artist short lived.

George Balanchine was the next great choreographer, an artist who possesses keen musical insight. Like Fokine, he had the good fortune to deal with composers like Prokofieff and Stravinsky in his more important assignments. The "Prodigal Son" with Prokofieff's fine score was one of the last creations staged by Diaghileff in Paris (1929). Of the list of the Stravinsky scores, Balanchine had the honor of devising the choreography for "Apollon Musagete", "Jeu de Cartes" and "Baiser de la Fée", all three for the American Ballet under the direction of Lincoln Kirstein and Edward Warburg in New York. Balanchine also adapted two of Stravinsky's scores which were not intended for ballet originally but were used with the composer's consent. The violin concerto was called "Balustrade", staged by the Original Ballet Russe in 1941, and "Danses Concertantes", staged for the Ballet Russe de Monte Carlo in 1944. The latter, with beautiful décor and costumes by Eugene Berman, and Stravinsky's very danceable score, is an exception to the rule, and had become a work of complete artistic unity.

Another choreographer who designed dance patterns to a Stravinsky score was Bronislava Nijinska, sister of the great Nijinsky. "Les Noces", with words and music by Stravinsky, was produced in Paris, 1923. It is unique in its musical construction, the orchestra consisting of four pianos and a group of percussion instruments, a chorus and four vocal soloists. A certain discrepancy of the primitive pagan story, and the almost geometrical way in which the masses are moved on stage kept the ballet from being a complete artistic success. More successful was Nijinska's adaptation of Ravel's "La Valse" (Paris, 1929).

Paris remained a center of activity, even after Diaghileff's death. Composers such as Milhaud, Poulenc, Honegger, Satie and Germaine Tailleferre contributed to the development of ballet.

The Swedish dancer-choreographer, Jean Borlin, who, incidentally, was the first choreographer to employ the services of an American composer (Cole Porter's "Within the Quota", the first ballet on an American theme, 1923) was greatly responsible for bringing the Avant-Garde to the fore. In "Les Maries de la Tour Eiffel", 1921, we find collaboration of not less than five young composers, members of the famous group of six: George Auric, Arthur Honegger, Darius Milhaud, Francis Poulenc and Germaine Tailleferre. The story of this ballet appears slightly eccentric, and is part of the trilogy, an experiment by Jean Cocteau, the other two parts being "Parade" and "Le Boeuf sur le Toit". Borlin also asked the young Darius Milhaud to write the score of his "Creation du Monde" (Paris, 1923). Milhaud also wrote the scores for "Salade", "Le Train Bleu", "Les Songes", "La Mort d'un Tyran", and "Saudades de Brazil". Following the trend of the influence created by the United States in the first post-war era, Milhaud was attracted to jazz and wrote a certain amount of music reflecting the idiom.

English ballet has contributed considerably to the development of young composers. With intelligent choreographers such as Ninette de Valois, Frederic Ashton and Marie Rambert, great opportunities were provided for the composers. Most representative is Vaughn Williams' score, "Job", originally in collaboration with Geoffrey Keynes. It was presented to, and rejected by Diaghileff. Williams had become resigned to the idea of using the score just as a concert suite until

Miss de Valois became interested and the ballet was produced in London, 1931.

One of the outstanding examples of fusion of dance and music is Miss de Valois' ballet "Checkmate", with score by Arthur Bliss, produced in Paris, 1937. The story, dealing with the figures of the checker board as human beings with human emotions, provides opportunities for a score with many facets of musical expression and Bliss makes the most of these splendid possibilities. The score was heard in New York at a Philharmonic Concert in 1940, with the composer conducting.

Frederick Ashton's most prominent work is "Façade", with the witty and brilliant score by William Walton. Though "Façade", like "Job", went through many stages before it reached its final shape, it is a work, not only solid in form, but probably the most humorous of all theatrical works; it should do away with the prejudice that English music is necessarily dry, for the score of "Façade" is one of the few pieces that has the power to create laughter when played as straight music in the concert hall. This same combination has recently created another sensation in a ballet called "Quest" which is based on the first book of Spenser's "Fairy Queen". The production was described as the terpsichorean event of the year 1942-43. According to Edwin Evans: The music is of particular interest as it embodies three different applications of variation-form. Action, and what film people would call "continuity" are treated in the traditional Wagnerian manner, with leading themes for the principal characters "metamorphosed" according to the circumstances unfolded in the story. But the choreographic variations of the "Seven Deadly Sins" are for once also variations in the musical sense — variations on a theme of which the primary form is not stated. And the concluding scene is constructed on a ground bass, not too slavishly adhered to but sufficiently persistent for the result to be called a "free passacaglia". This, like "Façade" is only an excursion into comedy.

It is only natural that American composers were slow in coming to the fore with original ballet music; for, aside from the tours of Diaghileff and Nijinsky during the first war, no considerable activities in ballet or modern dance took place in the United States until the early 1930's.

Therefore, curiously enough, two of the first ballets with music by Americans based on American themes were produced on European soil — "Within the Quota" by Cole Porter (Paris, 1923) and "Skyscrapers" by Carpenter (Munich, 1929).

"Within the Quota" was one of those courageous experiments of the Swedish Borlin when he led his company of "Ballet Suedois" through great success and equally great discussion in Paris. It was satire on American life of that period and Porter's music was satiric and exaggerated. At least that is the way it impressed its European listeners at that time.

The ballet "Skyscrapers" is the result of collaboration between the German choreographer Kroeller and John Alden Carpenter. Both of these ballets reflect the style of the early 20s. While "Within the Quota" is thoroughly and aggressively satiric, "Skyscrapers" is definitely serious, trying to convey a message of the kind in the opera "Machinist Hopkins" by Max Brand, or Křenek's early opera "Zwingburg", — the human soul being tortured by the tyranny of the machine. "Within the Quota'" has a cast which leaves little doubt as to the satirical intent of the ballet. It has an immigrant, a millionairess, a puritan, a colored gentleman, a jazz-baby, all of which have a grotesque angle to European eyes, just as the "Krauts" stand for exaggerated German character qualities. Hence, the first two American ballets are European in spirit although their music was composed by Americans.

In the United States, ballet is promoted by impresarios and the great concert agencies. This condition naturally results in a tendency of "Business first" which logically stifles serious creative forces. In the thirties, and until the outbreak of the Second World War, the Ballet Russe de Monte Carlo though returning every season, performed mostly European favorites.

An attempt to portray the American scene in ballet was "Union Pacific" (Philadelphia, 1934), with music by Nabokov and choreography by Massine. But Archibald MacLeish's book with its American theme (the building of the first transcontinental railroad) was the only thing that was American in the production. Both music and choreography were basically Russian, in spite of American tunes, which resulted in a complete lack of unity of ideas.

The influence of the musical comedy became apparent in this period. Choreographers concentrated on trying to be entertaining rather than following an artistic line. A typical example of this trend was "Ghost Town" (New York, 1939) by Marc Platoff, scored by Richard Rodgers: and then there was a third attempt to portray a certain historic period of the American scene in the ballet "Saratoga". This work by Massine with a score by Weinberger (New York, 1941) is American neither in dance, music, nor spirit.

Thus with the bigtime companies interested mainly in lucrative cross-country tours, the genuine creative output has been slim. Especially since the organizations were obliged to produce new productions here instead of in Europe because of the war.

Aside from "Rodeo" and "Fancy Free", no really important score has emerged, for the productions either employed adapted music or were outright revivals of older European ballets. So it was up to the smaller companies in the country to enlist the services of the American composer for truly American ballet music.

The forward looking Edward Warburg and Lincoln Kirstein realized the need for the fusion of the creative powers of musicians, choreographers, authors, and designers, the way Noverre had laid out the pattern about two hundred years ago, and thus the American Ballet came to life. Though the original organization was short-lived, Lincoln Kirstein and his Ballet Caravan which was an outgrowth of the American Ballet, carried on for quite a few seasons. It is to this organization that credit is due for the producing of significant original scores by American composers.

The first of this trend was "Yankee Clipper", scored by

Paul Bowles and choreographed by Eugene Loring (1937). "Filling Station" — with choreography by Lew Christensen (Hartford, Conn., 1938) has a witty score by Virgil Thomson which reflects the spirit and atmosphere of the American gasoline stations. And, where is there a better place to find characters of everyday life? The same years saw the première of "Billy the Kid" in Chicago, also under the Kirstein auspices. The story and choreography depict a historic character from the days of the great cattle-drives, which were to create so many of those types who were "evil in deed, yet good in heart". Aaron Copland's score is a piece of serious workmanship, inspired and dramatically tense. Rhythmically, it paves the way for "Rodeo", which is much gayer, though every bit as strong in a theatrical way.

Three years later in Rio de Janeiro (1941), Lew Christensen staged "Pastorela" with an original score by Paul Bowles. It is a kind of Nativity Play, as seen through the eyes of Mexican Indians, and Bowles actually used Mexican melodies as a basis for the score.

Two other American composers are represented in the choreography of Hans Veen. "The Incredible Flutist" (Boston, 1940), is the only theatre music by the extremely progressive New Englander, Walter Piston, and though the ballet leans slightly toward the atmosphere of "Petroushka", the music has retained strength of its own. It is one of the few American ballet scores to have been recorded by a major company to date. The most recent work of Veen is "Hudson River Legend" (Boston, 1944), scored by Josef Wagner. The "Legend of the Sleepy Hollow" is the basis for the ballet and the music follows along the romantic lines of Hadley and MacDowell.

Considerable music by American composers has been adapted for ballet. For example, Copland's "Salon Mexico" staged by Humphrey Weidman (1943). Charles Griffes' "White Peacock" found a choreographer in Adolf Bolm. Massine used sequences from Gershwin's music, employing the concerto as musical framework, to portray the characters of the New

Yorker. Just about every major Gershwin score has been choreographed by someone.

The WPA (Work Projects Administration), that so violently debated idea of the Roosevelt Administration, has its share in contributing to ballet in the United States, since together with the Music Project and Federal Theatre, there also was Federal Ballet. Ruth Page was the driving force in that project. The ballet "Frankie and Johnny", with an original score by Paul Moross, is something like a ballet version of the "Beggar's Opera", hiding its social significance behind a moral. The Moross music is based on native American themes.

Undoubtedly the two most significant scores to emerge from the major companies are "Rodeo" (Ballet Russe de Monte Carlo, 1942), and "Fancy Free" (Ballet Theatre, 1944). The former is a picture of the American Southwest. The choreography of Agnes de Mille and music of Aaron Copland are equally charming. This ballet was more successful than all the other attempts of the major companies to create an American work because it did not try to be American. It was American. It was honest, straight forward, without an eye peeking at the box-office. Just as Dvořak did not use spirituals in the "New World Symphony" but had absorbed their content, so Copland uses the rhythmic pattern of the cowboy tunes quoting them thematically. The result is a score which has all the drive necessary for the theatre, yet fully retaining the atmosphere of the Western landscape.

"Fancy Free" portrays New York, rather than America. Jerome Robbin's choreography employs steps from the dance-halls, and Leonard Bernstein's music pulls no punches in being close to the New York scene. The results are perfect, if somewhat gaudy.

The ill-fated "Ballet International", which after months and months of preparation had only one season (1944) in New York, produced two original scores. The first, a Dali concoction with Eglevsky's initial choreographic attempt, has a good score by Paul Bowles. But, unfortunately the music is completely overpowered by Dali. The second, Sebastian, on the other hand, is one step ahead to begin with since Gian-Carlo Menotti wrote the story as well as the music, and Edward Caton's choreography shows great respect for the score. While there is nothing in the music to put it in the "Petrushka" or "Daphnis and Chloe" class, it not only serves its purpose as a musical setting for a ballet, but it is also musically interesting.

The British choreographer, Antony Tudor, has contributed more to the discussion of music and ballet than anyone since the Diaghileff days with the exception, perhaps, of Massine's excursion into the symphonic field. However, outside of the fact that Tudor, like Massine, employs absolute music of the highest order for choreographic purposes, there is virtually no relationship between the two creators. Their approach is in direct opposition.

Tudor's ballets generally dwell on psychological studies of the complex characteristics of the human being. Frustration and psychoanalytical sexual problems are treated in an extremely delicate and subtle manner. He gives the inner emotions of his characters almost more importance than the actual dance movements; that is probably why he is able to use a type of music for dancing which would have been thought impossible by anyone before him. Two of his most arresting works "Lilac Garden" and "Pillar of Fire", contain hardly one fast movement, the music being Chausson's "Poème" and Schoenberg's "Transfigured Night", respectively. And in using the very lyric "Kindertotenlieder" by Gustav Mahler, he has expressed sorrow in the language of choreography as completely and as nobly as it is expressed in music.

All of Tudor's works produced by Ballet Theatre were conceived and set to music already in existence. Only his most recent work, "Undertow" (New York, April 1945), has an especially commissioned score, by the American William Schuman. Although composed expressly for the dance, it has as its main characteristic a noticeable absence of fast or rhythmic sections, — this makes it perfect for the languid movements by which Tudor gives characterization to figures of his psychological murder drama. Only in one moment of slight travesty does the music become danceable in the traditional sense. There is another instance when the mood of religious hymn tunes is the leading theme. Otherwise the music is purely abstract which is as it should be since the theme of the ballet deals with psychological problems.

The musical form of A B A corresponds with the form of the ballet, which is built on three parts: Prologue, The City, Epilogue. The musical form is directly related to the action according to the teachings of Noverre.

As a unity of dance and music this work is an interesting departure from the usual run of ballet scores as the rhythmic patterns are principally in the choreography, often in complete contrast to the sustained slow moving line of the score. This again shows that with a choreographer as highly developed intellectually as Tudor, it is not necessary for the dance to match the musical rhythm bar by bar. And in spite of the seeming contrasts in the rhythmic patterns of the dance as against those of the music an unusual blend of movement and music is achieved. This ballet is reminiscent of French impressionism: the music nestles gently without emotional exuberance to the psychology of the pantomimic events, — perhaps without the delicacy and dainty subtlety of Debussy's "Pelleas and Melisande". But this American impressionism of Schuman's might perhaps be able to forge ahead with the modern idea of ballet and build a dramatic unity out of an ideal conjunction of gesture and music. This association of a British choreographer and an American composer might perhaps be a guide-post for the future.

*   *   *

The establishment of national schools — above all the Slavic and all other peripheral nations — is an indication in music of the coming New Age. Just as in the Middle Ages the Mongol deluge drove the Slavic and Finno-Ugrian peoples before it and washed them up on the beach of European civilization, so the renaissance of these peripheral peoples preceded the great Russian revolution. These nations were nations of unknown quantities intellectually, of quite different type than the highly cultivated nations of old Europe. They are nations of workers and farmers. From this point of view the renaissance of the Poles, Czechs, Hungarians, Roumanians, and others, was only a prelude to the great Russian revolution. How does this thought fit into our history of dance music?

The music of the Baroque expressed the feeling and thought of the human being who felt a power above him, whether it was God's, the King's or the government's. The music of the classical composers on the other hand expressed the emotion and thought of the middle class that had become free and felt itself free. The romanticist felt that Europe's days were numbered. Pessimism and resignation were expressed as much in music as in the philosophy of Schopenhauer and Spengler.

An entirely new sense is found in the music of the new Eastern nations. There are melodies and rhythms of new unknown, anonymous masses. While already the music of the classicists and romanticists had lost contact with the people and floated in magnificent freedom over the clouds, — in the works of Smetana, Glinka and Bartók, we again feel the pulsating life of nations with their folk songs and dances. Almost all of these nations have something in common in rhythm, namely syncopation. There is no better symbol for revolutionary emotion and thought than syncopation, — the revolt of the unaccented beat against the accented. Syncopation is frequent in the Slavic dances of Dvořak, in Chopin's polonaises, and Hungarian rhythms of Bartók. But in modern American dance music it rules uncontestedly. In fact, it is a remarkable phenomenon that old European music was attacked from both the East and the West. Just as once the "syncopated" Sarabande and the erotic Fandango came out of the West to Europe, where they brought the blood of Baroque dancers to boil, so did American jazz throw Europeans of the twentieth century into a near frenzy. Both of the Americas in the twentieth century have, through the rhythms of the Negroes, related to those of the Near East, exerted the greatest influence upon dance music. Syncopation seems to be the rhythm of young, fresh nations, the rhythm of anonymous masses. The movements of the Negroes are impulsive, energetic and often angular. They differ essentially from those of the dominant class. These driving rhythms express the uninhibited vegetative life of this race, and the suggestive force of this new fascinating music conquered the American and European cities as once the Branle had won the French court, the Austrian "Weller" the court of Leopold I, the wild Canario, the exotic Saraband and undisciplined Volta the European Baroque courts and the Alpine Waltz and the village Polka high society of Paris and Vienna. Again it is the youthful melodies and masculine stamping rhythms of a new people which assert their seductive fascination. At the same time these melodies and rhythms are the reflex of the two Americas with their racial mixtures and unlimited energies. The effect of the jazz orchestra, therefore, with its uncompromising timbre defying every tradition, was sensational.

Paul Whiteman's orchestra was taken as a model and was copied by Sam Wooding, Vincent Lopez, and Jack Hylton; in Germany by Bernhard Etté, Marek Weber, Joseph Fuhs, and others.

From this orchestra a similar influence went out as once from the "petite bande" of Lully, which enraptured the dancers of the Parisian court balls, or from the Stamitz orchestra in Mannheim, or from Lanner's and Johann Strauss' orchestras. The choir effect of Whiteman's violins added a particular fascination. Predominance of the violin came to an end and passed to the hitherto unknown saxophone, or to other wind instruments. Whiteman's orchestra consisted of saxophones (soprano to bass) alternating with flutes, oboes and clarinets in A, B♭, E♭ and C, bass clarinets, trumpets (sometimes also French horns), trombones, tubas or string basses, suraphone, sousaphone, tympani of all kinds, two pianos, celeste and violins used only in particular passages to heighten the color, and banjos. The most important element, however, is the rhythmical section, to which, as we said above, two pianos belong, treated almost entirely as rhythmic instruments, further celeste, glockenspiel, chimes, vibraphone and xylophone. Players are required to "double", and the old tradition, according to which a player uses only one instrument throughout the whole piece, is done away with. Also the instrumental technique differs widely from the traditional one. The clarinet is often driven up to the higher sharp register and its tone qualities considerably changed by the fluttertongue. New registers of the trumpet's unbelievable portamenti, and glissandi of the trombones are uncovered by the "wow wow" revolutionary use of the mute. Improvising occupies a more prominent place. One instrument would carry the original melody while other instruments improvise counter-melodies. A new kind of jazz counterpoint develops. Counter-parts to be carried out strictly, no longer are used, but short imitations, peculiar abbreviations of the theme, sudden bits of melody like ironic caricatures, as if the instruments were "ribbing" each other, are characteristic of jazz. The filling out of the smaller intervals with glissandi and portamenti reminds one of the quarter tones of Arabian music, of the harsh, grotesque sounds of Chinese and Javanese music. The negation of harmony was evidence that jazz had begun an offensive against European music. The most important dance form of jazz is the "fox trot". Other forms have been the Charleston, Black Bottom, One-step, the American Tango, Habanera, Milonga, Argentino, the antiquated Boston and the English Waltz may be considered as related. The form of the dance pieces, as a rule, is the two-part song form, consisting of "verse" (strophe), and chorus (refrain), thirty-two bars.* The "chorus" is the actual instrument for rhythmic effect, for the various drums and rhythm instruments. There is no limit set to imagination!

The forerunner of jazz was the "rag", which itself has connections with the earlier minstrel show tunes, the "cake walk" and the "buck-and-wing" of the period from 1840 on.

---

* The blues in their original forms had mostly 12-beat phrases.

"Turkey in the Straw" is an example of the latter. Since syncopation appears quite frequent in English, and particularly in Irish popular music also, English and Irish songs and dances were frequently adapted to the syncopated exaggerations and improvisations which the American Negroes liked, and with which they combine the rhythmic gesturing and ecstatic shouts in the primitive bands in the early period of jazz. Here I should like to quote a passage from the description by Prince Bernhard of Saxony-Weimar of his travels in 1825 in the United States, and the dance music at a ball in Columbia, South Carolina. "The music consisted," so the Prince writes, "of two violins and a tambourine. This tambourine was struck with a terrible energy. The two others scraped the violin in the truest sense of the word. One of them cried out the figures, imitating with his body all the motions of the dance . . ."

"Ragtime" already shows polyrhythmic forms found among the African Negroes (use of melodic motives comprising groups of three or six notes in conflict with the 2/4 or 4/4 meter which, by giving different distributions of the notes with respect to the normal accentuation of the measure, produces a form of syncopation sometimes called "secondary rag" or "polyrhythm". Apel: Harvard Dictionary of Music). "Secondary rag" is here the opposite of "primary rag", by which one may understand the different syncopations which do not develop by simultaneous playing of various rhythms, but are "linear". Particularly the "blues" which developed around 1900 are typical Negro music. Here we find also the seventh chords so characteristic of the later period of jazz — they seek no resolution and need none — subdominant in character, often with a minor third and the parallel fourths and fifths which in Bach's times hurt the ear so much but today are so titillating — also sevenths and seconds — the so-called "barber shop harmonies". These parallel movements are traditional in the work songs and religious songs of the American Negroes and are connected with the heterophonic formations as we found them among primitive peoples and the Asiatic nations. While white musicians like Whiteman, Ted Lewis and Guy Lombardo

developed jazz as a concert form and stylized and commercial-
ized it, its original form by no means died out in the smaller
instrumental groups of from four to seven men. This original
form received new significance in hot jazz above all through
the Negro trumpeter and "scat singer" Louis Armstrong, which
differed sharply from the already conventional type of "sweet"
or "symphonic jazz". The elements of "hot jazz" are short
phrases, fragments of melody, mocking old systems of rhythm,
fragments into which the old melody seems to have been dissolved, and which are carried mostly by the vibratos of the
clarinet, the saxophone, the trombone and even the piano.
The imitation of the voice, the coarse or "dirty" tone — again
a regression to primitive music in opposition to the civilized
tempered tone system — is likewise an ingredient of this music,
just as the melodic independence of both hands on the piano
and the habit of now beating all four beats with the rhythm
instead of one and three or two and four. A kind of hypnotic
effect is the consequence of this rhythm. Even more important
is the increasing significance of improvisation again reminding
one of the primitive forms of playing music. It gains importance in the last phase of jazz, in "boogy-woogy", which
goes back to the Kansas City style of the thirties. Characteristic of this style is the "riff" the technique of short melodically
rhythmic ostinato forms which the band, or in the case of the
piano the left hand, plays while the solo instrument or the
right hand improvises. This "ostinato" is sharply "dotted"
and reminds one strongly of the ostinato themes of the seventeenth and eighteenth centuries which likewise were based on
the simplest melodic formulas (descending tetrachord, etc.).
They, too, were often strongly dotted in rhythm. This becomes
of more interest to us when we realize that also those old
ostinato dances (Chaconne, Passacaglia, Folia), were imported from the West Indies to Europe. The riff changes the
pitch or the exact melodic form of a melody, while it keeps the
general character, the "Maquam" — as the oriental musician
would say. But that also reminds one of music of oriental
and primitive peoples. These last forms of dance music are

closely connected with the spirit of modern society. We find in them that atmosphere of "civilized barbarity" which we see in another form in the art of Bartók and Stravinsky. The names of the dances which seem to have been taken over by both high and low class are "Swingtime", "Menuet", "La Conga", "La Bomba", "Snake Hips", the "Shim-Sham", "Shimmy", the "Westchester", "Suzi Q", "Rumba", "Peabody", "Grapevine Waltz", "Swing Waltz". The names, to a certain degree, go back to ancient dances. The "Rumba" in some way is connected with the old "Rotta"; the "Peabody" with the "Pavane". The great variability of the dance steps can be traced back to certain basic forms just as in the case of the "boogy-woogy" and the melody of the "riff". The "jitterbug" in its variant forms reminds one strikingly of the old "Moresca". It is the expression of the tremendous vitality of the Negroes and whoever has seen original Negro dancers must be aware of the fact that Harlem and the other Negro sections of American cities have given a new direction to dance music and have had a tremendous effect upon the influence of music in general.

From about 1935 on with the rise of the clarinetist Benny Goodman and the brothers Jimmy and Tommy Dorsey, swing came into style, a continuation of the "hot jazz" tradition. The word "jazz" seems to refer to the style of playing, to the subtle syncopated rubato. Everything was "swung", from the folk song to Mozart and Wagner. Neither Debussy nor Brahms were spared. Swing orchestras were formed with entirely new instruments, (vibraharp, electric guitar) and old instruments came into new use (harpsichord, celeste). Unbelievable precision of ensemble playing was attained, as well as an exquisite cultivation of solo work, so that swing emancipated itself from dance music, just as had that ballet music at the time of Lully, Rameau, Handel and Bach, whose dance music really had little to do with actual dancing. The jazz and swing composers have been reproached with the fact that they impiously violated the melodies of the classicists. Nowhere does African-American-European racial mixture appear so clearly as in the jazzed-up classical melodies. But this "jazzing" is nothing new. Let us remember the "Basse Danse" in which the melodic skeleton was distorted according to need; and in the age of the waltz entire operatic arias were arranged as waltzes, polkas and quadrilles. Even Mozart had nothing against it when in 1787 at a Prague ball he found his "Figaro" melodies transformed into German dances and contres. (He probably would only have smiled over the jazzing up of his C major sonata!)

The element of caricature in jazz and its successors is in fact highly essential for the revolutionary character of the new dance. We should remember that musical currents from the depths of the masses have expressed themselves by preference in mocking the artistic forms of the higher dominant classes. For instance, let us take the "Beggar's Opera" or the Opera Buffa, and also the German operetta, where a coloratura aria as a rule, is to travesty grand opera.

The origin of the name "jazz" is obscure. Some trace it back to the abbreviated given name of the Negro musician Jazzbo Brown, whose compositions aroused lively interest in the Chicago of 1915. According to another point of view, the name is supposed to come from the verb, jazz, to give chase to. Less plausible is the explanation that the word comes from the French word jaser, meaning to chat, a word which the Negroes of Louisiana and South Carolina are supposed to have taken from the French colonists. There is another much less delicate explanation of that word, which is popular among jazz-players. The significance of jazz for art music is known. When Louis Gruenberg's "Daniel Jazz" appeared at one of the international musical festivals in Europe, people were at first shocked. Today people have gotten used to his "Jazz Berries", and Gershwin's "Rhapsody in Blue" is evaluated in Europe now as the most genuine expression of American feeling. To be sure Gershwin was not the first one who introduced jazz into art music. Stravinsky's "Piano Rag Music" dated 1920, Milhaud's "La Création du Monde", composed in 1923, and other jazz compositions are of an earlier date. Nevertheless the 12th of February, 1924, is a turning point in American musical history, when Paul Whiteman first produced Gershwin's "Rhapsody in Blue", a shot that was heard around the world, as John Tasker Howard expresses himself in David Ewen's "Modern Composers". Frederick Jacobi in his essay "America's Popular Music" (Modern Music 1941), remarks quite correctly that America's popular music "occupies the place held by the music of Offenbach in the sixties, and that of Johann Strauss in the eighties, except for the fact that the world of today, being so much more unified (in some ways) than was the world of seventy years ago, its range of popularity, both geographically and numerically, is far greater than was that of its beloved predecessors".

The young Viennese Wilhelm Grosz (who died in New York in 1939), expressed the essentials of jazz strongly in his Opus No. 7, as did likewise Paul Hindemith with the "fox trot" in the closing movement of his Chamber Music Suite Op. 24. Hindemith in his Klavier Suite "1922" occupied himself with the new forms of dance music, and Stravinsky wrote a "rag-time" for eleven solo instruments. Milhaud's "Trois Rag Caprices" are from the point of view of modern dance history likewise remarkable, so are Alfredo Casella's "Five Pieces for String Quartet", the last number of which is a fox trot.

The Prague musician Erwin Schulhoff too was inclined toward the new dance music. His jazz studies (Charleston, Blue, Tango and Toccata on the Shimmy "Kitten on the Keys") are particularly noteworthy. Křenek has jazz in his opera "Johnny spielt auf", and Kurt Weill used it in his "Dreigroschenoper". Also Bohuslav Martinu in his "Esquisses de Danses" has taken jazz rhythms over. In many of his dances he combines Czech folkloristic material with elements of jazz. Jazz style is found also in John Alden Carpenter's "Concertino for Piano and Orchestra" (1915) (Ragtime rhythm), in Eric Satie's "Ballet Parade" (Rag-time du Paquebot), in Stravinsky's "Histoire du soldat", in the latter's composition "Ragtime for eleven instruments", in Milhaud's Ballet "Le boeuf sur le toit", in Aaron Copland's "Concerto for Piano and Orchestra", in

Ravel's "Sonata for Violin and Piano", in Constant Lambert's "Rio Grande" for voices and orchestra and in many others.

*   *   *

The demolition of harmonic in favor of more melodic and rhythmic thought is a result of increasing extra-European (American and Eastern) influence. It is characteristic that a Slav, Aloys Haba, who sought most radically to break down the diatonic system through the creation of quarter-tone music, (and he felt that he had to support his music also, not only theoretically but also philosophically), enlisted the aid of the Arabic system of smallest intervals. The Arabian Music Congress in Cairo in 1932 accepted his theory. Further, and in a different manner, (particularly by Heinrich Berl in his book "Das Judentum in der Musik"), it was stated that above all Jewish musicians were attacking the old system of European harmony. Arnold Schoenberg's twelve-tone system is nothing else but the negation of the old classic and romantic harmony of tension in favor of an absolute dissonance as it were. The "leading tone" is looked upon as antiquated. The melody goes its own way without regard to any resulting loss of harmonic and contrapuntal unity, and follows only the rules of melody line.

Eastern- and new Western music have something in common: it is the denial of the importance of music as a means of psychology. In its place, ecstatic tuneful music is to be set — music for the sake of itself. Let us look at the difference between a romantic Strauss Waltz and a "Boogy-woogy"!

It must not be forgotten that with the development of the National Schools of the Czechs, Poles, Russians and Hungarians, further elements of Eastern origin were introduced into European music. They have brought new ways of creation. These peripheral nations whose melodies and dances reveal their Eastern origin, have exerted a similar influence as American "Jazz". The latter is based on Negro culture and therefore — again through its African origin — related to the culture of the Near East. The predominance of rhythm and the continuing destruction of the old European tone-system are both evident in modern dance music.

The music of the 19th century was still European.

The music of the 20th century is no longer European. Just as Europe lost its monopoly in so many ways to America and the East so also in the field of music, and particularly in dance music. The latter was bound to give up its place of honor — owned by Europe so far — to other countries of the world.

The Slavic peoples of the East and the Western peoples of the Americas will be those who shall create and develop both dance music and dance in the days to come.

INDEX OF NAMES

INDEX

OF DANCES AND DANCE FORMS

357

BIBLIOGRAPHY

Abert, Hermann
"W. A. Mozart", 1919
Abert, Hermann
"J. G. Noverre and his influence
on ballet music". (Year book 1908,
Peters)
Adler, Guido
"Handbuch der Musikgeschichte",
1930
Ambros, Aug. Wilhelm
"History of Music" (especially Vol.
IV, revised by H. Leichtentritt,
1909)
Ambros, Aug. Wilhelm
"Carneval und Tanz in alter Zeit"
(Bunte Blaetter, 1872)
Arbeau, Th.
"Orchésographie", 1588.
Armstrong, Louis
"Swing that Music", 1936
Aubry, P.
"Estampies et Danses Royales",
1907

Baldus, Herbert
"Indianerstudien im nordoestlichen
Chaco", 1931
Baresel, Alfr.
"Jazz Book", 1926
Bartók, B.
"Hungarian Peasant Music" (Mu-
sical Quarterly XIX)
Basile, G. B.
"Il Pentamerone" (edited by Lieb-
recht, 1846)
Beaumont, W.
"Complete Book of Ballets", 1937,
1942
Becking, Gustav
"Der Rhythmus als historische Er-

kenntnisquelle", 1928
Besseler, Heinrich
"Musik des Mittelalters und der
Renaissance"
Bie, Oskar
"Der Tanz" 1919
Blasis, Ch.
"Code complet de la danse", 1830
Blume, F.
"Studien zur Vorgeschichte der Or-
chestersuite im 15ten und 16ten
Jahrhundert", 1925
Boehme, Franz Magnus
"Geschichte des Tanzes in Deutsch-
land", 1886
Böhn, Max
"Der Tanz", 1925
Bolte, Johannes
"Zur Geschichte des Tanzes" (Ale-
mannia XVIII), 1890
Braun, Lisbeth
"Die Balletkomposition von Joseph
Starzer" ("Studien zur Musikwis-
senschaft")
Bücher, Karl
"Arbeit und Rhythmus", 1909
Bücken, Ernst
"Musik des 19. Jahrhunderts bis
zur Moderne"
Bücken, Ernst
"Musik des Rokokos und der Klas-
sik"
Burckhard, Jacob
"Die Kultur der Renaissance in
Italien" (7. Aufl.), 1899

Casanova, Giacomo
"Memoirs" (Conrad), 1907
Castiglione, Bald.
"Il Corteggiano", 1514

366   BIBLIOGRAPHY

Chambers
   "The Medieval Stage", 1903
Chase, G.
   "The Music of Spain", 1941
Commenda, Hans
   "Der Landla" ("Heimatgaue")
   1923
Condamin, G.
   "La Suite Instrumentale", 1905
Czerwinski, Albert
   "Brevier der Tanzkunst", 1879
Czerwinski, Albert
   "Die Taenze des 16. Jahrhunderts"

Dancing Master, The
   1709
Danckert, Werner
   "Geschichte der Gigue", 1924
Darwin, Charles
   "On the origin of species", 1859
Decsey, Ernst
   "Johann Strauss", 1922
"Denkmaeler
   der Tonkunst in Bayern"
"Denkmaeler
   der Tonkunst in Oesterreich" (Ed-
   ited by Guido Adler)
"Denkmaeler
   deutcher Tonkunst"

Ecorcheville, Jules
   "Vingt suites d'orchestre", 1906
Ehrenfels, Christ.
   "Ueber Gestaltsqualitaeten", 1922
Einstein. Alfred
   "Das Neue Musiklexicon", 1926
Einstein, Alfred
   "Mozart", 1945
Einstein, Alfred
   "Chronologisch - thematisches Ver-
   zeichnis saemtlicher Tonwerke W.
   A. Mozarts" (Dr. Ludwig Ritter,
   Köchel) 1937
Eitner, R.
   "Taenze des 15. bis 17. Jahrhun-
   derts" (Monatshefte fuer Musik-
   geschichte" VII. Beilage)

Feuillet
   "L'Allemande", 1701
Feuillet et Dezais
   "Choréographie, ou l'art de décrire
   la danse", 1699
Fischer, Carl von
   "Grieg's Harmonik und das nord-
   laendische Folklore", 1938
Fox Strangways, A. H.
   "Music of Hindostan", 1914
Friedenthal, Albert
   "Musik, Tanz und Dichtung bei
   den Kreolen Amerikas", 1913

Geiringer, Karl
   "Paul Peurl - Studien zur Musik-
   wissenschaft"
Gerheuser, Ludwig
   "Jacob Scheiffelhut und seine Ins-
   trumentalmusik", 1931
Goldberg, Isaac
   "George Gershwin, 1931
Gombosi, Otto
   "About Dance and Dance Music
   in the Late Middle Ages" (Musical
   Quarterly, 1941)
Goode, G.
   "The Book of Ballets", 1939
Gradenwitz, P.
   "Joh. Stamitz's Leben", 1935
Grimm, Melchior
   "Le petit Prophète de Boehmisch-
   broda", 1753
Grove's
   "Dictionary of Music and Musi-
   cians", 1945

Haas, Robert
   "Musik des Barocks"
Haas, Robert
   "Die Wiener Ballet - Pantomime im
   18. Jahrhundert und Gluck's Don
   Juan" ("Studien zur Musikwissen-
   schaft)
Haas, Robert
   "Die Musik in der Wiener Stegreif-
   komoedie" ("Studien zur Musik-
   wissenschaft")

Haas, Robert
"Die musikalische Auffuehrungs-praxis" (Bücken, "Handbuch der Musikwissenschaft")

Haensel, Christ. Gottl.
"Allerneueste, Anweisung zur Aeus-serlichen Moral", 1755

Henseler, Ant.
"J. Offenbach", 1930

Herzog, G.
"Research in Primitive and Folk Music in U.S.A.", 1936

Heuss, Alfr.
"Die Instrumentalstuecke des "Or-feo" (Sammelbaende der Intern. Musikgesellschaft, 1903)

Hobson, W.
"American Jazz Music", 1939

Hornbostel, Otto von
"Musik des Orients", (Collection of recordings)

Howard, J. T.
"Our American Music", 1931

Howard, J. T.
"Our Contemporary Composers" 1941

Idelsohn, A. Z.
"Gesaenge der orientalischen Se-phardim", 1923
"Jewish Music in its historical de-velopment", 1929

Junk, V.
Handbuch des Tanzes", 1930

Kahl, Willi
"Das lyrische Klavierstueck Schu-berts und seiner Vorgaenger seit 1810" (Archiv f. Musikwissenschaft 1921)

Kinkeldey, Otto
"A Jewish dancing master of the Renaissance", 1929

Komma, K. M.
"Joh. Zach und die Czechischen Musiker im deutschen Umbruch des 18. Jahrhunderts", 1938

Kretzschmar, Hermann
"Geschichte der Oper", 1919

Lach, Robert
"Zur Geschichte des Gesellschafts-tanzes im 18. Jahrhundert", 1920

Lachmann, Robert
"Musik des Orients", 1929

Lachmann, Robert
"Musik der ausser - europaeischen Voelker" (Handbuch der Musik-wissenschaft)

Lambranzi, G. di
"Neue und curieuse Theatralische Tantz - Schul" 1717 (New English Edition, 1928)

Lang, Paul Henry
"Music in Western Civilization", 1941

Leichtentritt, Hugo
"Haendel", 1924

Long, E. B. and McKee
"A Bibliography of Music for the Dance", 1936

Magriel, Paul D.
"A Bibliography of Dancing", 1936

Mannhardt, W.
"Wald - und Feldkulte", 1904

Mattheson, Johann
"Der vollkommene Capellmeister", 1739

Mattheson, Johann
"Das neu - eroeffnete Orchester", 1713

Mendelssohn, Ignaz
"Zur Entwicklung des Walzers" ("Studien zur Musikwissenschaft", 13)

Menéstrier, C.
"Des représentations en musique anciennes et modernes", 1681

Merian, W.
"Der Tanz in den deutschen Ta-bulaturbuechern des 16. Jahrhun-derts", 1927

Mersmann, Hans
"Moderne Musik" (Handbuch der

Musikwissenschaft)
Meyer - Luebke, Wilhelm
"Romanisch - Etymologisches Woer-
terbuch", 1911, 1930
Michel, Arthur
"The Earliest Dance Manuals",
1945
"Modern Music"
Published by the "League of Com-
posers"
Moser, H. J.
"Deutsche Musikgeschichte", 1923,
1924
Muenster, Johannes von
"Tanzfest der Toechter Sieben",
1594

Nef, Karl
"Zur Geschichte der deutschen In-
strumentalmusik in der zweiten
Haelfte des 17. Jahrh., 1902
Nef, Karl
"Geschichte der Sinfonie und der
Suite", 1921
Negri, Cesare
"Nuove inventioni di balli", 1604
Negri, Cesare
"Le grazie d'amore", 1580
Nejedlý, Zdeněk
"Magister Zavis und seine Schule"
(Sammelbaende der Intern. Musik-
gesellschaft, VII)
Nettl, Paul
"Das Wiener Barocklied", 1934
Nettl, Paul
"Traces of the Negroid in the
Mauresque of the 16th and 17th
centuries", (Phylon, 1944)
Nettl, Paul
"Music und Tanz bei Casanova",
1924
Nettl, Paul
"Musik - Barock in Boehmen und
Maehren", 1927
Nettl, Paul
"Alte juedische Spielleute und Mu-
siker", 1927
Nettl, Paul

"Schubert's Czech Predecessors"
(Music & Letters, XXIII)
Nettl, Paul
"Die Bergamaska" (Zeitschrift f.
Musikwissenschaft, V)
Nettl, Paul
"Ein verschollenes Tournier - Bal-
let von M. A. Cesti" (Zeitschrift
f. Musikwissenschaft, VIII)
Nettl, Paul
"La Musica en la Danza", 1945
Nettl, Paul
"Tanz and Tanzmusik" in Adler's
"Handbuch der Musikgeschichte",
1930
Nettl, Paul
"Equestrian Ballets of the Baroque
Period" (Musical Quarterly, 1933)
Nettl, Paul
"Heinrich Franz Biber" (Sudeten-
deutsche Lebensbilder, 1926)
Nettl, Paul
"Mozart in Boehmen", 1938
Nettl, Paul
"Die Wiener Tanzkomposition in
der zweiten Haefte des 17. Jhdts."
(Studien zur Musikwissenschaft, 8)
Nettl, Paul
"Zur Vorgeschichte der sueddeut-
schen Taenze" ("Bulletin de la So-
cieté Union Musicologique", 1923)
Nettl, Paul
"Birth of the Waltz" (Dance In-
dex, 1946)
Nettl, Paul
"Beitrag zur Geschichte des deut-
schen Singballets" (Zeitschrift f.
Musikwissenschaft, 6)
"Neues Taschenbuch
zum geselligen Vergnuegen", 1801
Niedecker, Hans
"Jean Georges Noverre"
Norlind, Tobias
"Zur Geschichte der polnischen
Taenze" (Sammelbaende der In-
tern. Musikgesellsch., 1911)
Norlind, Tobias
"Zur Geschichte der Suite" (Sam-

melbaende der Intern. Musikgesellschaft., VII)
Noverre, J. G.
"Lettres sur la danse et sur les
ballets", 1760

Oberst, Guenther
"Englische Orchestersuiten um
1600", 1929

Pohl, C. F.
"Haydn" (Botstiber III)
Porter, E.
"Music through the Dance", 1937
Praetorius, Michael
"Syntagma Musicum", 1615-1619
Praetorius, Michael
"Terpsichore", 1612
Prunières, Henri
"Claudio Monteverdi", 1924
Prunières, Henri
"Le Ballet de Cour en France",
1914
Pulver, J.
"The Ancient Dance Forms" (Pro-
ceedings of the Musical Associa-
tion, XXXIX)

Rank, Otto
"Der Mythus von der Geburt des
Helden", 1909
Ratzel, Friedr.
"Voelkerkunde", 1885-1888
Reese, Gustave
"Music in the Middle Ages", 1940
Riemann, Hugo
"Musiklexikon", 1929
Riemann, Hugo
"Handbuch der Musikgeschichte",
1904-1913
Rietsch, Heinr.
"Joh. Jos. Fux's Concentus" (Stu-
dien zur Musikwissenschaft IV)
Robitschek, Alfred
"Der Kotillon", 1925
Rohloff, Ernst
"Studien zum Musiktraktat des Jo-
hannes de Grocheo", 1930

Rossmann, W.
"Ueber die Tarantella in Capri"
(Allgem. musikal. Zeitung, 1880)
Rousseau, J. J.
"Dictionnaire de Musique", 1768
Rychnovsky, Ernst
"Smetana", 1924

Sachs, Curt
"History of Musical Instruments",
1940
Sachs, Curt
"Anthologie Sonore" (Collection
of recordings)
Sachs, Curt
"2000 Jahre Musik auf der Schall-
platte"
Sachs, Curt
"Geist und Werden der Musik-
instrumente", 1929
Sachs, Curt
"Eine Weltgeschichte des Tanzes",
1933
Sandberger, Adolf
"Roland Lassus' Beziehungen zur
italienischen Literatur" (Sammel-
baende der Intern. Musikgesellsch.
V)
Sargeant, Winthrop
"Jazz", 1946
Scharlitt, Bernh.
"Chopin", 1919
Schein, Joh. Herm.
"Banchetto Musicale", 1617 (Edited
by A. Pruefer)
Schindler, Ant.
"Biographie von Ludwig von Bee-
thoven", 1871
Scholz, Hans
"Johann Sigismund Kusser", 1911
Schottky and Ziska
"Oesterreichische Volklieder", 1819
Schrade, Leo
"Taenze aus einer anonymen itali-
enischen Tabulatur", 1551 (Zeit-
schrift f. Musikwissenschaft X)
Schurtz, Heinrich
"Altersklassen und Maennerbuen-

370   B I B L I O G R A P H Y

de", 1902
Sharp, Cecil J.
"The Country Dance Book", 1909-
1911
Sharp, Cecil J.
"The Dance", 1924
Sharp, E.
"Story of the Dance", 1928
Slonimsky, Nicolas
"Music of Latin America", 1945
Sonner, Rudolf
"Musik und Tanz", 1930
Sourek, Otokar and Stefan, Paul
"Dvořak", 1935
Spencer, Herbert
"Principles of Psychology", 1870-
1872
Spitta, Philipp
"J. S. Bach" 1873, 1880
Stefan, Paul
"Franz Schubert", 1928
Stumpf, Karl
"Die Anfaenge der Musik", 1911
Stumpf, Karl
"Tonpsychologie" 1883, 1890
Stumpf, Karl (with Hornbostel)
"Beitraege zur Akustik und Mu-
sikwissenschaft" (from 1922)
Szabolcsi, B.
"Probleme der alten ungarischen
Musikgeschichte" (Zeitschrift f.
Musikwissenschaft VII & VIII)

Tappert, Wilhelm

"Sang und Klang aus alter Zeit",
1906
Taubert, Gottfried
"Rechtschaffner Tantzmeister", 1717
Thayer, A. W.
"Ludwig van Beethoven's Leben"
(3. Auflage von Hugo Riemann)
1917
Tuerk, Daniel Gottlob
"Neue Klavier Schule", 1798

Ungarelli, G.
"Le vecchie Danze Italiane", 1894

Voss, R.
"Der Tanz und seine Geschichte",
1885

Waldau, Alfred
"Boehmische Nationaltaenze", 1859,
1860
Wellesz, Egon
"Die Opern und Oratorien in
Wien von 1660-1708" (Studien zur
Musikwissenschaft, 6)
Winterstein, Alfred
"Der Ursprung der Tragoedie",
1925
Wolf, Joh.
"Die Taenze des Mittelalters"
(Archiv f. Musikwissenschaft I)
Wundt, Wilhelm
"Voelkerpsychologie", 1911